SHI

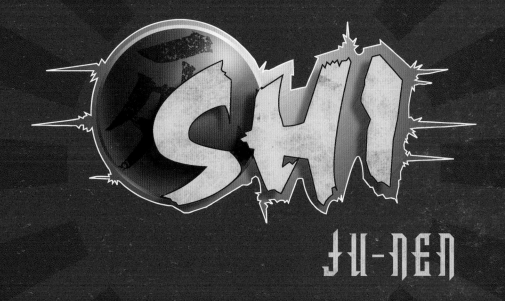

JU-NEN

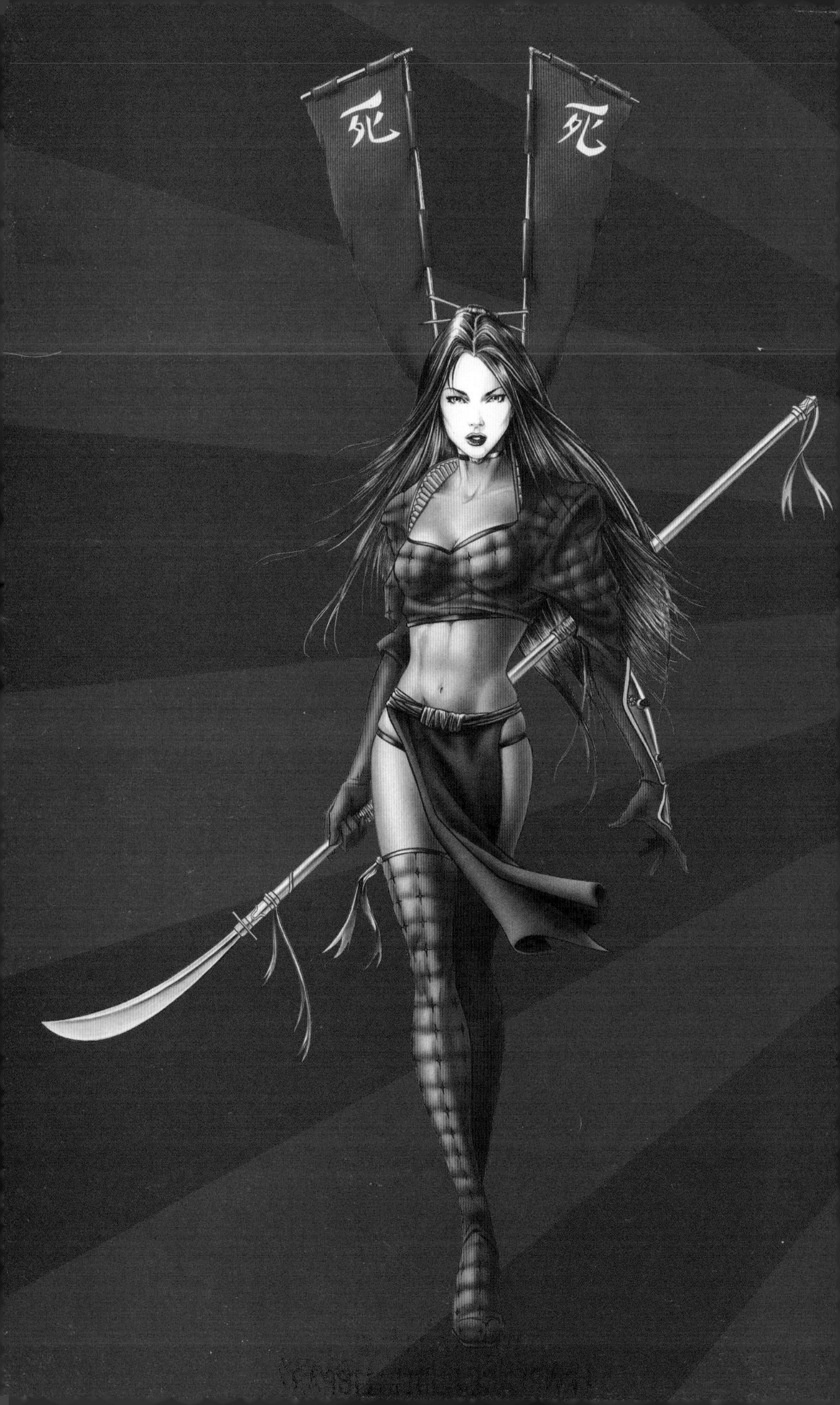
死
死

SHI

JU-NEN

STORY AND ILLUSTRATION BY

BILLY TUCCI

—

COVER BY

BILLY TUCCI AND MARK SPARACIO

DARK HORSE BOOKS™

LAWRENCE PUBLIC LIBRARY

PUBLISHER

Mike Richardson

DESIGNER

Ben Brown

SHI: JU-NEN™ & ©2005 William Elliott Tucci. Dark Horse Books™ is a trademark of Dark Horse Comics, Inc. Dark Horse Comics® is a trademark of Dark Horse Comics, Inc., registered in various categories and countries. All rights reserved. No portion of this publication may be reproduced or transmitted, in any form or by any means, without the express written permission of Dark Horse Comics, Inc. Names, characters, places, and incidents featured in this publication either are the product of the author's imagination or are used fictitiously. Any resemblance to actual persons (living or dead), events, institutions, or locales, without satiric intent, is coincidental.

This book collects issues 1 through 4 of the Dark Horse comic-book series *Shi: Ju-nen*.

Dark Horse Books
A division of Dark Horse Comics, Inc.
10956 SE Main Street
Milwaukie, OR 97222

darkhorse.com
crusadefinearts.com

To find a comics shop in your area,
call the Comic Shop Locator Service
toll-free at (888) 266-4226.

First edition: February 2006
ISBN: 1-59307-451-4

1 3 5 7 9 10 8 6 4 2

Printed in China

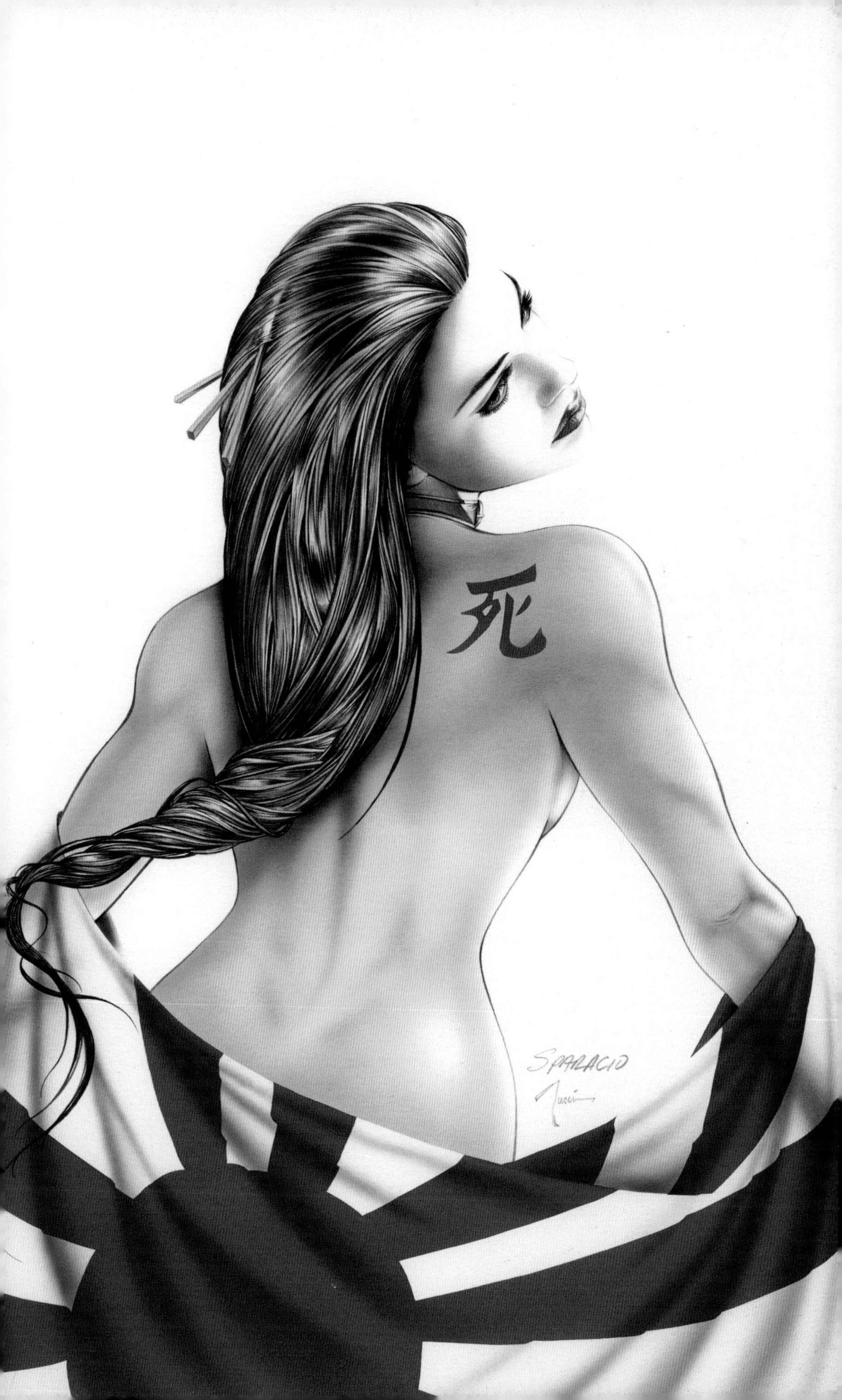
死
SPARACIO

STORY AND ILLUSTRATION
Billy Tucci

COLORS
Brett K. Smith

COLOR FLATS
John Wilson

LETTERING
Marshall Dillon

ART SCANNING AND CLEANUP
Jason Fitzpatrick

BACKGROUND ASSISTS
Mike Kenzine

COVER
Billy Tucci and Mark Sparacio

ORIGINAL FASHIONS
Anna Sui

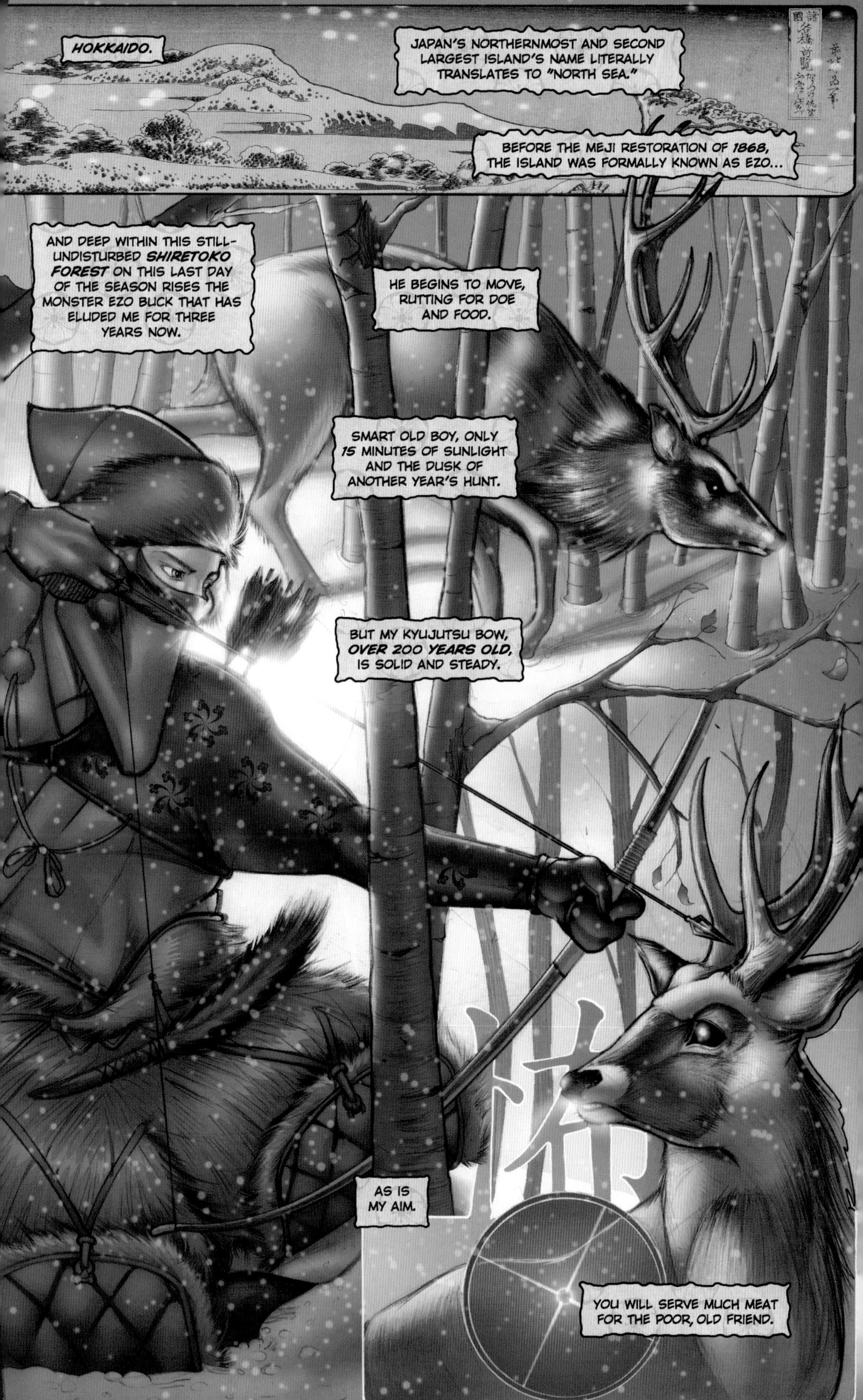
HOKKAIDO.
JAPAN'S NORTHERNMOST AND SECOND LARGEST ISLAND'S NAME LITERALLY TRANSLATES TO "NORTH SEA."
BEFORE THE MEJI RESTORATION OF 1868, THE ISLAND WAS FORMALLY KNOWN AS EZO...
AND DEEP WITHIN THIS STILL-UNDISTURBED SHIRETOKO FOREST ON THIS LAST DAY OF THE SEASON RISES THE MONSTER EZO BUCK THAT HAS ELUDED ME FOR THREE YEARS NOW.
HE BEGINS TO MOVE, RUTTING FOR DOE AND FOOD.
SMART OLD BOY, ONLY 15 MINUTES OF SUNLIGHT AND THE DUSK OF ANOTHER YEAR'S HUNT.
BUT MY KYUJUTSU BOW, OVER 200 YEARS OLD, IS SOLID AND STEADY.
AS IS MY AIM.
YOU WILL SERVE MUCH MEAT FOR THE POOR, OLD FRIEND.

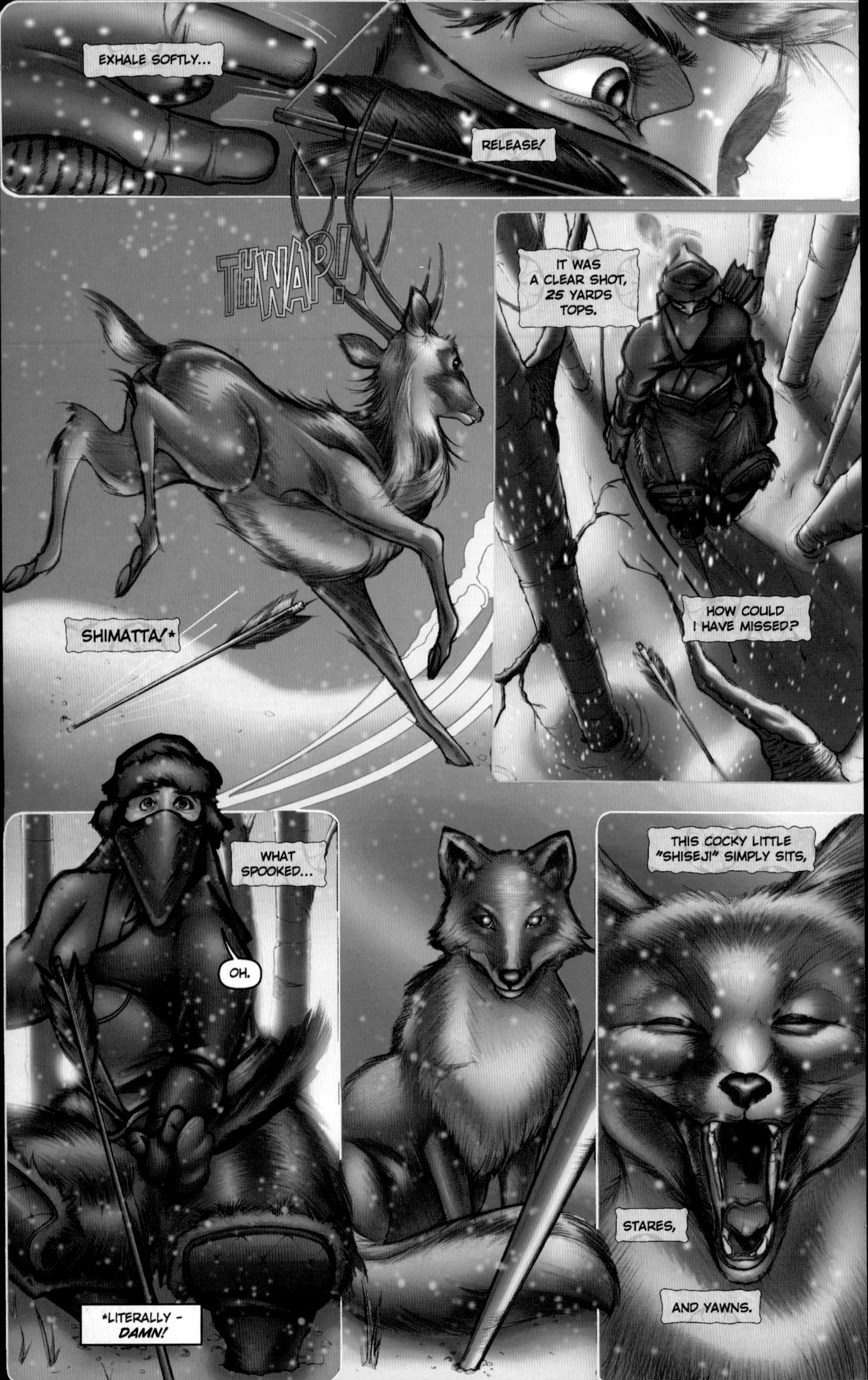
EXHALE SOFTLY...
RELEASE!
THWAP!
SHIMATTA!*
IT WAS A CLEAR SHOT, 25 YARDS TOPS.
HOW COULD I HAVE MISSED?
WHAT SPOOKED...
OH.
*LITERALLY - DAMN!
THIS COCKY LITTLE "SHISEJI" SIMPLY SITS,
STARES,
AND YAWNS.

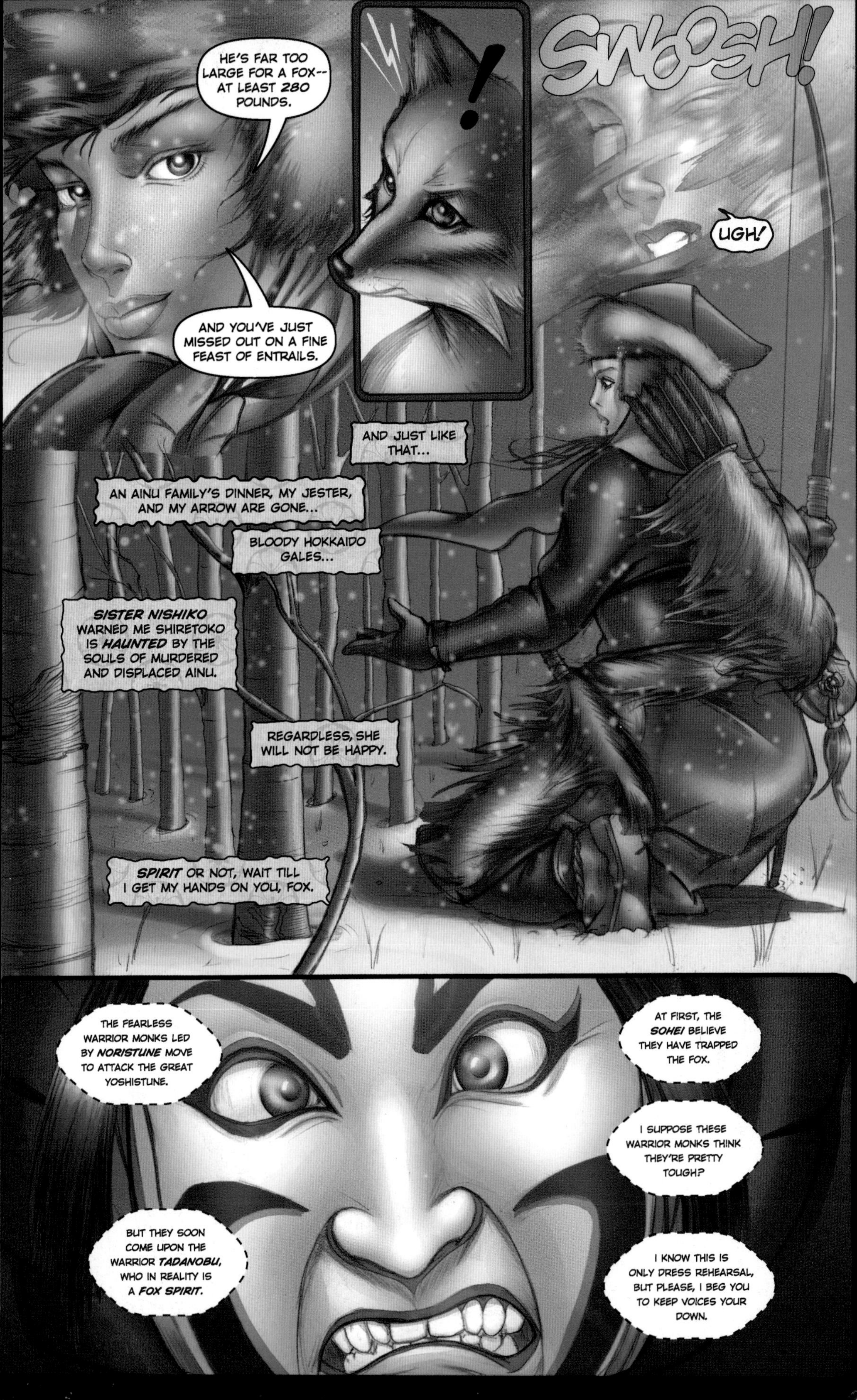

HE'S FAR TOO LARGE FOR A FOX-- AT LEAST 280 POUNDS.
AND YOU'VE JUST MISSED OUT ON A FINE FEAST OF ENTRAILS.
!
SWOOSH!
UGH!
AND JUST LIKE THAT...
AN AINU FAMILY'S DINNER, MY JESTER, AND MY ARROW ARE GONE...
BLOODY HOKKAIDO GALES...
SISTER NISHIKO WARNED ME SHIRETOKO IS HAUNTED BY THE SOULS OF MURDERED AND DISPLACED AINU.
REGARDLESS, SHE WILL NOT BE HAPPY.
SPIRIT OR NOT, WAIT TILL I GET MY HANDS ON YOU, FOX.
THE FEARLESS WARRIOR MONKS LED BY NORISTUNE MOVE TO ATTACK THE GREAT YOSHISTUNE.
AT FIRST, THE SOHEI BELIEVE THEY HAVE TRAPPED THE FOX.
I SUPPOSE THESE WARRIOR MONKS THINK THEY'RE PRETTY TOUGH?
BUT THEY SOON COME UPON THE WARRIOR TADANOBU, WHO IN REALITY IS A FOX SPIRIT.
I KNOW THIS IS ONLY DRESS REHEARSAL, BUT PLEASE, I BEG YOU TO KEEP VOICES YOUR DOWN.

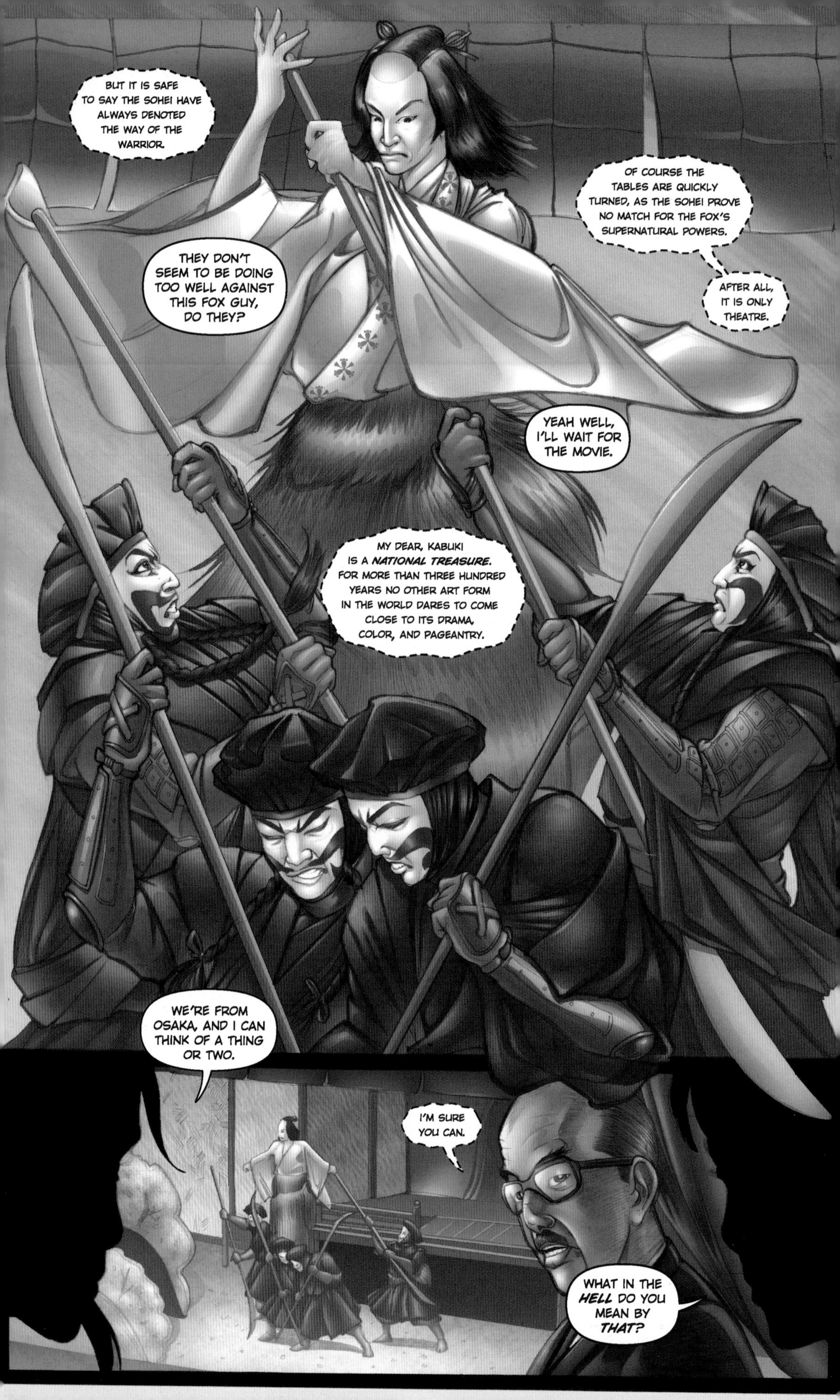
BUT IT IS SAFE TO SAY THE SOHEI HAVE ALWAYS DENOTED THE WAY OF THE WARRIOR.
THEY DON'T SEEM TO BE DOING TOO WELL AGAINST THIS FOX GUY, DO THEY?
OF COURSE THE TABLES ARE QUICKLY TURNED, AS THE SOHEI PROVE NO MATCH FOR THE FOX'S SUPERNATURAL POWERS.
AFTER ALL, IT IS ONLY THEATRE.
YEAH WELL, I'LL WAIT FOR THE MOVIE.
MY DEAR, KABUKI IS A ***NATIONAL TREASURE.*** FOR MORE THAN THREE HUNDRED YEARS NO OTHER ART FORM IN THE WORLD DARES TO COME CLOSE TO ITS DRAMA, COLOR, AND PAGEANTRY.
WE'RE FROM OSAKA, AND I CAN THINK OF A THING OR TWO.
I'M SURE YOU CAN.
WHAT IN THE ***HELL*** DO YOU MEAN BY ***THAT?***

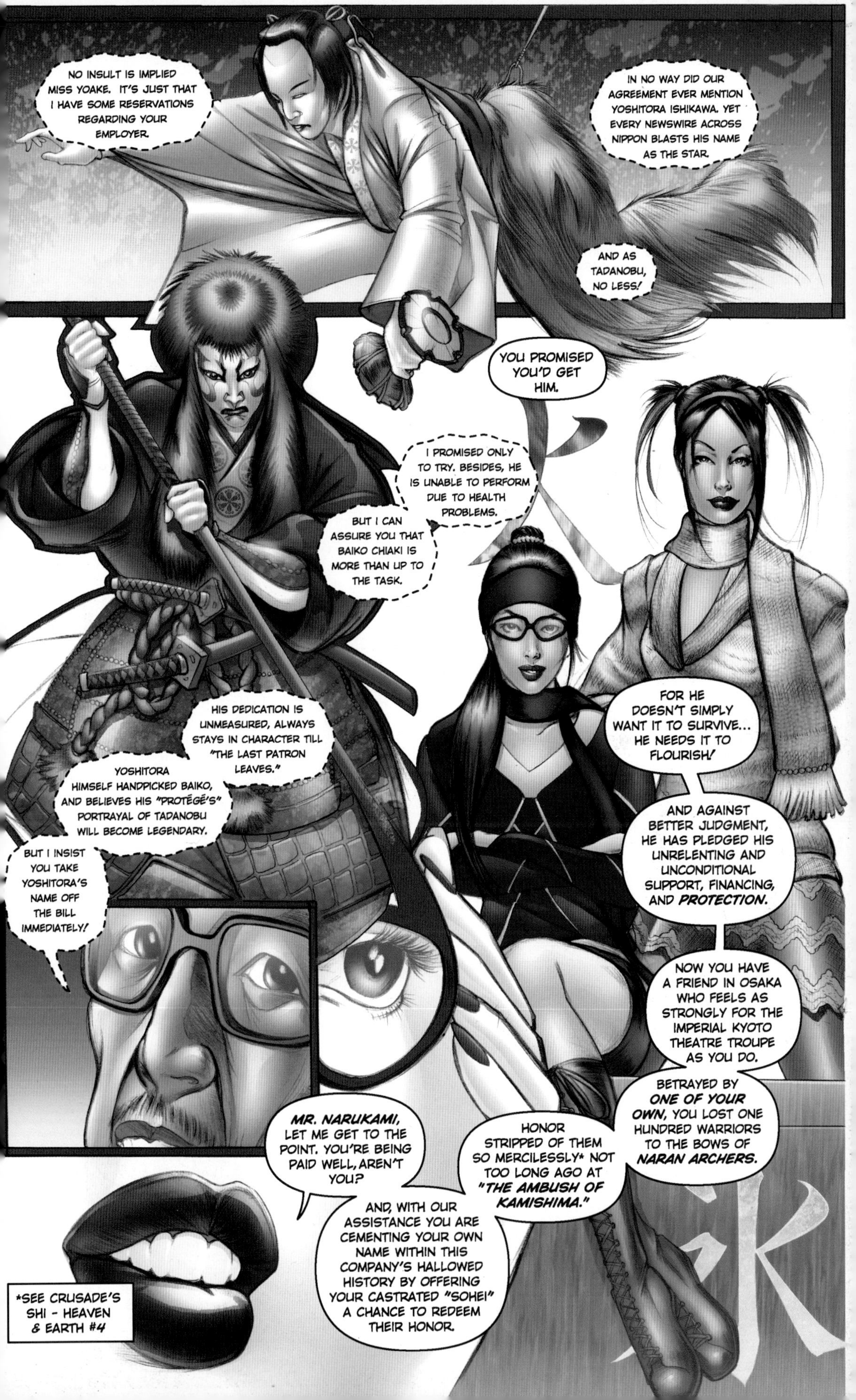
NO INSULT IS IMPLIED MISS YOAKE. IT'S JUST THAT I HAVE SOME RESERVATIONS REGARDING YOUR EMPLOYER.
IN NO WAY DID OUR AGREEMENT EVER MENTION YOSHITORA ISHIKAWA. YET EVERY NEWSWIRE ACROSS NIPPON BLASTS HIS NAME AS THE STAR.
AND AS TADANOBU, NO LESS!
YOU PROMISED YOU'D GET HIM.
I PROMISED ONLY TO TRY. BESIDES, HE IS UNABLE TO PERFORM DUE TO HEALTH PROBLEMS.
BUT I CAN ASSURE YOU THAT BAIKO CHIAKI IS MORE THAN UP TO THE TASK.
HIS DEDICATION IS UNMEASURED, ALWAYS STAYS IN CHARACTER TILL "THE LAST PATRON LEAVES."
YOSHITORA HIMSELF HANDPICKED BAIKO, AND BELIEVES HIS "PROTÉGÉ'S" PORTRAYAL OF TADANOBU WILL BECOME LEGENDARY.
BUT I INSIST YOU TAKE YOSHITORA'S NAME OFF THE BILL IMMEDIATELY!
MR. NARUKAMI, LET ME GET TO THE POINT. YOU'RE BEING PAID WELL, AREN'T YOU?
AND, WITH OUR ASSISTANCE YOU ARE CEMENTING YOUR OWN NAME WITHIN THIS COMPANY'S HALLOWED HISTORY BY OFFERING YOUR CASTRATED "SOHEI" A CHANCE TO REDEEM THEIR HONOR.
HONOR STRIPPED OF THEM SO MERCILESSLY* NOT TOO LONG AGO AT "THE AMBUSH OF KAMISHIMA."
BETRAYED BY ONE OF YOUR OWN, YOU LOST ONE HUNDRED WARRIORS TO THE BOWS OF NARAN ARCHERS.
NOW YOU HAVE A FRIEND IN OSAKA WHO FEELS AS STRONGLY FOR THE IMPERIAL KYOTO THEATRE TROUPE AS YOU DO.
FOR HE DOESN'T SIMPLY WANT IT TO SURVIVE... HE NEEDS IT TO FLOURISH!
AND AGAINST BETTER JUDGMENT, HE HAS PLEDGED HIS UNRELENTING AND UNCONDITIONAL SUPPORT, FINANCING, AND PROTECTION.
*SEE CRUSADE'S SHI - HEAVEN & EARTH #4

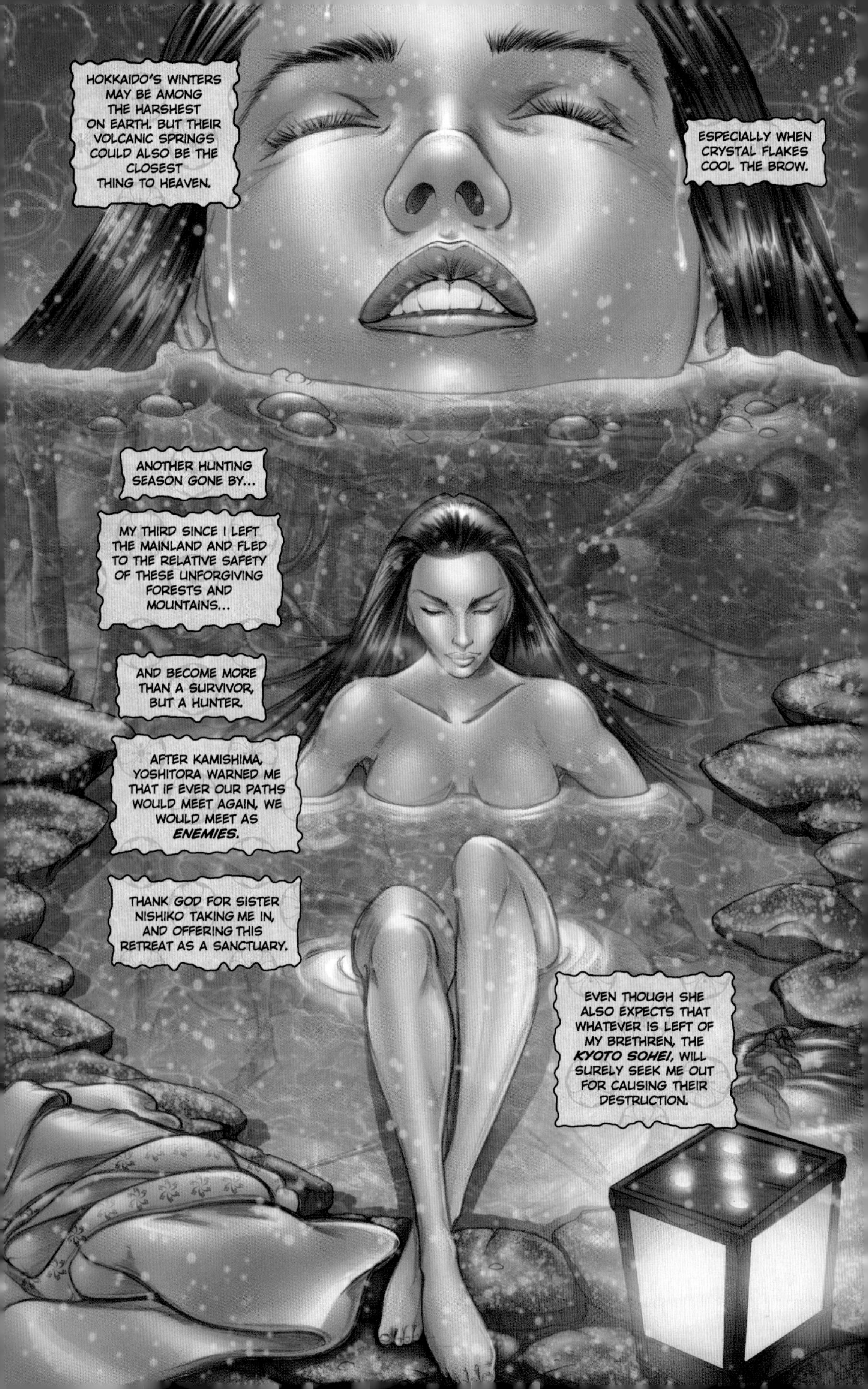
HOKKAIDO'S WINTERS MAY BE AMONG THE HARSHEST ON EARTH. BUT THEIR VOLCANIC SPRINGS COULD ALSO BE THE CLOSEST THING TO HEAVEN.
ESPECIALLY WHEN CRYSTAL FLAKES COOL THE BROW.
ANOTHER HUNTING SEASON GONE BY...
MY THIRD SINCE I LEFT THE MAINLAND AND FLED TO THE RELATIVE SAFETY OF THESE UNFORGIVING FORESTS AND MOUNTAINS...
AND BECOME MORE THAN A SURVIVOR, BUT A HUNTER.
AFTER KAMISHIMA, YOSHITORA WARNED ME THAT IF EVER OUR PATHS WOULD MEET AGAIN, WE WOULD MEET AS ***ENEMIES.***
THANK GOD FOR SISTER NISHIKO TAKING ME IN, AND OFFERING THIS RETREAT AS A SANCTUARY.
EVEN THOUGH SHE ALSO EXPECTS THAT WHATEVER IS LEFT OF MY BRETHREN, THE ***KYOTO SOHEI,*** WILL SURELY SEEK ME OUT FOR CAUSING THEIR DESTRUCTION.

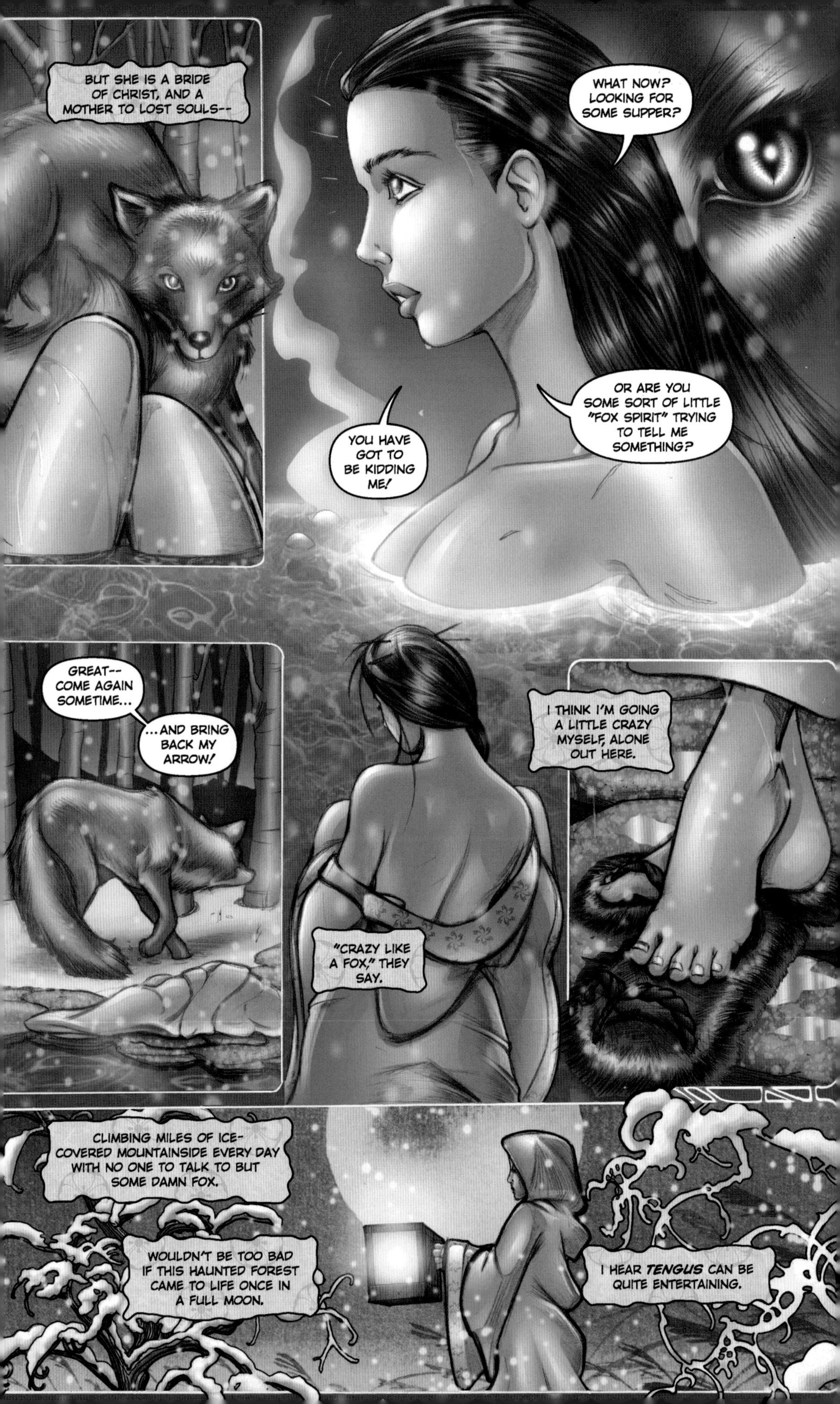

BUT SHE IS A BRIDE OF CHRIST, AND A MOTHER TO LOST SOULS--
WHAT NOW? LOOKING FOR SOME SUPPER?
YOU HAVE GOT TO BE KIDDING ME!
OR ARE YOU SOME SORT OF LITTLE "FOX SPIRIT" TRYING TO TELL ME SOMETHING?
GREAT-- COME AGAIN SOMETIME...
...AND BRING BACK MY ARROW!
"CRAZY LIKE A FOX," THEY SAY.
I THINK I'M GOING A LITTLE CRAZY MYSELF, ALONE OUT HERE.
CLIMBING MILES OF ICE-COVERED MOUNTAINSIDE EVERY DAY WITH NO ONE TO TALK TO BUT SOME DAMN FOX.
WOULDN'T BE TOO BAD IF THIS HAUNTED FOREST CAME TO LIFE ONCE IN A FULL MOON.
I HEAR *TENGUS* CAN BE QUITE ENTERTAINING.

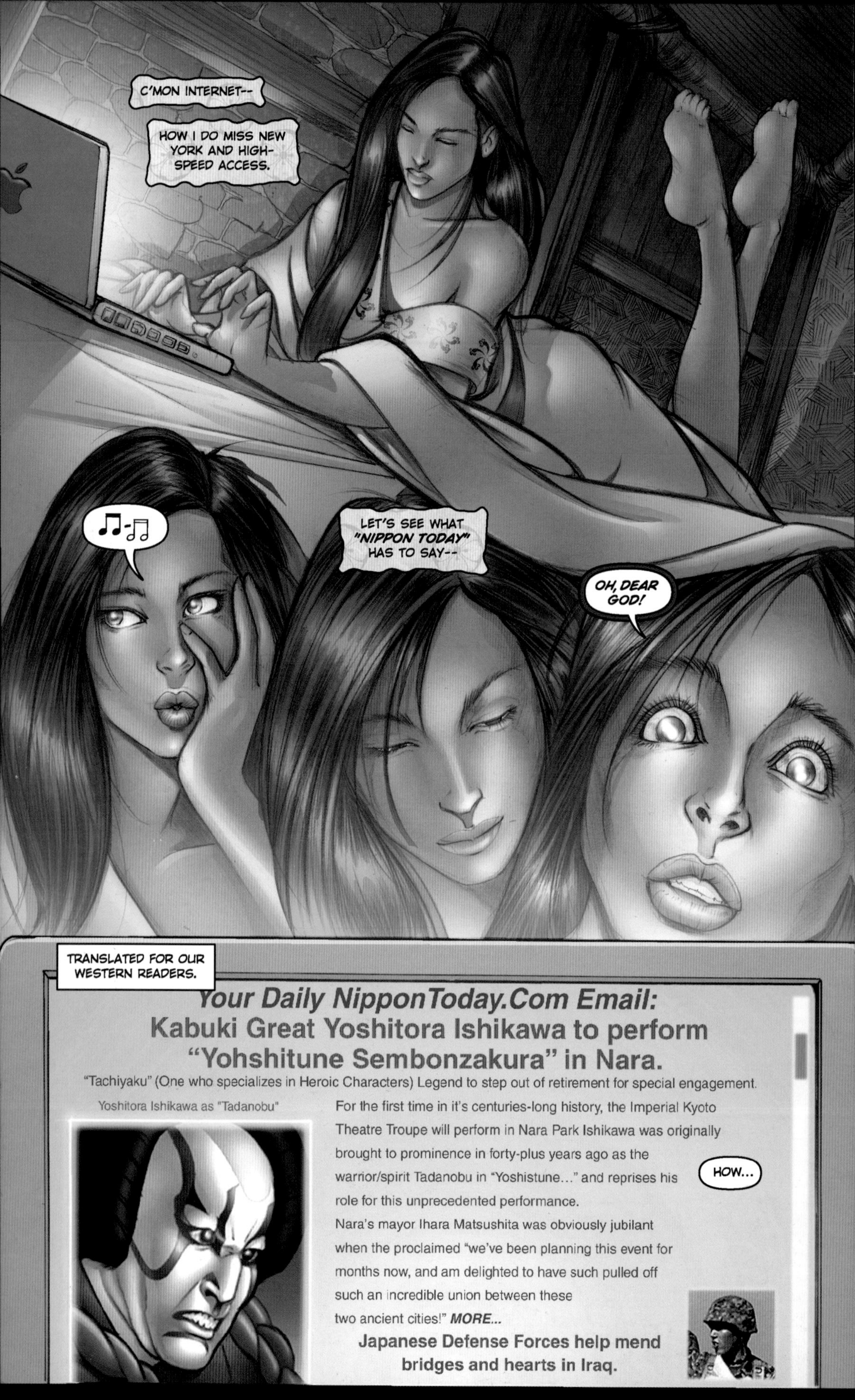
C'MON INTERNET--
HOW I DO MISS NEW YORK AND HIGH-SPEED ACCESS.
♫-♫
LET'S SEE WHAT "NIPPON TODAY" HAS TO SAY--
OH, DEAR GOD!
TRANSLATED FOR OUR WESTERN READERS.
Your Daily NipponToday.Com Email:
Kabuki Great Yoshitora Ishikawa to perform "Yohshitune Sembonzakura" in Nara.
"Tachiyaku" (One who specializes in Heroic Characters) Legend to step out of retirement for special engagement.
Yoshitora Ishikawa as "Tadanobu"
For the first time in it's centuries-long history, the Imperial Kyoto Theatre Troupe will perform in Nara Park Ishikawa was originally brought to prominence in forty-plus years ago as the warrior/spirit Tadanobu in "Yoshistune..." and reprises his role for this unprecedented performance.
Nara's mayor Ihara Matsushita was obviously jubilant when the proclaimed "we've been planning this event for months now, and am delighted to have such pulled off such an incredible union between these two ancient cities!" MORE...
HOW...
Japanese Defense Forces help mend bridges and hearts in Iraq.

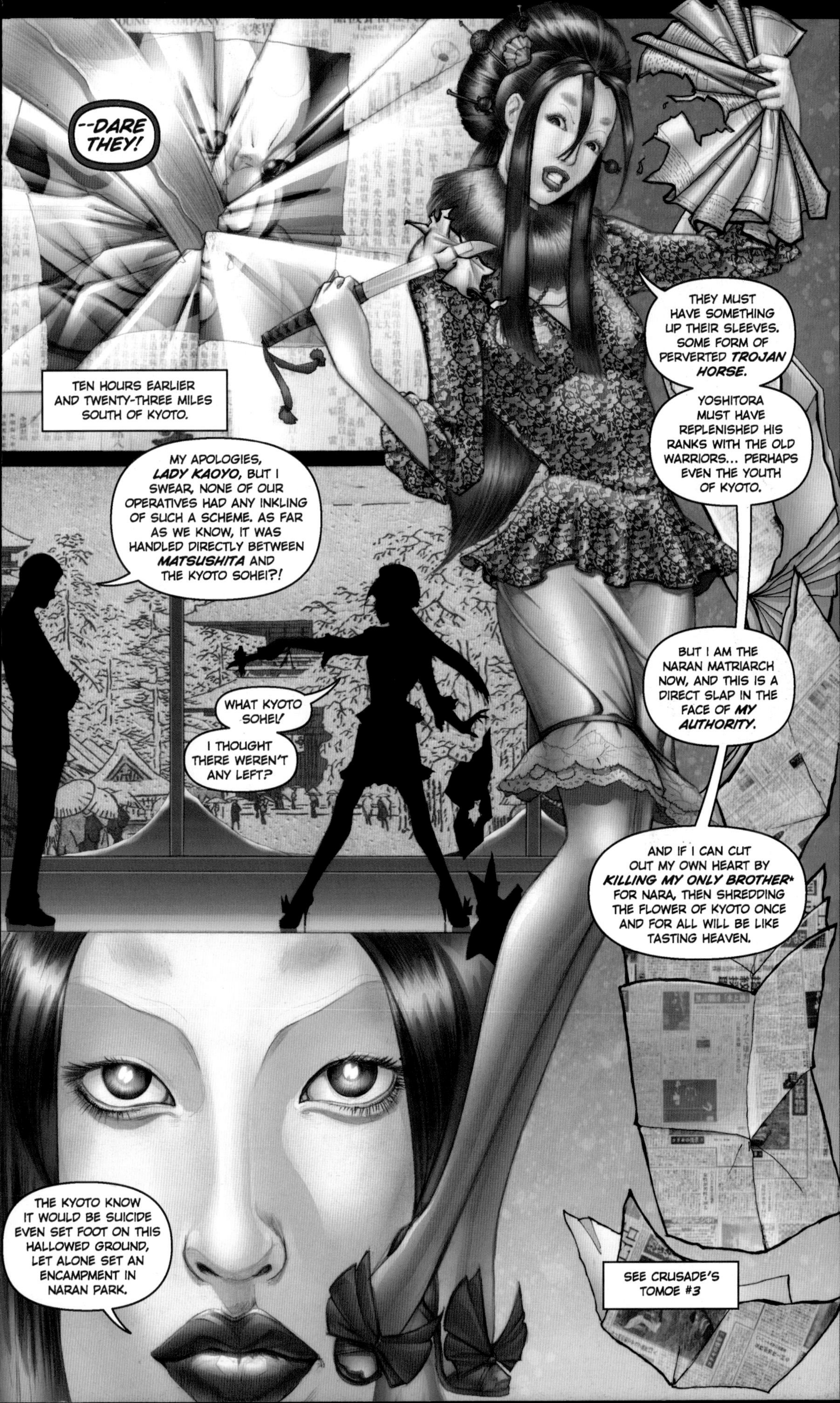
--DARE THEY!
TEN HOURS EARLIER AND TWENTY-THREE MILES SOUTH OF KYOTO.
THEY MUST HAVE SOMETHING UP THEIR SLEEVES. SOME FORM OF PERVERTED TROJAN HORSE.
YOSHITORA MUST HAVE REPLENISHED HIS RANKS WITH THE OLD WARRIORS... PERHAPS EVEN THE YOUTH OF KYOTO.
MY APOLOGIES, LADY KAOYO, BUT I SWEAR, NONE OF OUR OPERATIVES HAD ANY INKLING OF SUCH A SCHEME. AS FAR AS WE KNOW, IT WAS HANDLED DIRECTLY BETWEEN MATSUSHITA AND THE KYOTO SOHEI?!
WHAT KYOTO SOHEI!
I THOUGHT THERE WEREN'T ANY LEFT?
BUT I AM THE NARAN MATRIARCH NOW, AND THIS IS A DIRECT SLAP IN THE FACE OF MY AUTHORITY.
AND IF I CAN CUT OUT MY OWN HEART BY KILLING MY ONLY BROTHER* FOR NARA, THEN SHREDDING THE FLOWER OF KYOTO ONCE AND FOR ALL WILL BE LIKE TASTING HEAVEN.
THE KYOTO KNOW IT WOULD BE SUICIDE EVEN SET FOOT ON THIS HALLOWED GROUND, LET ALONE SET AN ENCAMPMENT IN NARAN PARK.
SEE CRUSADE'S TOMOE #3

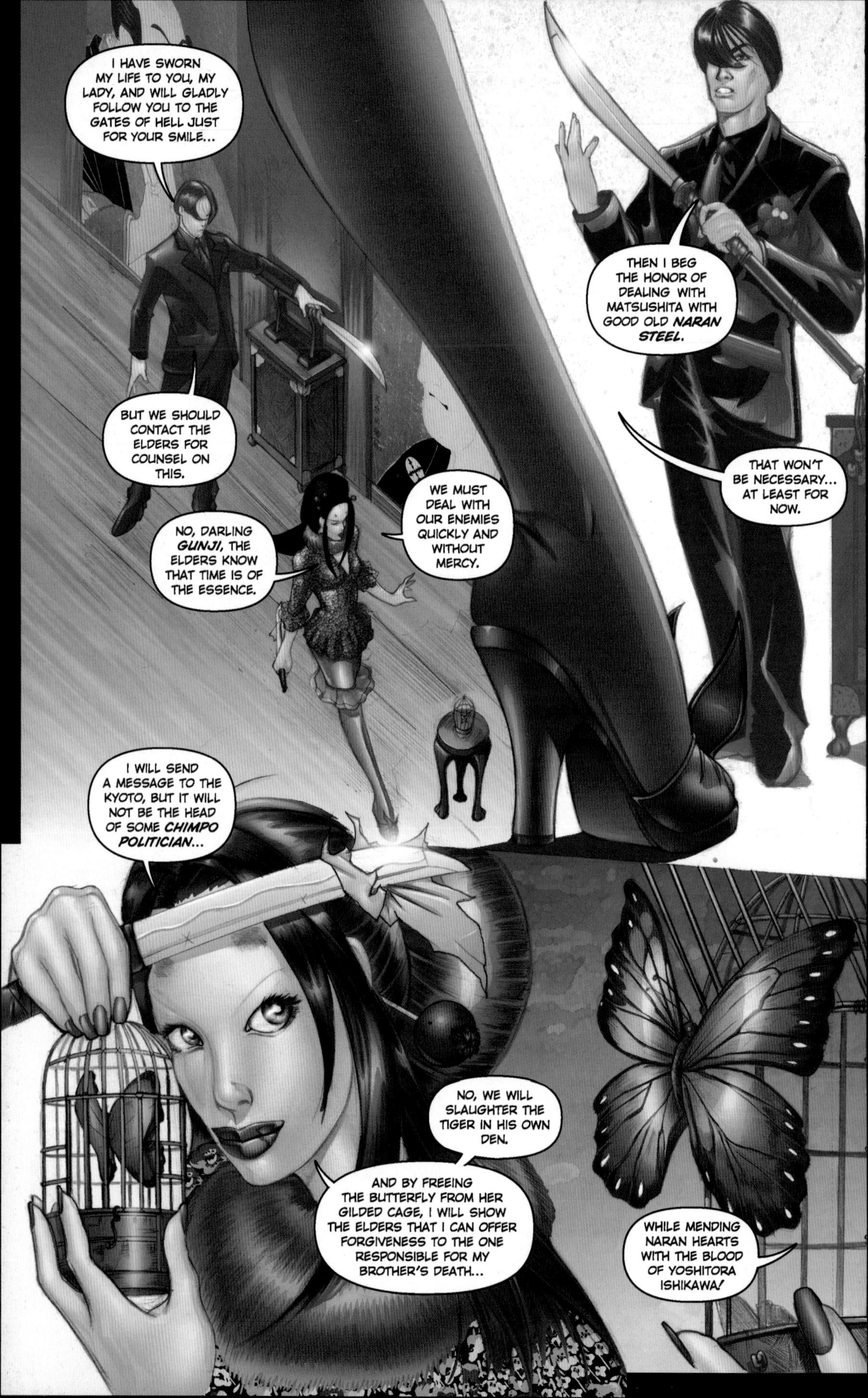
I HAVE SWORN MY LIFE TO YOU, MY LADY, AND WILL GLADLY FOLLOW YOU TO THE GATES OF HELL JUST FOR YOUR SMILE...
BUT WE SHOULD CONTACT THE ELDERS FOR COUNSEL ON THIS.
NO, DARLING GUNJI, THE ELDERS KNOW THAT TIME IS OF THE ESSENCE.
WE MUST DEAL WITH OUR ENEMIES QUICKLY AND WITHOUT MERCY.
THEN I BEG THE HONOR OF DEALING WITH MATSUSHITA WITH GOOD OLD NARAN STEEL.
THAT WON'T BE NECESSARY... AT LEAST FOR NOW.
I WILL SEND A MESSAGE TO THE KYOTO, BUT IT WILL NOT BE THE HEAD OF SOME CHIMPO POLITICIAN...
NO, WE WILL SLAUGHTER THE TIGER IN HIS OWN DEN.
AND BY FREEING THE BUTTERFLY FROM HER GILDED CAGE, I WILL SHOW THE ELDERS THAT I CAN OFFER FORGIVENESS TO THE ONE RESPONSIBLE FOR MY BROTHER'S DEATH...
WHILE MENDING NARAN HEARTS WITH THE BLOOD OF YOSHITORA ISHIKAWA!

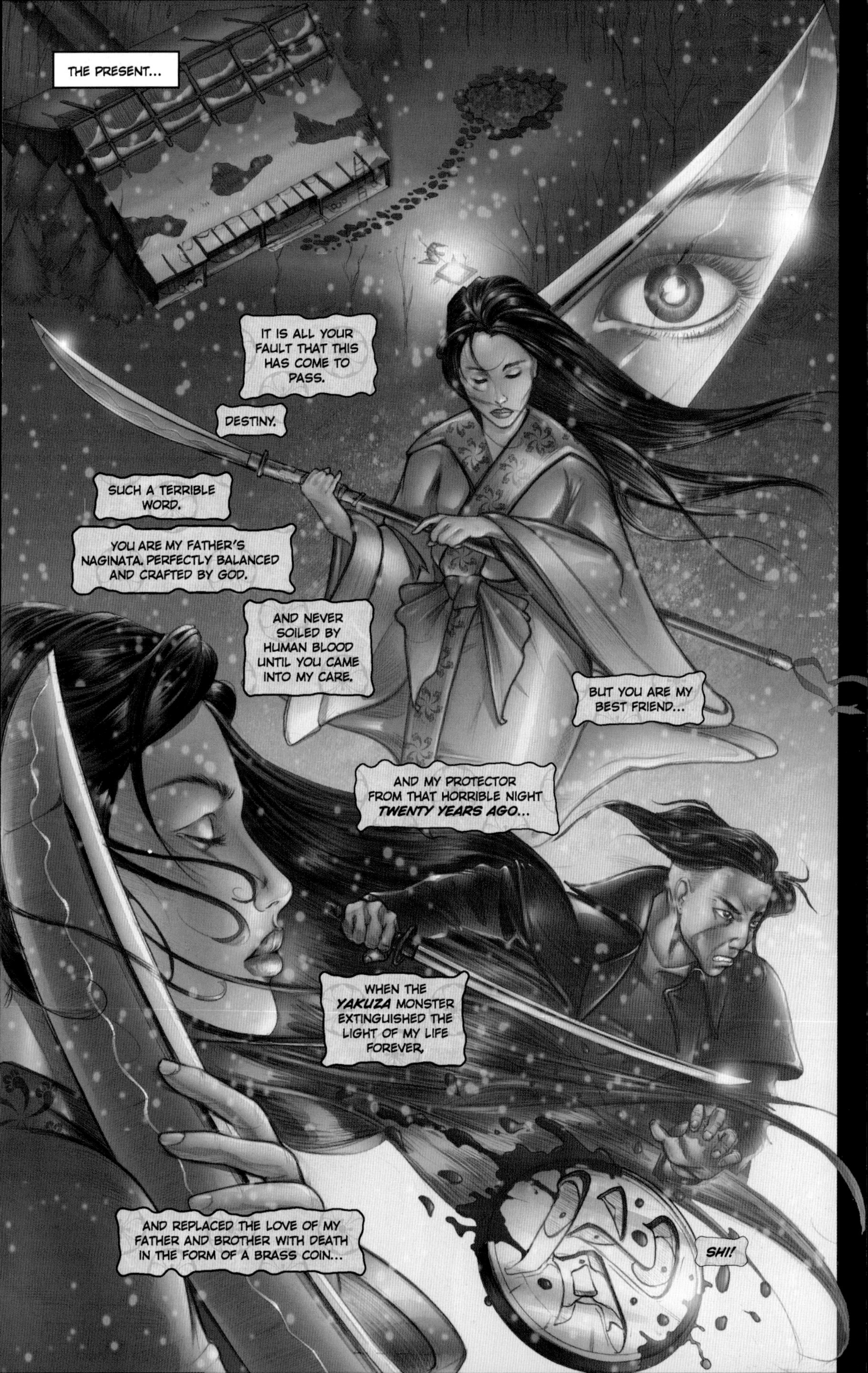
THE PRESENT...
IT IS ALL YOUR FAULT THAT THIS HAS COME TO PASS.
DESTINY.
SUCH A TERRIBLE WORD.
YOU ARE MY FATHER'S NAGINATA. PERFECTLY BALANCED AND CRAFTED BY GOD.
AND NEVER SOILED BY HUMAN BLOOD UNTIL YOU CAME INTO MY CARE.
BUT YOU ARE MY BEST FRIEND...
AND MY PROTECTOR FROM THAT HORRIBLE NIGHT *TWENTY YEARS AGO...*
WHEN THE *YAKUZA* MONSTER EXTINGUISHED THE LIGHT OF MY LIFE FOREVER,
AND REPLACED THE LOVE OF MY FATHER AND BROTHER WITH DEATH IN THE FORM OF A BRASS COIN...
SHI!

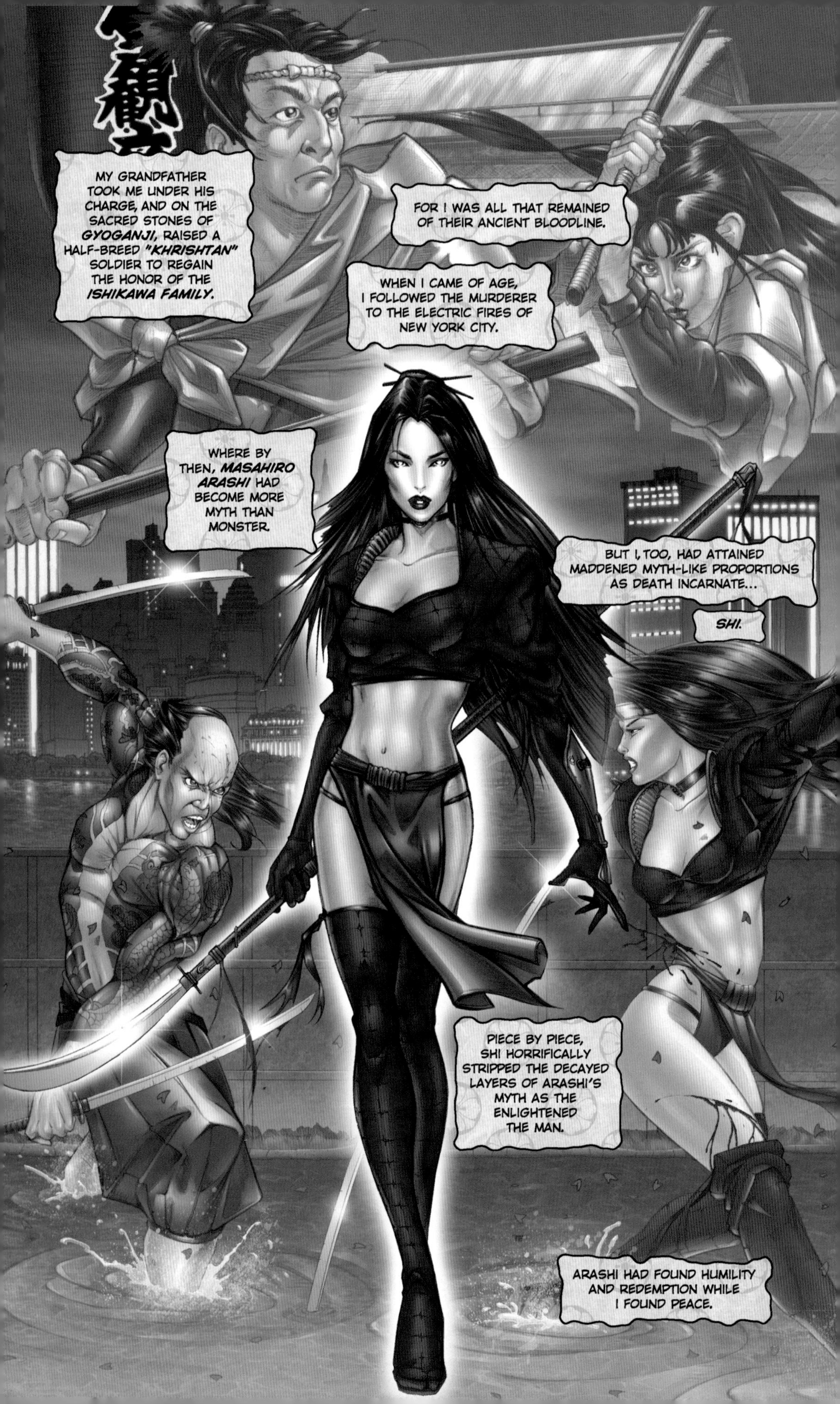
MY GRANDFATHER TOOK ME UNDER HIS CHARGE, AND ON THE SACRED STONES OF *GYOGANJI,* RAISED A HALF-BREED *"KHRISHTAN"* SOLDIER TO REGAIN THE HONOR OF THE *ISHIKAWA FAMILY.*
FOR I WAS ALL THAT REMAINED OF THEIR ANCIENT BLOODLINE.
WHEN I CAME OF AGE, I FOLLOWED THE MURDERER TO THE ELECTRIC FIRES OF NEW YORK CITY.
WHERE BY THEN, *MASAHIRO ARASHI* HAD BECOME MORE MYTH THAN MONSTER.
BUT I, TOO, HAD ATTAINED MADDENED MYTH-LIKE PROPORTIONS AS DEATH INCARNATE...
SHI.
PIECE BY PIECE, SHI HORRIFICALLY STRIPPED THE DECAYED LAYERS OF ARASHI'S MYTH AS THE ENLIGHTENED THE MAN.
ARASHI HAD FOUND HUMILITY AND REDEMPTION WHILE I FOUND PEACE.

BUT FATE, LIKE DESTINY, IS INDEED CRUEL, AND LOVES THE BLOOD OF INNOCENTS.
THE RESULTS OF MY VICTORIOUS ACTIONS AGAINST ARASHI SOWED DIVISION IN THE RANKS OF YOSHITORA'S KYOTO SOHEI.
WITH MANY OF THE YOUNGER, MORE IMPRESSIONABLE WARRIORS SEEKING CHRISTIANITY...
AFTER ALL, IT WAS MY "FAITH" THAT MADE ME LEGEND.
AND MY MOTHER *CATHERINE*, A PRISONER.
WITH THE HELP OF MY BEST FRIEND *TOMOE*, I WAS ABLE TO SAVE HER LIFE...
BUT THE PRICE PAID FOR AN ALLIANCE WITH NARA'S MOST CUNNING WARRIOR WAS OVER *100* KYOTO BROTHERS AND SISTERS SLAUGHTERED AT *KAMISHIMA*.
CRACK!
WHAT WAS THAT?

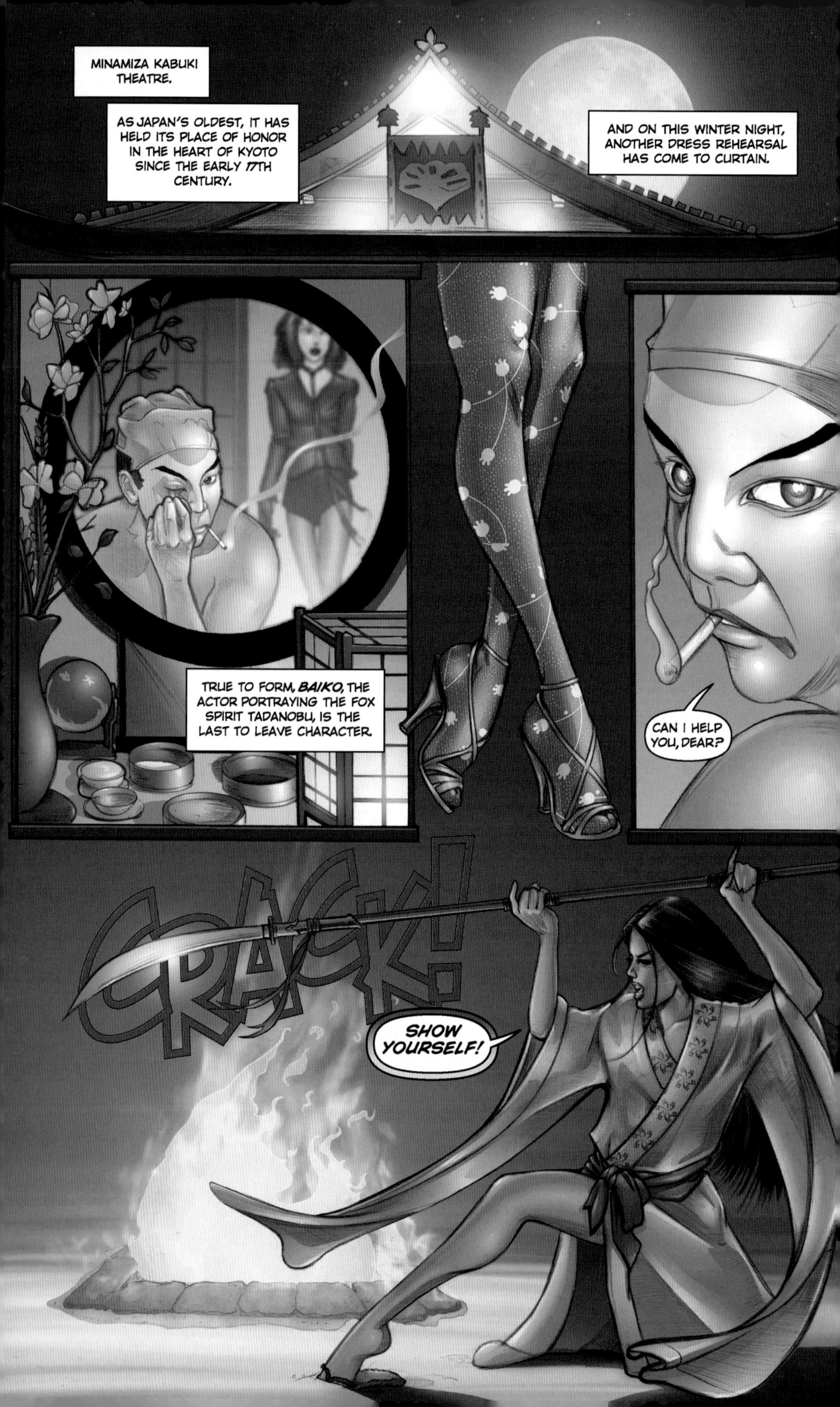
MINAMIZA KABUKI THEATRE.
AS JAPAN'S OLDEST, IT HAS HELD ITS PLACE OF HONOR IN THE HEART OF KYOTO SINCE THE EARLY 17TH CENTURY.
AND ON THIS WINTER NIGHT, ANOTHER DRESS REHEARSAL HAS COME TO CURTAIN.
TRUE TO FORM, BAIKO, THE ACTOR PORTRAYING THE FOX SPIRIT TADANOBU, IS THE LAST TO LEAVE CHARACTER.
CAN I HELP YOU, DEAR?
CRACK!
SHOW YOURSELF!

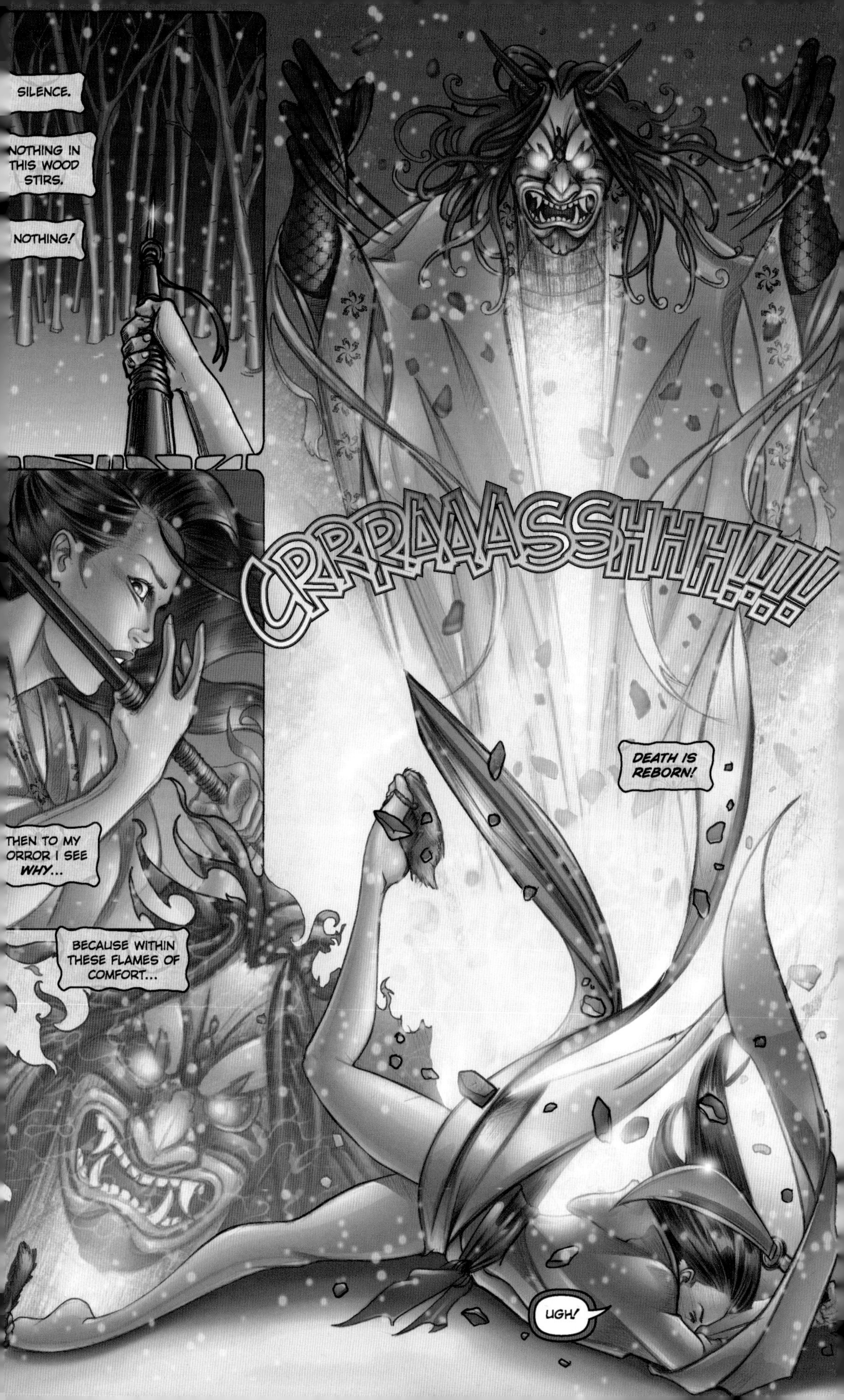
SILENCE.
NOTHING IN THIS WOOD STIRS.
NOTHING!
THEN TO MY ORROR I SEE WHY...
BECAUSE WITHIN THESE FLAMES OF COMFORT...
CRRRAAASSHHHH!!!!
DEATH IS REBORN!
UGH!

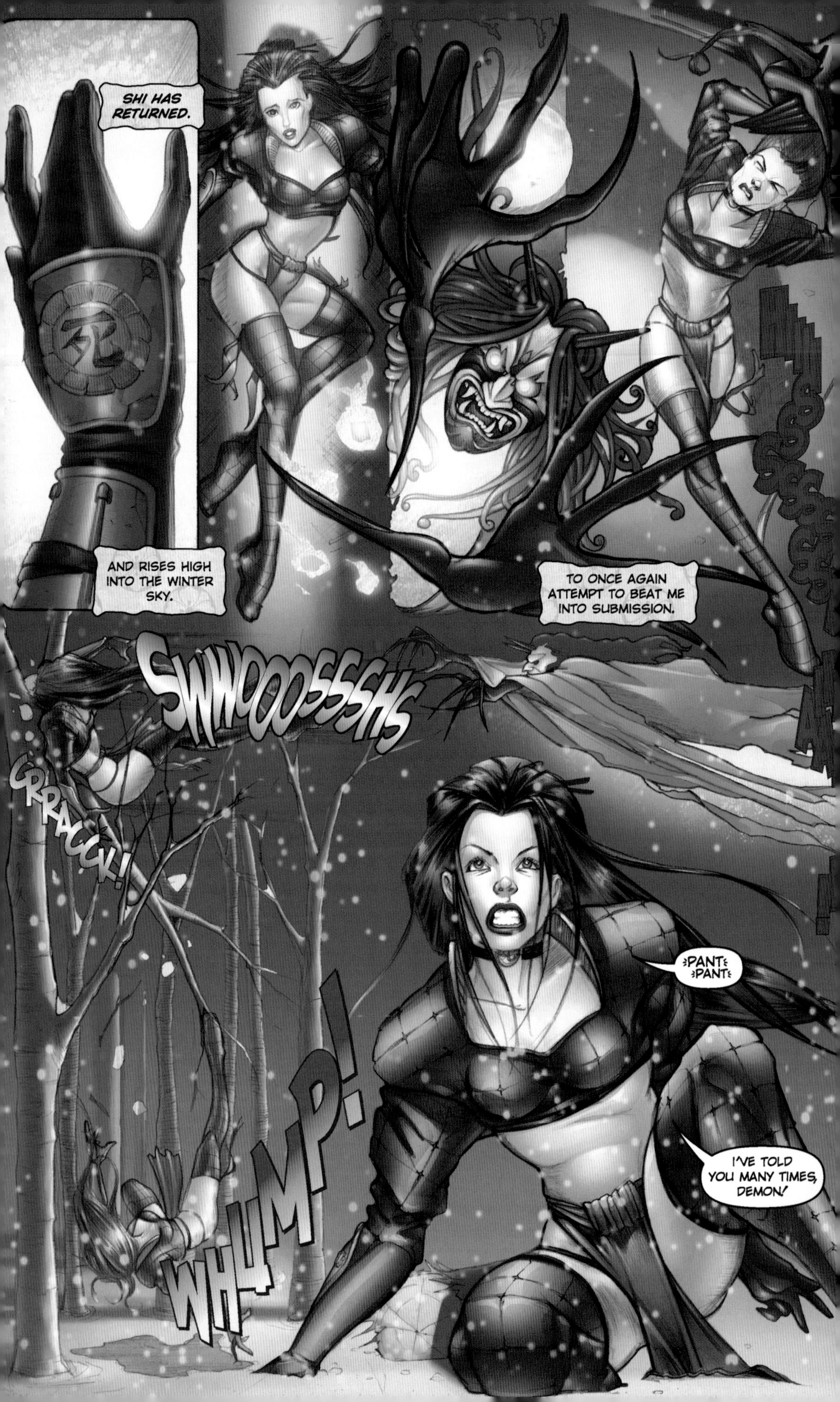
SHI HAS RETURNED.
AND RISES HIGH INTO THE WINTER SKY.
TO ONCE AGAIN ATTEMPT TO BEAT ME INTO SUBMISSION.
SWWOOOSSSSHS
CRRACCCK!
WHUMP!
PANT PANT
I'VE TOLD YOU MANY TIMES, DEMON!

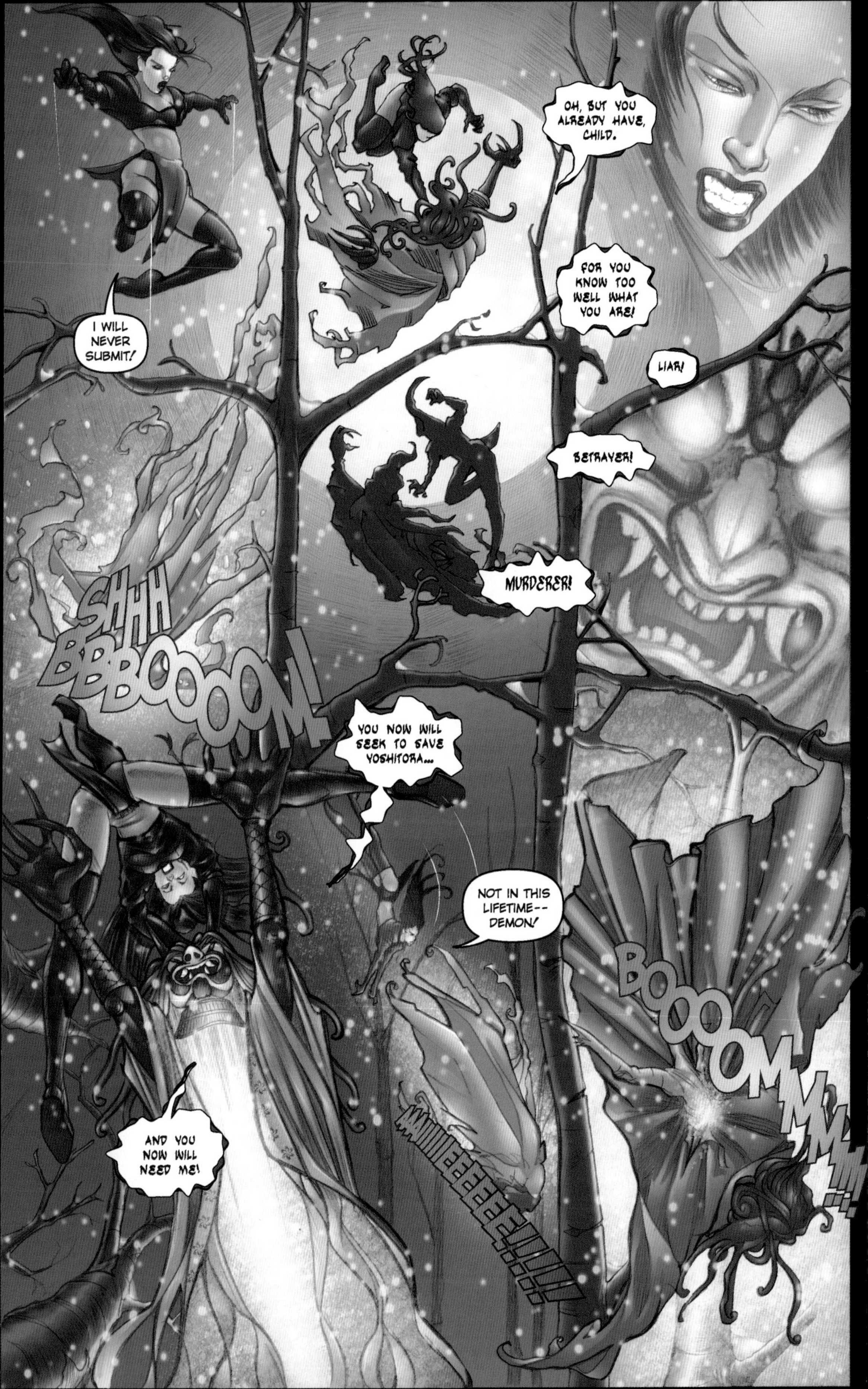
I WILL NEVER SUBMIT!
OH, BUT YOU ALREADY HAVE, CHILD.
FOR YOU KNOW TOO WELL WHAT YOU ARE!
LIAR!
BETRAYER!
MURDERER!
SHHH BBBOOOOOM!
YOU NOW WILL SEEK TO SAVE YOSHITORA...
NOT IN THIS LIFETIME--DEMON!
BOOOOMMM...
AND YOU NOW WILL NEED ME!

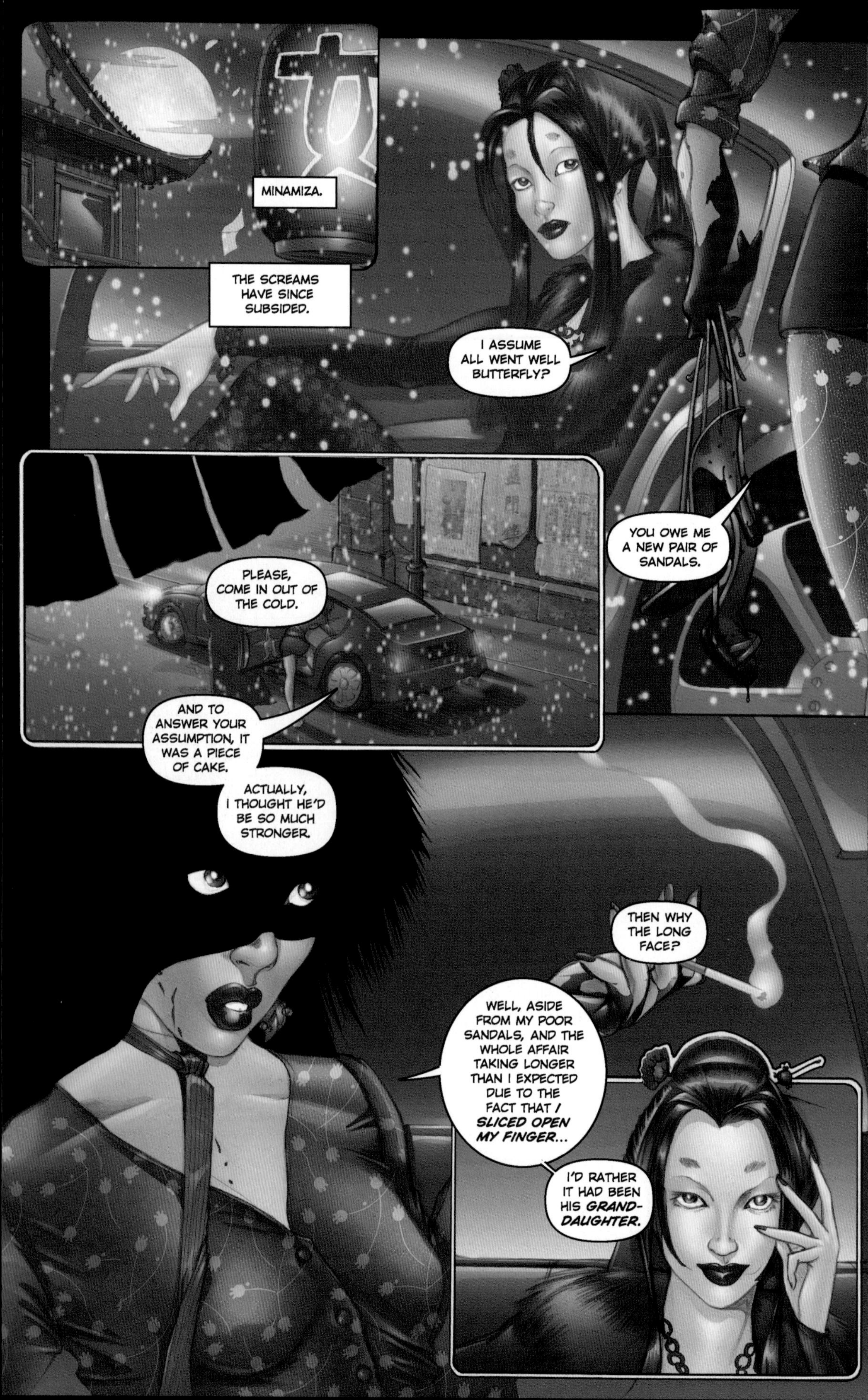

MINAMIZA.
THE SCREAMS HAVE SINCE SUBSIDED.
I ASSUME ALL WENT WELL BUTTERFLY?
YOU OWE ME A NEW PAIR OF SANDALS.
PLEASE, COME IN OUT OF THE COLD.
AND TO ANSWER YOUR ASSUMPTION, IT WAS A PIECE OF CAKE.
ACTUALLY, I THOUGHT HE'D BE SO MUCH STRONGER.
THEN WHY THE LONG FACE?
WELL, ASIDE FROM MY POOR SANDALS, AND THE WHOLE AFFAIR TAKING LONGER THAN I EXPECTED DUE TO THE FACT THAT *I SLICED OPEN MY FINGER...*
I'D RATHER IT HAD BEEN HIS *GRAND-DAUGHTER.*

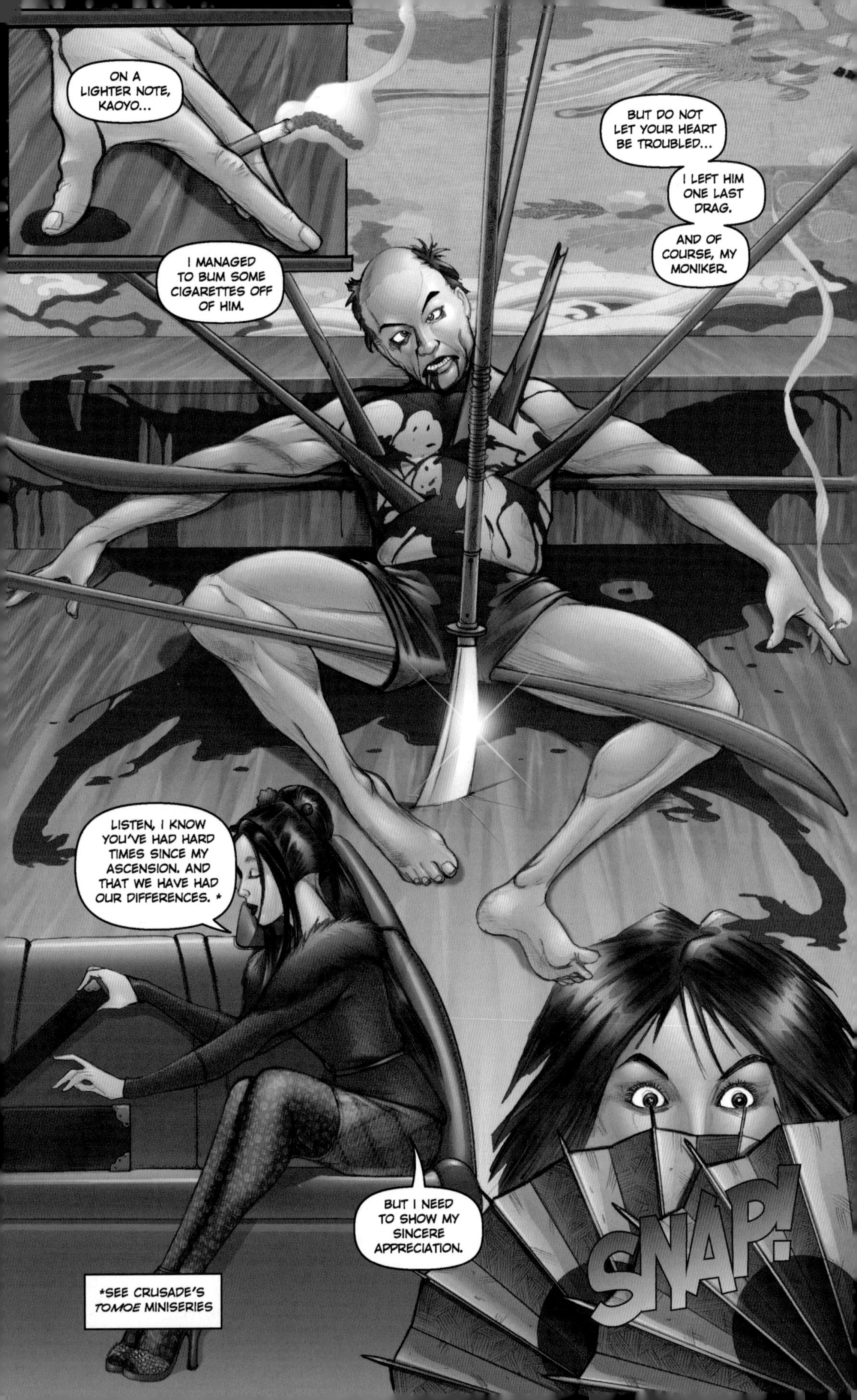
ON A LIGHTER NOTE, KAOYO...
I MANAGED TO BUM SOME CIGARETTES OFF OF HIM.
BUT DO NOT LET YOUR HEART BE TROUBLED...
I LEFT HIM ONE LAST DRAG.
AND OF COURSE, MY MONIKER.
LISTEN, I KNOW YOU'VE HAD HARD TIMES SINCE MY ASCENSION. AND THAT WE HAVE HAD OUR DIFFERENCES. *
BUT I NEED TO SHOW MY SINCERE APPRECIATION.
SNAP!
*SEE CRUSADE'S *TOMOE* MINISERIES

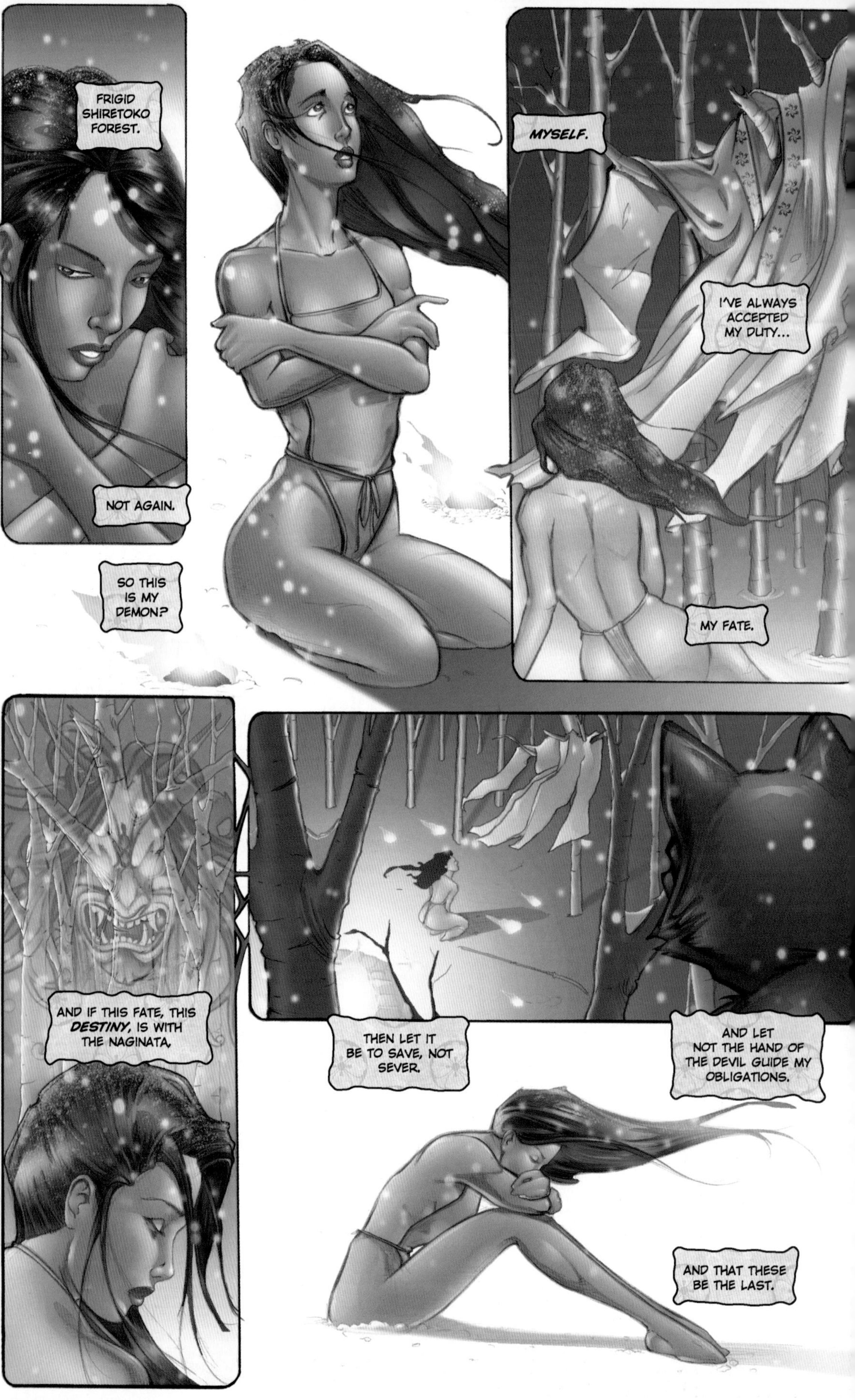
FRIGID SHIRETOKO FOREST.
NOT AGAIN.
SO THIS IS MY DEMON?
MYSELF.
I'VE ALWAYS ACCEPTED MY DUTY...
MY FATE.
AND IF THIS FATE, THIS *DESTINY*, IS WITH THE NAGINATA,
THEN LET IT BE TO SAVE, NOT SEVER.
AND LET NOT THE HAND OF THE DEVIL GUIDE MY OBLIGATIONS.
AND THAT THESE BE THE LAST.

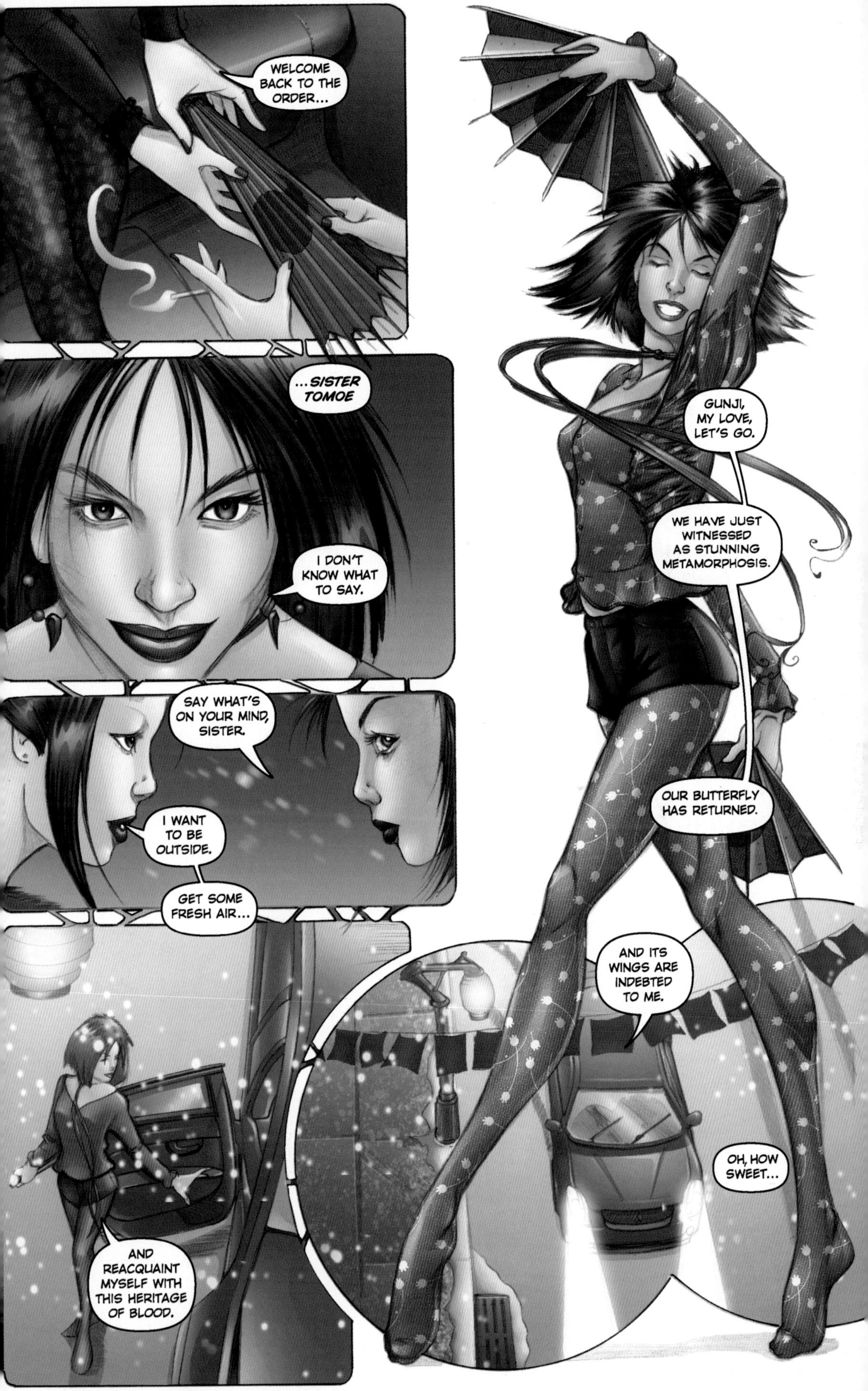
WELCOME BACK TO THE ORDER...
...SISTER TOMOE
I DON'T KNOW WHAT TO SAY.
SAY WHAT'S ON YOUR MIND, SISTER.
I WANT TO BE OUTSIDE.
GET SOME FRESH AIR...
AND REACQUAINT MYSELF WITH THIS HERITAGE OF BLOOD.
GUNJI, MY LOVE, LET'S GO.
WE HAVE JUST WITNESSED AS STUNNING METAMORPHOSIS.
OUR BUTTERFLY HAS RETURNED.
AND ITS WINGS ARE INDEBTED TO ME.
OH, HOW SWEET...

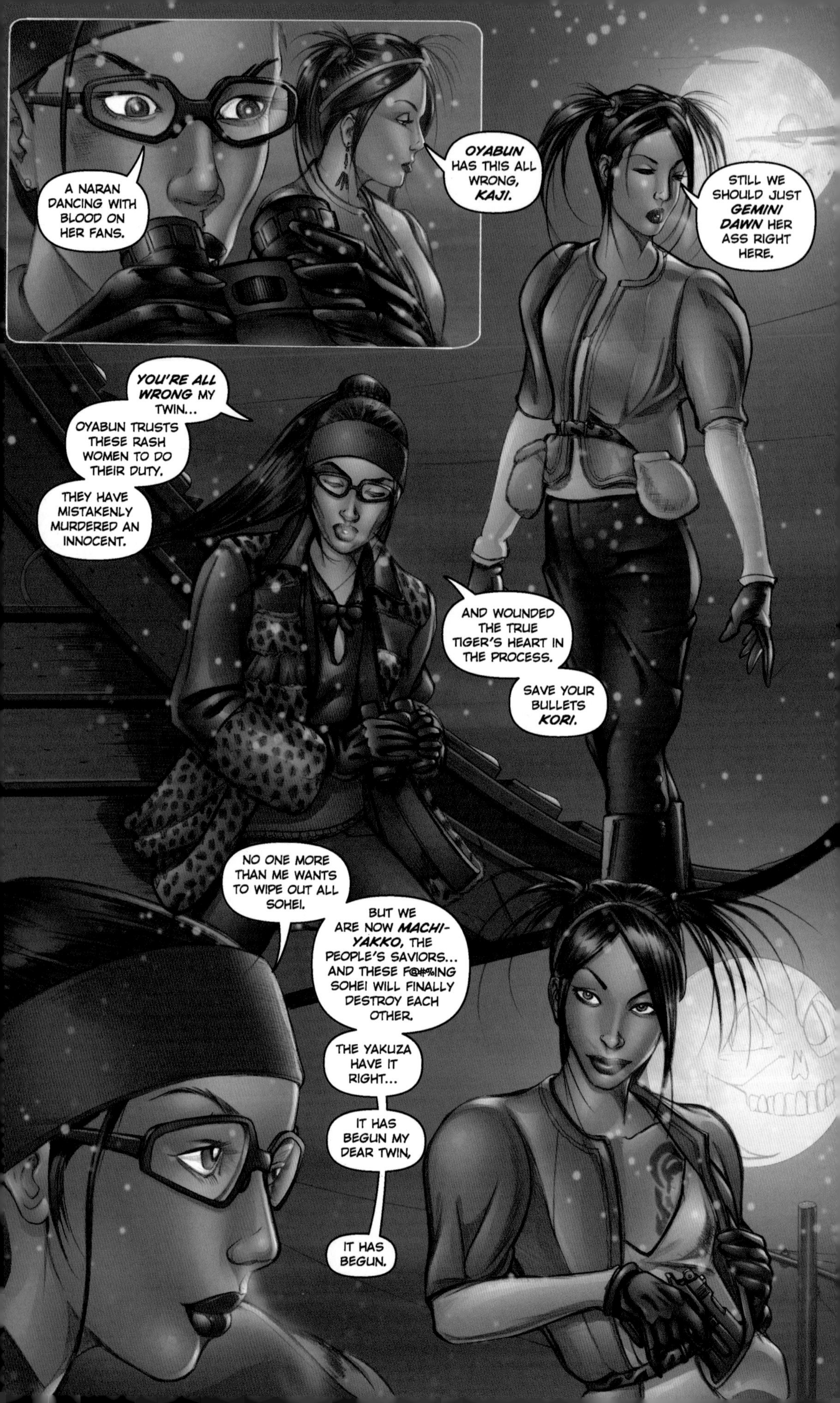
A NARAN DANCING WITH BLOOD ON HER FANS.
OYABUN HAS THIS ALL WRONG, KAJI.
STILL WE SHOULD JUST GEMINI DAWN HER ASS RIGHT HERE.
YOU'RE ALL WRONG MY TWIN...
OYABUN TRUSTS THESE RASH WOMEN TO DO THEIR DUTY.
THEY HAVE MISTAKENLY MURDERED AN INNOCENT.
AND WOUNDED THE TRUE TIGER'S HEART IN THE PROCESS.
SAVE YOUR BULLETS KORI.
NO ONE MORE THAN ME WANTS TO WIPE OUT ALL SOHEI.
BUT WE ARE NOW MACHI-YAKKO, THE PEOPLE'S SAVIORS... AND THESE F@#%ING SOHEI WILL FINALLY DESTROY EACH OTHER.
THE YAKUZA HAVE IT RIGHT...
IT HAS BEGUN MY DEAR TWIN,
IT HAS BEGUN.

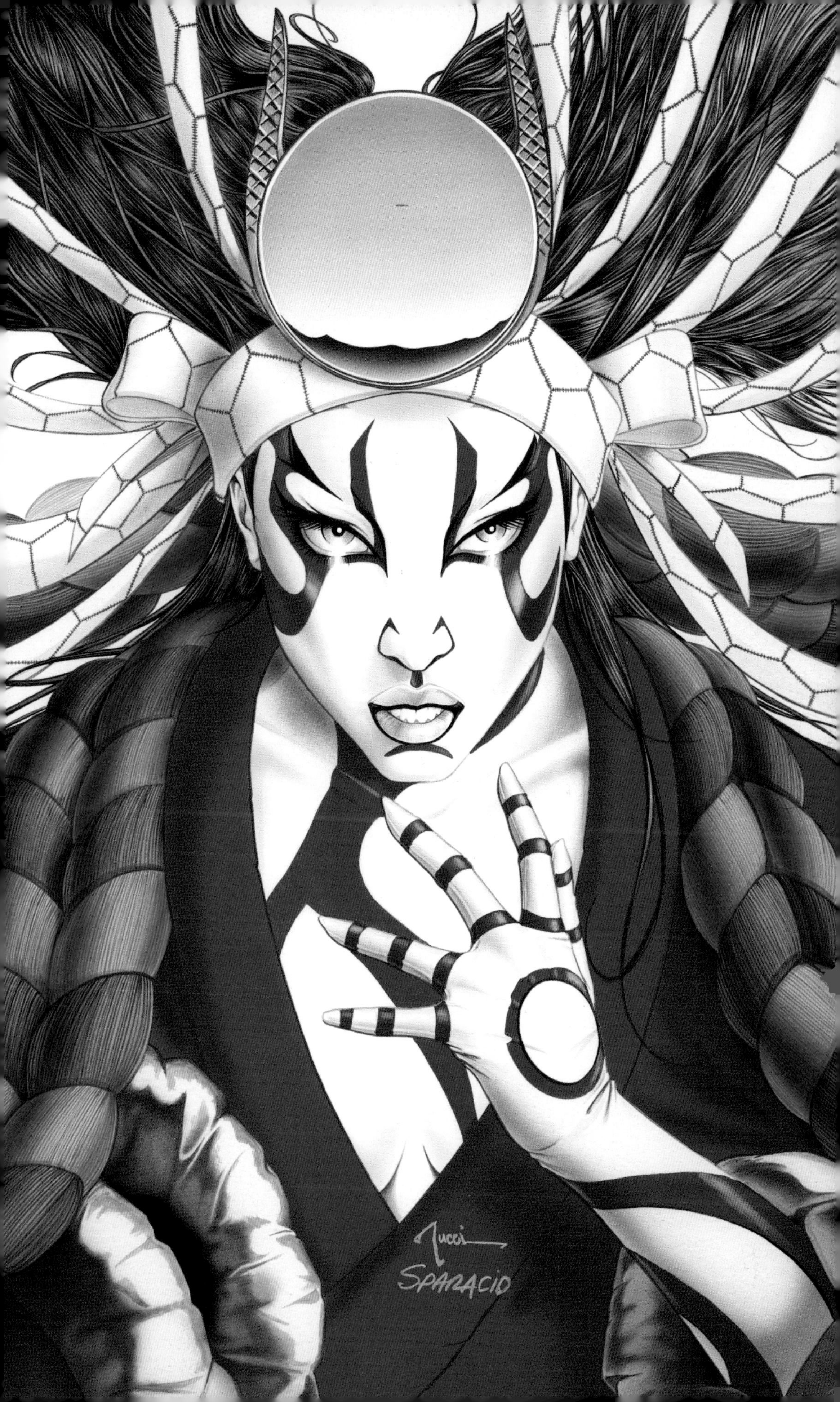
Tucci
SPARACIO

STORY, SCRIPT, AND ILLUSTRATION
BILLY TUCCI

SCRIPT
J.C. VAUGHN

COLORS
BRETT R. SMITH

COLOR FLATS
JOHN WILSON

LETTERING
MARSHALL DILLON

ART SCANNING AND CLEANUP
KRISTEN PURDY AND MIKE KENZINE

COVER
BILLY TUCCI AND MARK SPARACIO

ORIGINAL FASHIONS
ANNA SUI

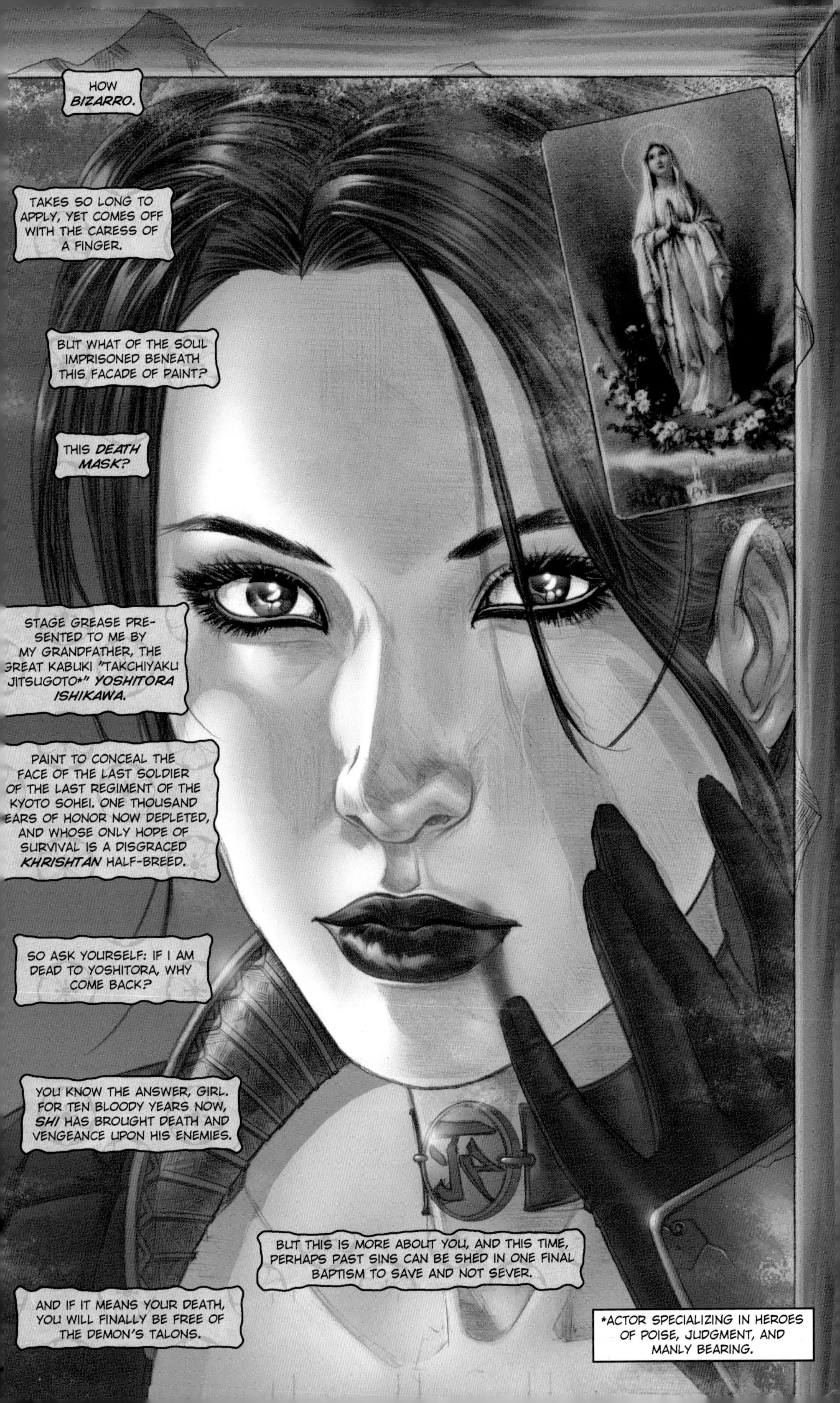
HOW BIZARRO.
TAKES SO LONG TO APPLY, YET COMES OFF WITH THE CARESS OF A FINGER.
BUT WHAT OF THE SOUL IMPRISONED BENEATH THIS FACADE OF PAINT?
THIS DEATH MASK?
STAGE GREASE PRESENTED TO ME BY MY GRANDFATHER, THE GREAT KABUKI "TAKCHIYAKU JITSUGOTO*" YOSHITORA ISHIKAWA.
PAINT TO CONCEAL THE FACE OF THE LAST SOLDIER OF THE LAST REGIMENT OF THE KYOTO SOHEI. ONE THOUSAND YEARS OF HONOR NOW DEPLETED, AND WHOSE ONLY HOPE OF SURVIVAL IS A DISGRACED KHRISHTAN HALF-BREED.
SO ASK YOURSELF: IF I AM DEAD TO YOSHITORA, WHY COME BACK?
YOU KNOW THE ANSWER, GIRL. FOR TEN BLOODY YEARS NOW, SHI HAS BROUGHT DEATH AND VENGEANCE UPON HIS ENEMIES.
BUT THIS IS MORE ABOUT YOU, AND THIS TIME, PERHAPS PAST SINS CAN BE SHED IN ONE FINAL BAPTISM TO SAVE AND NOT SEVER.
AND IF IT MEANS YOUR DEATH, YOU WILL FINALLY BE FREE OF THE DEMON'S TALONS.
*ACTOR SPECIALIZING IN HEROES OF POISE, JUDGMENT, AND MANLY BEARING.

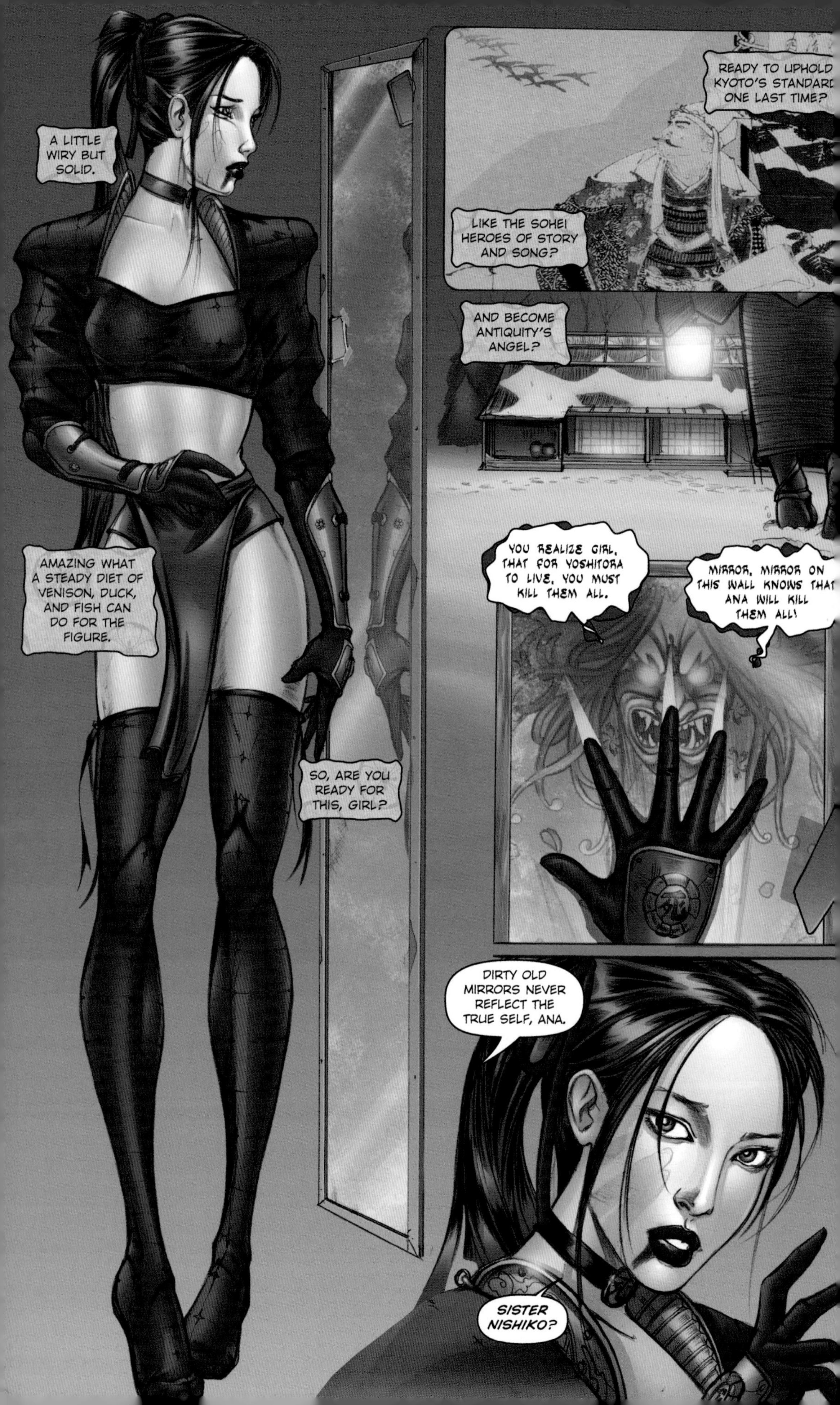
A LITTLE WIRY BUT SOLID.
AMAZING WHAT A STEADY DIET OF VENISON, DUCK, AND FISH CAN DO FOR THE FIGURE.
SO, ARE YOU READY FOR THIS, GIRL?
READY TO UPHOLD KYOTO'S STANDARD ONE LAST TIME?
LIKE THE SOHEI HEROES OF STORY AND SONG?
AND BECOME ANTIQUITY'S ANGEL?
YOU REALIZE GIRL, THAT FOR YOSHITORA TO LIVE, YOU MUST KILL THEM ALL.
MIRROR, MIRROR ON THIS WALL KNOWS THAT ANA WILL KILL THEM ALL!
DIRTY OLD MIRRORS NEVER REFLECT THE TRUE SELF, ANA.
SISTER NISHIKO?

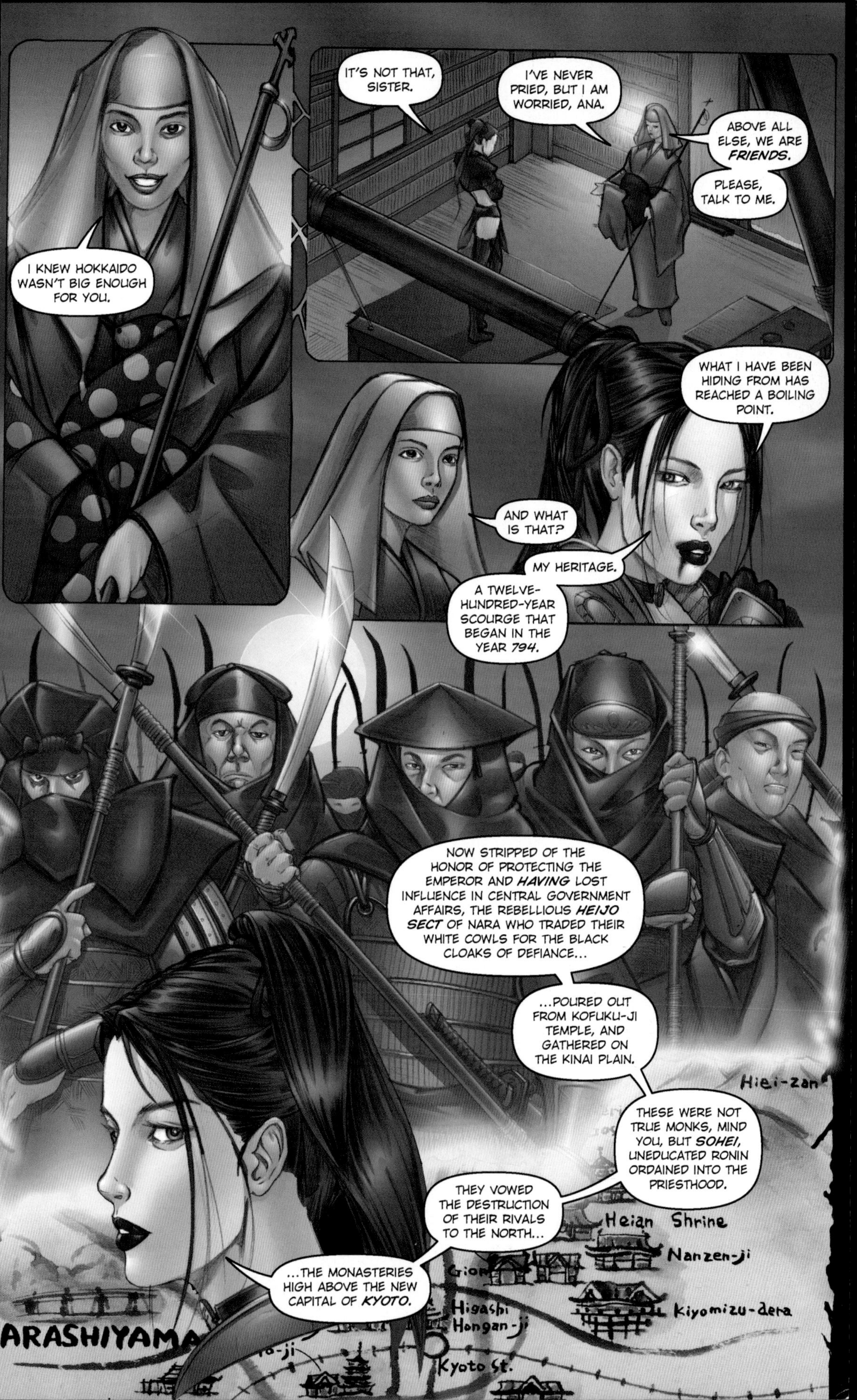
I KNEW HOKKAIDO WASN'T BIG ENOUGH FOR YOU.
IT'S NOT THAT, SISTER.
I'VE NEVER PRIED, BUT I AM WORRIED, ANA.
ABOVE ALL ELSE, WE ARE *FRIENDS*.
PLEASE, TALK TO ME.
WHAT I HAVE BEEN HIDING FROM HAS REACHED A BOILING POINT.
AND WHAT IS THAT?
MY HERITAGE.
A TWELVE-HUNDRED-YEAR SCOURGE THAT BEGAN IN THE YEAR *794*.
NOW STRIPPED OF THE HONOR OF PROTECTING THE EMPEROR AND *HAVING* LOST INFLUENCE IN CENTRAL GOVERNMENT AFFAIRS, THE REBELLIOUS *HEIJO SECT* OF NARA WHO TRADED THEIR WHITE COWLS FOR THE BLACK CLOAKS OF DEFIANCE...
...POURED OUT FROM KOFUKU-JI TEMPLE, AND GATHERED ON THE KINAI PLAIN.
THESE WERE NOT TRUE MONKS, MIND YOU, BUT *SOHEI*, UNEDUCATED RONIN ORDAINED INTO THE PRIESTHOOD.
THEY VOWED THE DESTRUCTION OF THEIR RIVALS TO THE NORTH...
...THE MONASTERIES HIGH ABOVE THE NEW CAPITAL OF *KYOTO*.
Hiei-zan
Heian Shrine
Nanzen-ji
Kiyomizu-dera
Higashi Hongan-ji
Kyoto St.
ARASHIYAMA

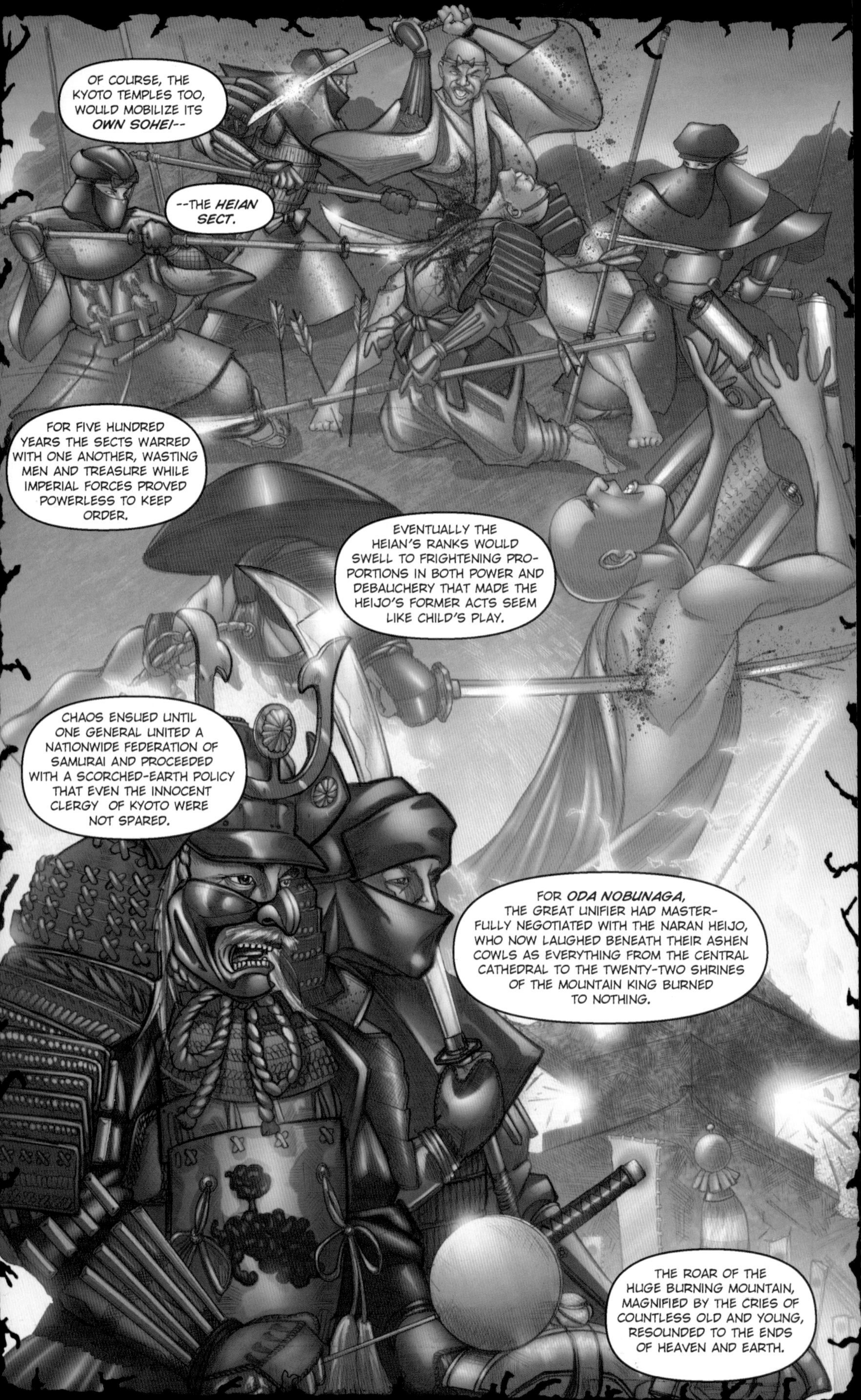

OF COURSE, THE KYOTO TEMPLES TOO, WOULD MOBILIZE ITS *OWN SOHEI*--
--THE *HEIAN SECT*.
FOR FIVE HUNDRED YEARS THE SECTS WARRED WITH ONE ANOTHER, WASTING MEN AND TREASURE WHILE IMPERIAL FORCES PROVED POWERLESS TO KEEP ORDER.
EVENTUALLY THE HEIAN'S RANKS WOULD SWELL TO FRIGHTENING PRO-PORTIONS IN BOTH POWER AND DEBAUCHERY THAT MADE THE HEIJO'S FORMER ACTS SEEM LIKE CHILD'S PLAY.
CHAOS ENSUED UNTIL ONE GENERAL UNITED A NATIONWIDE FEDERATION OF SAMURAI AND PROCEEDED WITH A SCORCHED-EARTH POLICY THAT EVEN THE INNOCENT CLERGY OF KYOTO WERE NOT SPARED.
FOR *ODA NOBUNAGA,* THE GREAT UNIFIER HAD MASTER-FULLY NEGOTIATED WITH THE NARAN HEIJO, WHO NOW LAUGHED BENEATH THEIR ASHEN COWLS AS EVERYTHING FROM THE CENTRAL CATHEDRAL TO THE TWENTY-TWO SHRINES OF THE MOUNTAIN KING BURNED TO NOTHING.
THE ROAR OF THE HUGE BURNING MOUNTAIN, MAGNIFIED BY THE CRIES OF COUNTLESS OLD AND YOUNG, RESOUNDED TO THE ENDS OF HEAVEN AND EARTH.

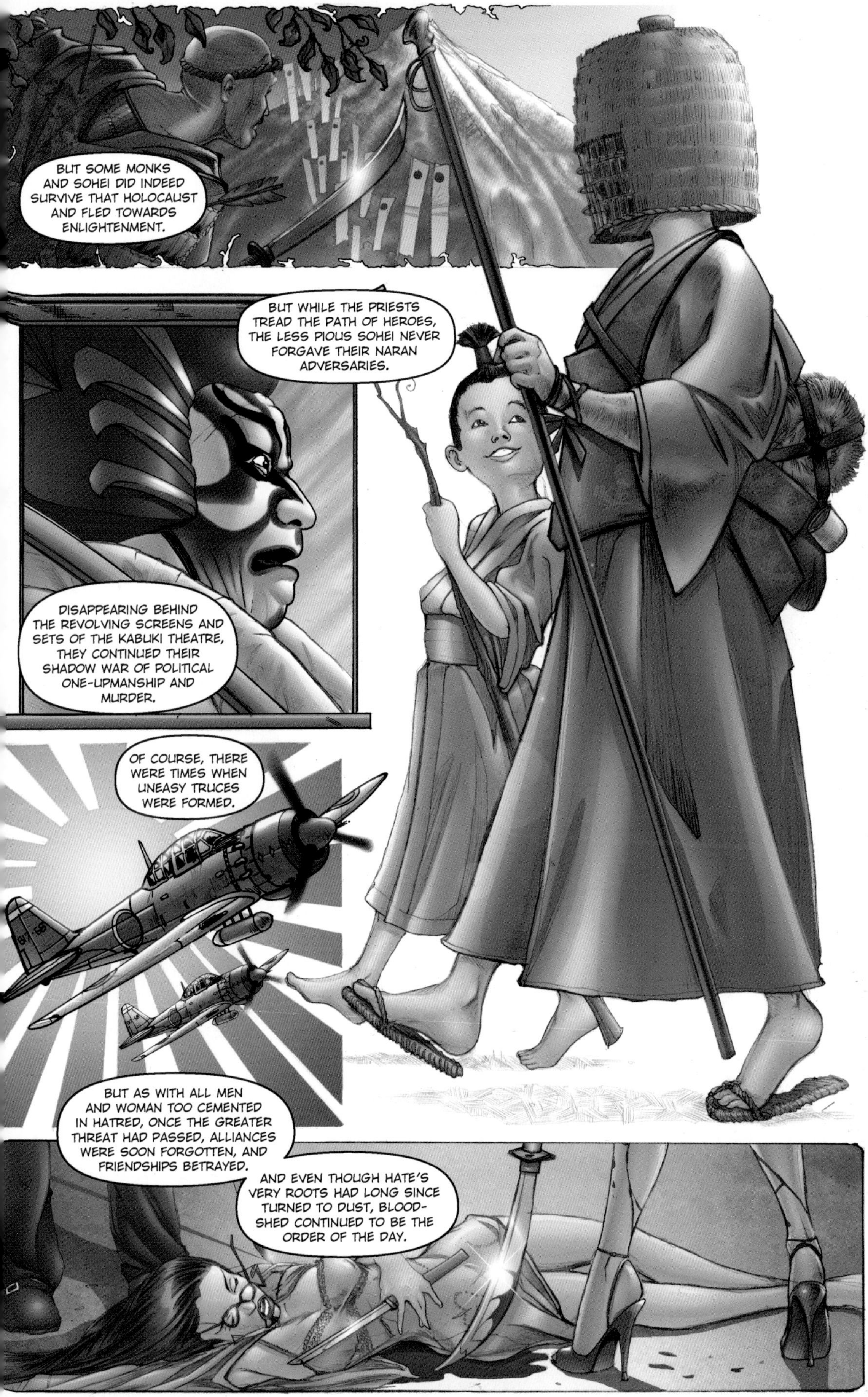

BUT SOME MONKS AND SOHEI DID INDEED SURVIVE THAT HOLOCAUST AND FLED TOWARDS ENLIGHTENMENT.
BUT WHILE THE PRIESTS TREAD THE PATH OF HEROES, THE LESS PIOUS SOHEI NEVER FORGAVE THEIR NARAN ADVERSARIES.
DISAPPEARING BEHIND THE REVOLVING SCREENS AND SETS OF THE KABUKI THEATRE, THEY CONTINUED THEIR SHADOW WAR OF POLITICAL ONE-UPMANSHIP AND MURDER.
OF COURSE, THERE WERE TIMES WHEN UNEASY TRUCES WERE FORMED.
BUT AS WITH ALL MEN AND WOMAN TOO CEMENTED IN HATRED, ONCE THE GREATER THREAT HAD PASSED, ALLIANCES WERE SOON FORGOTTEN, AND FRIENDSHIPS BETRAYED.
AND EVEN THOUGH HATE'S VERY ROOTS HAD LONG SINCE TURNED TO DUST, BLOOD-SHED CONTINUED TO BE THE ORDER OF THE DAY.

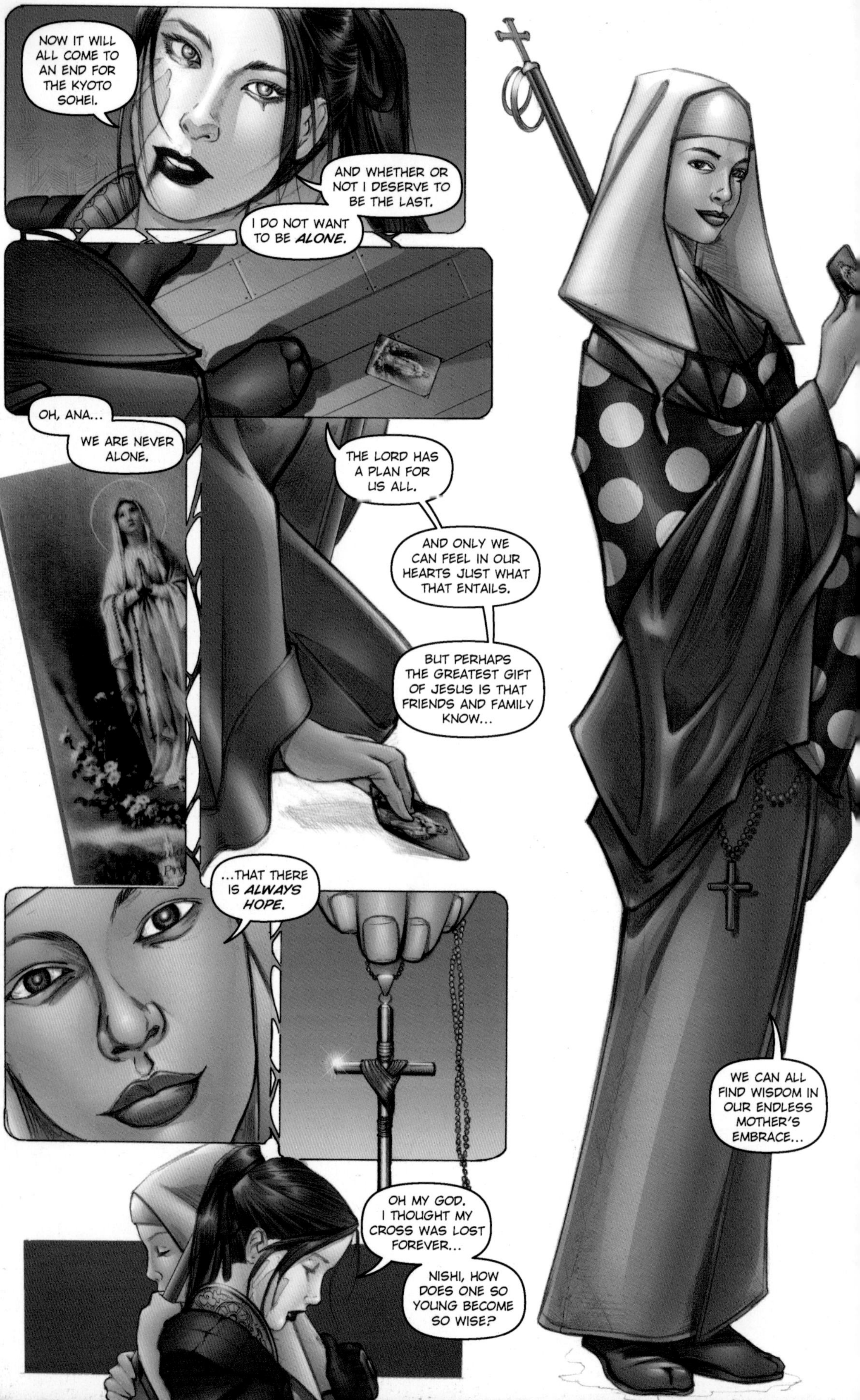
NOW IT WILL ALL COME TO AN END FOR THE KYOTO SOHEI.
AND WHETHER OR NOT I DESERVE TO BE THE LAST.
I DO NOT WANT TO BE ***ALONE.***
OH, ANA...
WE ARE NEVER ALONE.
THE LORD HAS A PLAN FOR US ALL.
AND ONLY WE CAN FEEL IN OUR HEARTS JUST WHAT THAT ENTAILS.
BUT PERHAPS THE GREATEST GIFT OF JESUS IS THAT FRIENDS AND FAMILY KNOW...
...THAT THERE IS ***ALWAYS HOPE.***
OH MY GOD. I THOUGHT MY CROSS WAS LOST FOREVER...
NISHI, HOW DOES ONE SO YOUNG BECOME SO WISE?
WE CAN ALL FIND WISDOM IN OUR ENDLESS MOTHER'S EMBRACE...

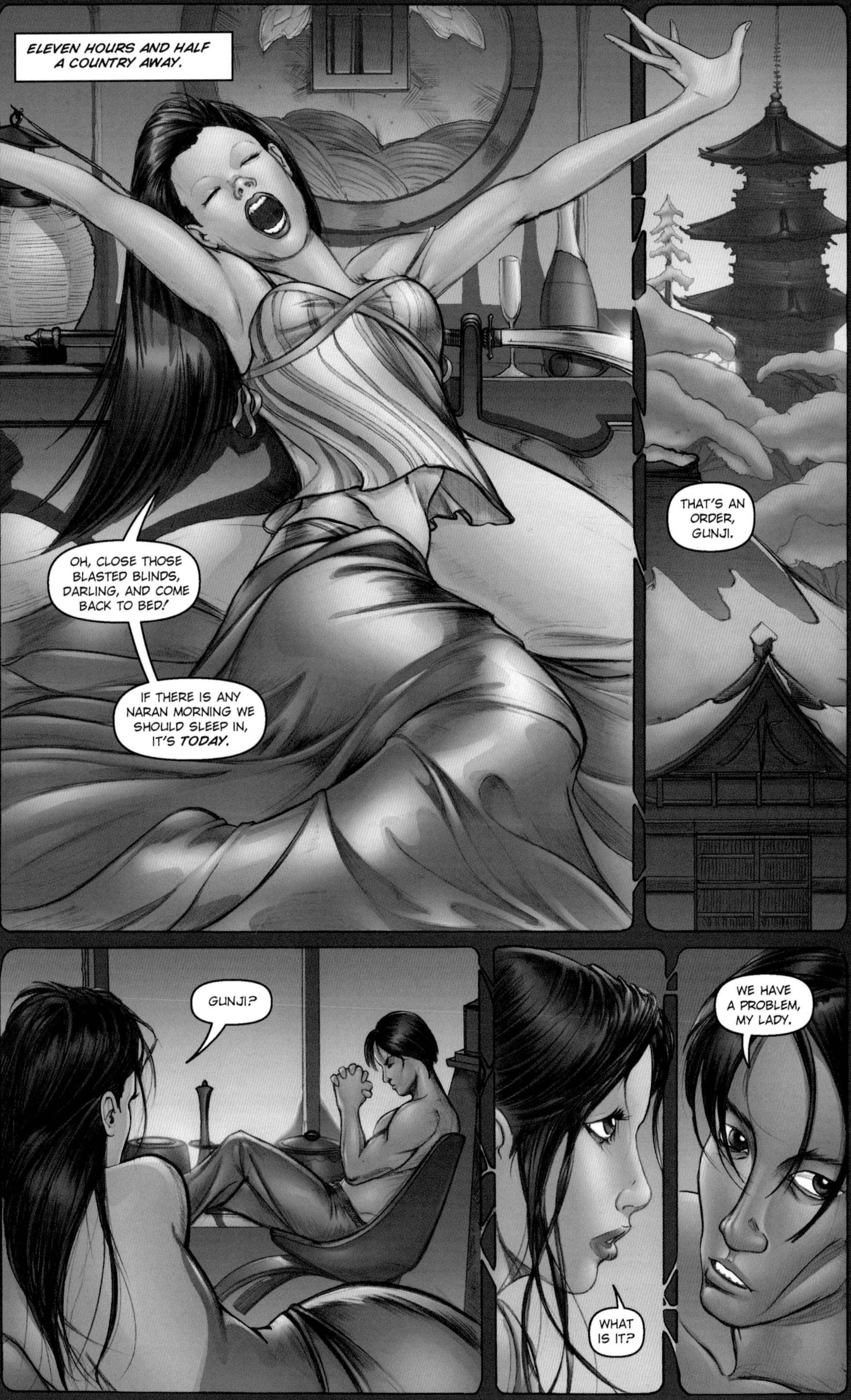
ELEVEN HOURS AND HALF A COUNTRY AWAY.
OH, CLOSE THOSE BLASTED BLINDS, DARLING, AND COME BACK TO BED!
IF THERE IS ANY NARAN MORNING WE SHOULD SLEEP IN, IT'S *TODAY.*
THAT'S AN ORDER, GUNJI.
GUNJI?
WHAT IS IT?
WE HAVE A PROBLEM, MY LADY.

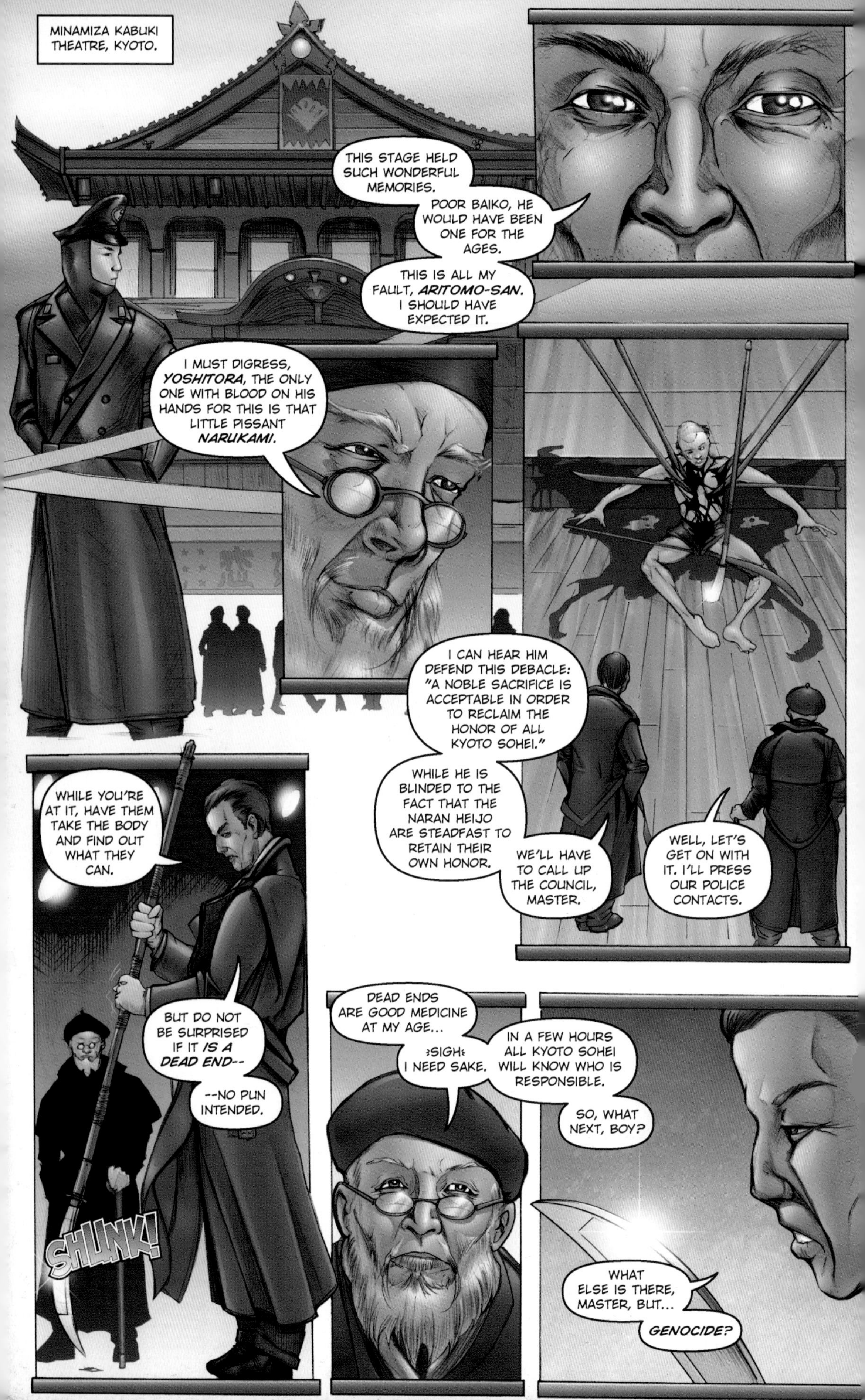
MINAMIZA KABUKI THEATRE, KYOTO.
THIS STAGE HELD SUCH WONDERFUL MEMORIES.
POOR BAIKO, HE WOULD HAVE BEEN ONE FOR THE AGES.
THIS IS ALL MY FAULT, *ARITOMO-SAN*. I SHOULD HAVE EXPECTED IT.
I MUST DIGRESS, *YOSHITORA*, THE ONLY ONE WITH BLOOD ON HIS HANDS FOR THIS IS THAT LITTLE PISSANT *NARUKAMI*.
I CAN HEAR HIM DEFEND THIS DEBACLE: "A NOBLE SACRIFICE IS ACCEPTABLE IN ORDER TO RECLAIM THE HONOR OF ALL KYOTO SOHEI."
WHILE HE IS BLINDED TO THE FACT THAT THE NARAN HEIJO ARE STEADFAST TO RETAIN THEIR OWN HONOR.
WE'LL HAVE TO CALL UP THE COUNCIL, MASTER.
WELL, LET'S GET ON WITH IT. I'LL PRESS OUR POLICE CONTACTS.
WHILE YOU'RE AT IT, HAVE THEM TAKE THE BODY AND FIND OUT WHAT THEY CAN.
BUT DO NOT BE SURPRISED IF IT *IS A DEAD END*--
--NO PUN INTENDED.
SHUNK!
DEAD ENDS ARE GOOD MEDICINE AT MY AGE...
SIGH I NEED SAKE.
IN A FEW HOURS ALL KYOTO SOHEI WILL KNOW WHO IS RESPONSIBLE.
SO, WHAT NEXT, BOY?
WHAT ELSE IS THERE, MASTER, BUT...
GENOCIDE?

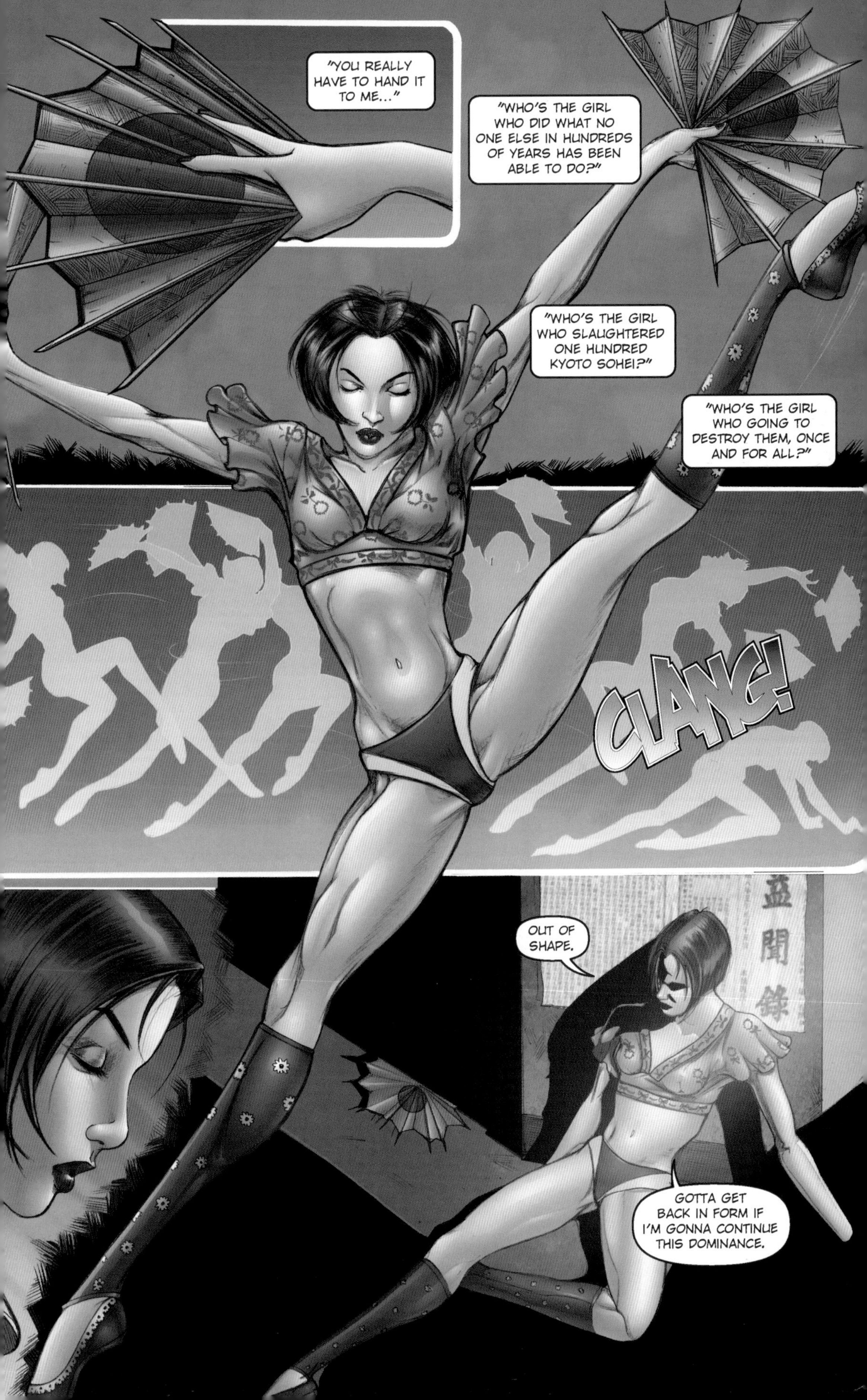
"YOU REALLY HAVE TO HAND IT TO ME..."
"WHO'S THE GIRL WHO DID WHAT NO ONE ELSE IN HUNDREDS OF YEARS HAS BEEN ABLE TO DO?"
"WHO'S THE GIRL WHO SLAUGHTERED ONE HUNDRED KYOTO SOHEI?"
"WHO'S THE GIRL WHO GOING TO DESTROY THEM, ONCE AND FOR ALL?"
CLANG!
OUT OF SHAPE.
GOTTA GET BACK IN FORM IF I'M GONNA CONTINUE THIS DOMINANCE.

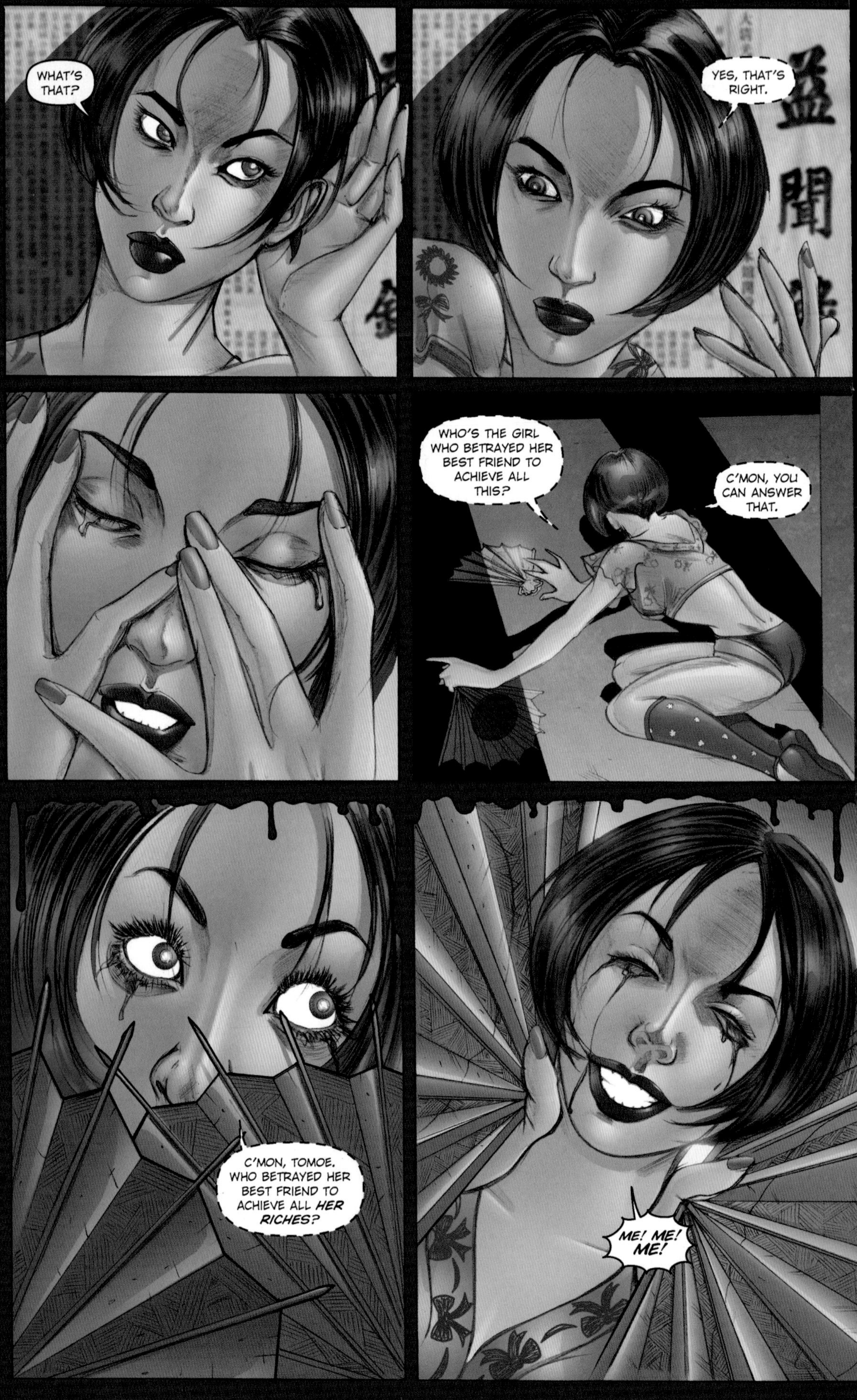
WHAT'S THAT?
YES, THAT'S RIGHT.
WHO'S THE GIRL WHO BETRAYED HER BEST FRIEND TO ACHIEVE ALL THIS?
C'MON, YOU CAN ANSWER THAT.
C'MON, TOMOE. WHO BETRAYED HER BEST FRIEND TO ACHIEVE ALL HER RICHES?
ME! ME! ME!

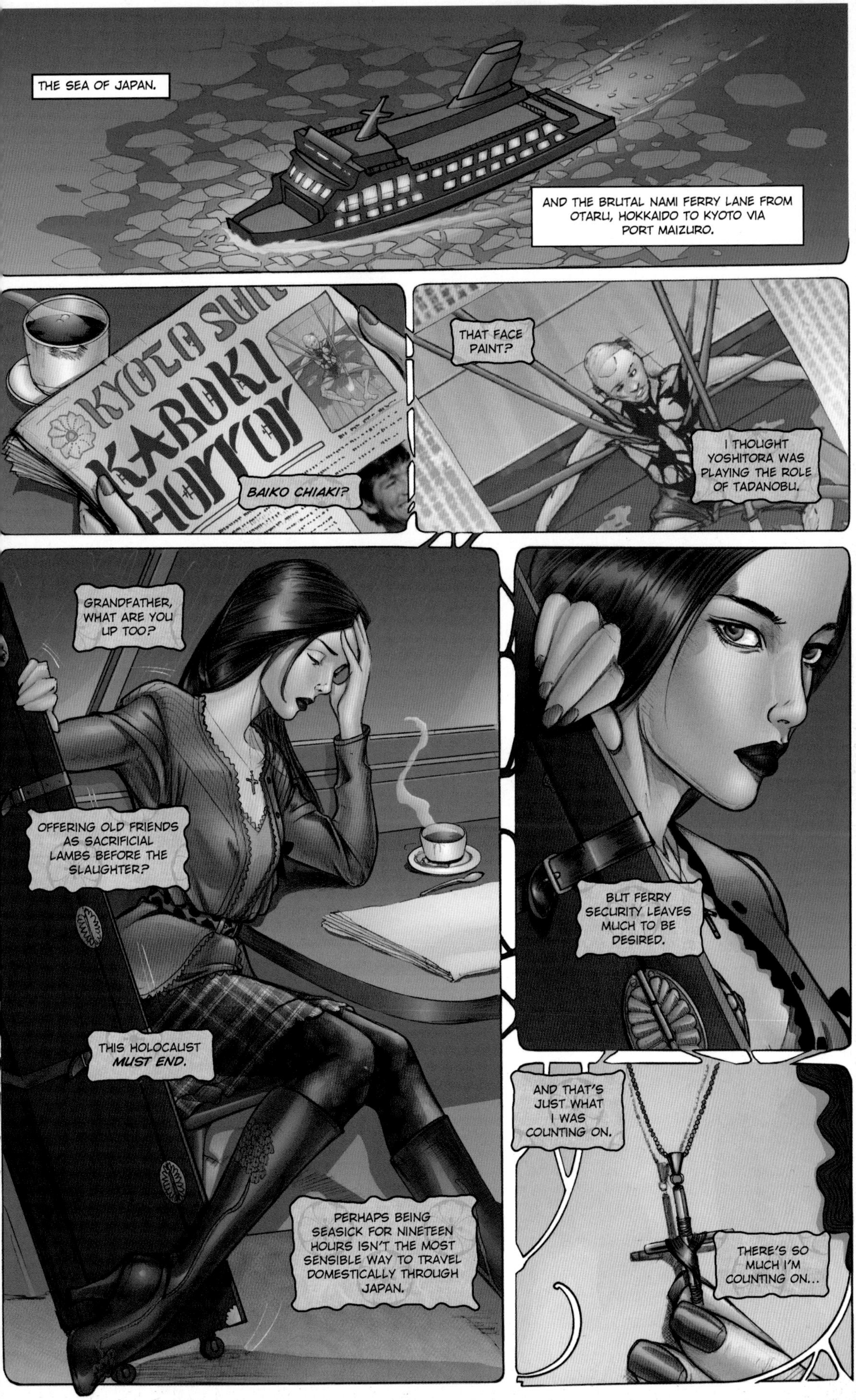
THE SEA OF JAPAN.
AND THE BRUTAL NAMI FERRY LANE FROM OTARU, HOKKAIDO TO KYOTO VIA PORT MAIZURO.
KYOTO SUN
KABUKI HORROR
BAIKO CHIAKI?
THAT FACE PAINT?
I THOUGHT YOSHITORA WAS PLAYING THE ROLE OF TADANOBU.
GRANDFATHER, WHAT ARE YOU UP TOO?
OFFERING OLD FRIENDS AS SACRIFICIAL LAMBS BEFORE THE SLAUGHTER?
THIS HOLOCAUST *MUST END.*
PERHAPS BEING SEASICK FOR NINETEEN HOURS ISN'T THE MOST SENSIBLE WAY TO TRAVEL DOMESTICALLY THROUGH JAPAN.
BUT FERRY SECURITY LEAVES MUCH TO BE DESIRED.
AND THAT'S JUST WHAT I WAS COUNTING ON.
THERE'S SO MUCH I'M COUNTING ON...

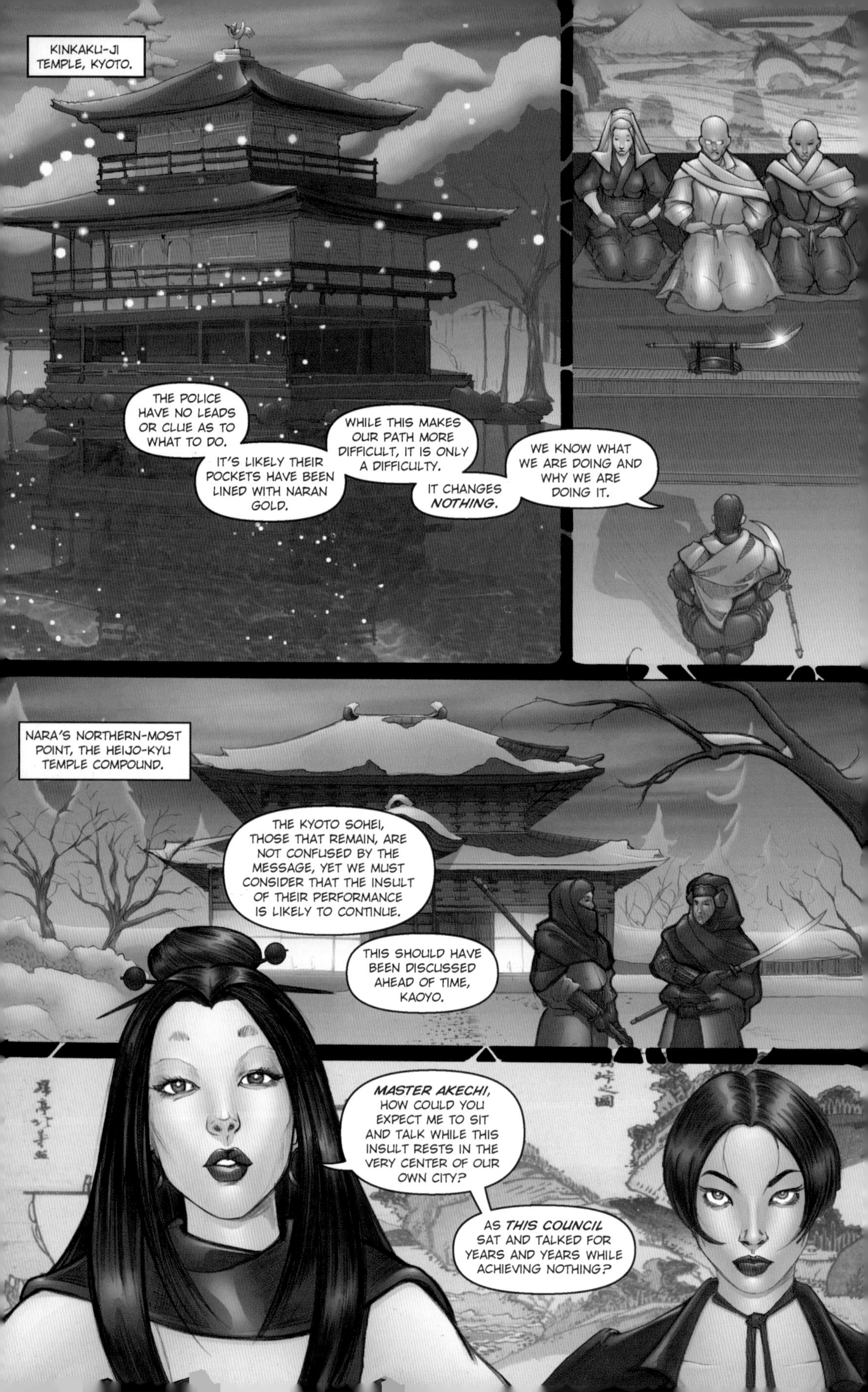
KINKAKU-JI TEMPLE, KYOTO.
THE POLICE HAVE NO LEADS OR CLUE AS TO WHAT TO DO.
IT'S LIKELY THEIR POCKETS HAVE BEEN LINED WITH NARAN GOLD.
WHILE THIS MAKES OUR PATH MORE DIFFICULT, IT IS ONLY A DIFFICULTY.
IT CHANGES *NOTHING*.
WE KNOW WHAT WE ARE DOING AND WHY WE ARE DOING IT.
NARA'S NORTHERN-MOST POINT, THE HEIJO-KYU TEMPLE COMPOUND.
THE KYOTO SOHEI, THOSE THAT REMAIN, ARE NOT CONFUSED BY THE MESSAGE, YET WE MUST CONSIDER THAT THE INSULT OF THEIR PERFORMANCE IS LIKELY TO CONTINUE.
THIS SHOULD HAVE BEEN DISCUSSED AHEAD OF TIME, KAOYO.
MASTER AKECHI, HOW COULD YOU EXPECT ME TO SIT AND TALK WHILE THIS INSULT RESTS IN THE VERY CENTER OF OUR OWN CITY?
AS *THIS COUNCIL* SAT AND TALKED FOR YEARS AND YEARS WHILE ACHIEVING NOTHING?

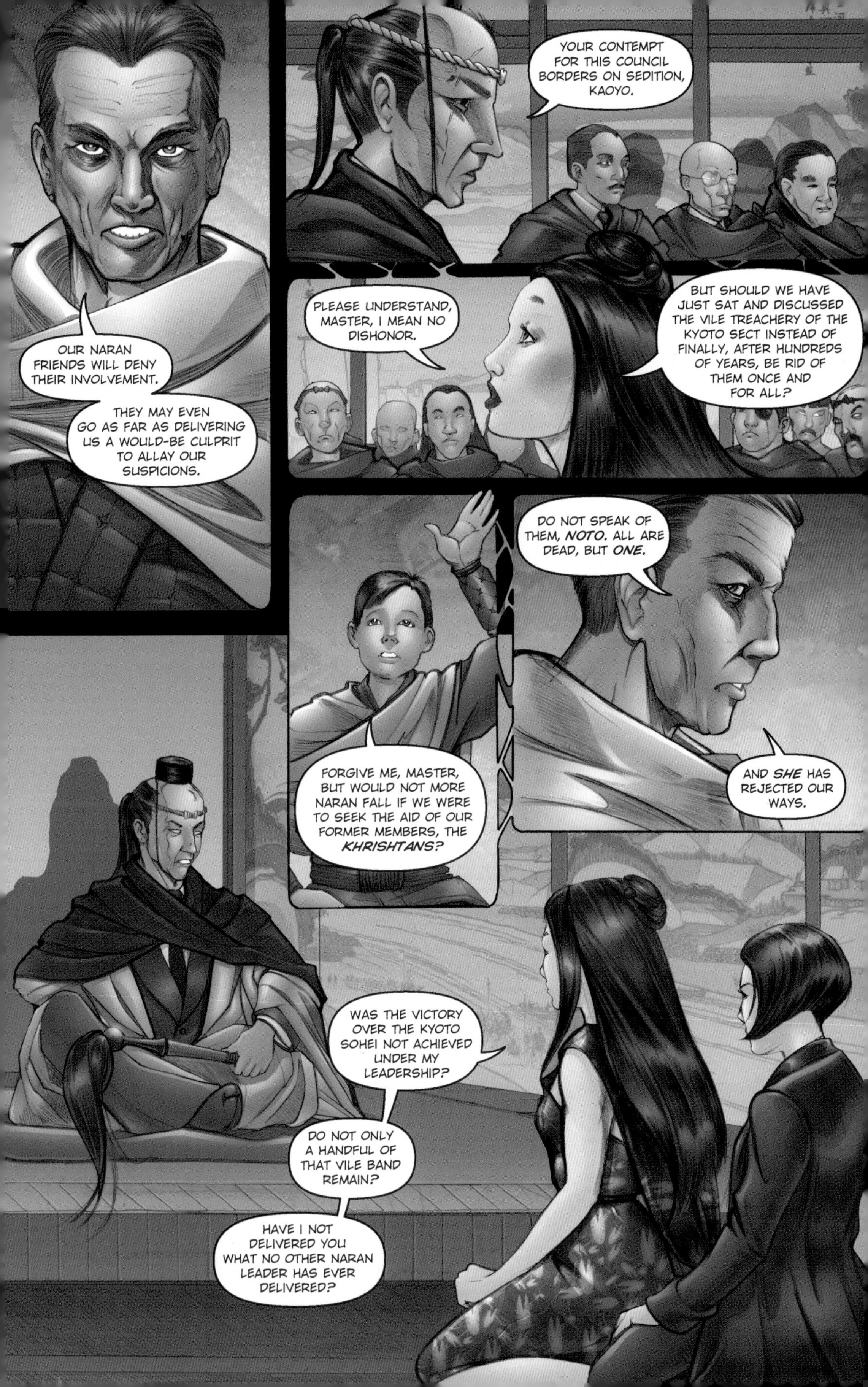
OUR NARAN FRIENDS WILL DENY THEIR INVOLVEMENT.
THEY MAY EVEN GO AS FAR AS DELIVERING US A WOULD-BE CULPRIT TO ALLAY OUR SUSPICIONS.
YOUR CONTEMPT FOR THIS COUNCIL BORDERS ON SEDITION, KAOYO.
PLEASE UNDERSTAND, MASTER, I MEAN NO DISHONOR.
BUT SHOULD WE HAVE JUST SAT AND DISCUSSED THE VILE TREACHERY OF THE KYOTO SECT INSTEAD OF FINALLY, AFTER HUNDREDS OF YEARS, BE RID OF THEM ONCE AND FOR ALL?
FORGIVE ME, MASTER, BUT WOULD NOT MORE NARAN FALL IF WE WERE TO SEEK THE AID OF OUR FORMER MEMBERS, THE ***KHRISHTANS?***
DO NOT SPEAK OF THEM, ***NOTO.*** ALL ARE DEAD, BUT ***ONE.***
AND ***SHE*** HAS REJECTED OUR WAYS.
WAS THE VICTORY OVER THE KYOTO SOHEI NOT ACHIEVED UNDER MY LEADERSHIP?
DO NOT ONLY A HANDFUL OF THAT VILE BAND REMAIN?
HAVE I NOT DELIVERED YOU WHAT NO OTHER NARAN LEADER HAS EVER DELIVERED?

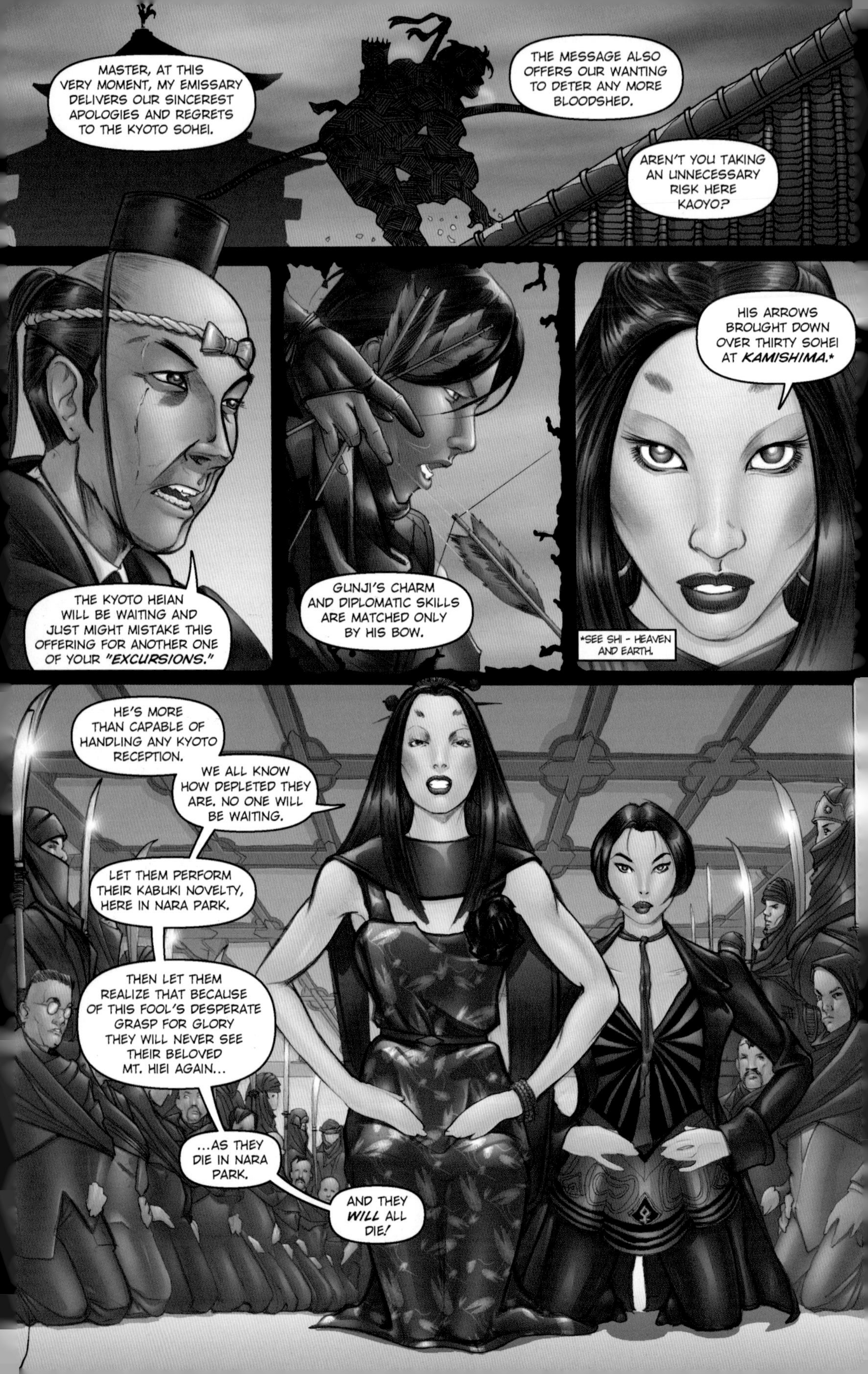
MASTER, AT THIS VERY MOMENT, MY EMISSARY DELIVERS OUR SINCEREST APOLOGIES AND REGRETS TO THE KYOTO SOHEI.
THE MESSAGE ALSO OFFERS OUR WANTING TO DETER ANY MORE BLOODSHED.
AREN'T YOU TAKING AN UNNECESSARY RISK HERE KAOYO?
THE KYOTO HEIAN WILL BE WAITING AND JUST MIGHT MISTAKE THIS OFFERING FOR ANOTHER ONE OF YOUR "EXCURSIONS."
GUNJI'S CHARM AND DIPLOMATIC SKILLS ARE MATCHED ONLY BY HIS BOW.
HIS ARROWS BROUGHT DOWN OVER THIRTY SOHEI AT KAMISHIMA.*
*SEE SHI - HEAVEN AND EARTH.
HE'S MORE THAN CAPABLE OF HANDLING ANY KYOTO RECEPTION.
WE ALL KNOW HOW DEPLETED THEY ARE. NO ONE WILL BE WAITING.
LET THEM PERFORM THEIR KABUKI NOVELTY, HERE IN NARA PARK.
THEN LET THEM REALIZE THAT BECAUSE OF THIS FOOL'S DESPERATE GRASP FOR GLORY THEY WILL NEVER SEE THEIR BELOVED MT. HIEI AGAIN...
...AS THEY DIE IN NARA PARK.
AND THEY WILL ALL DIE!

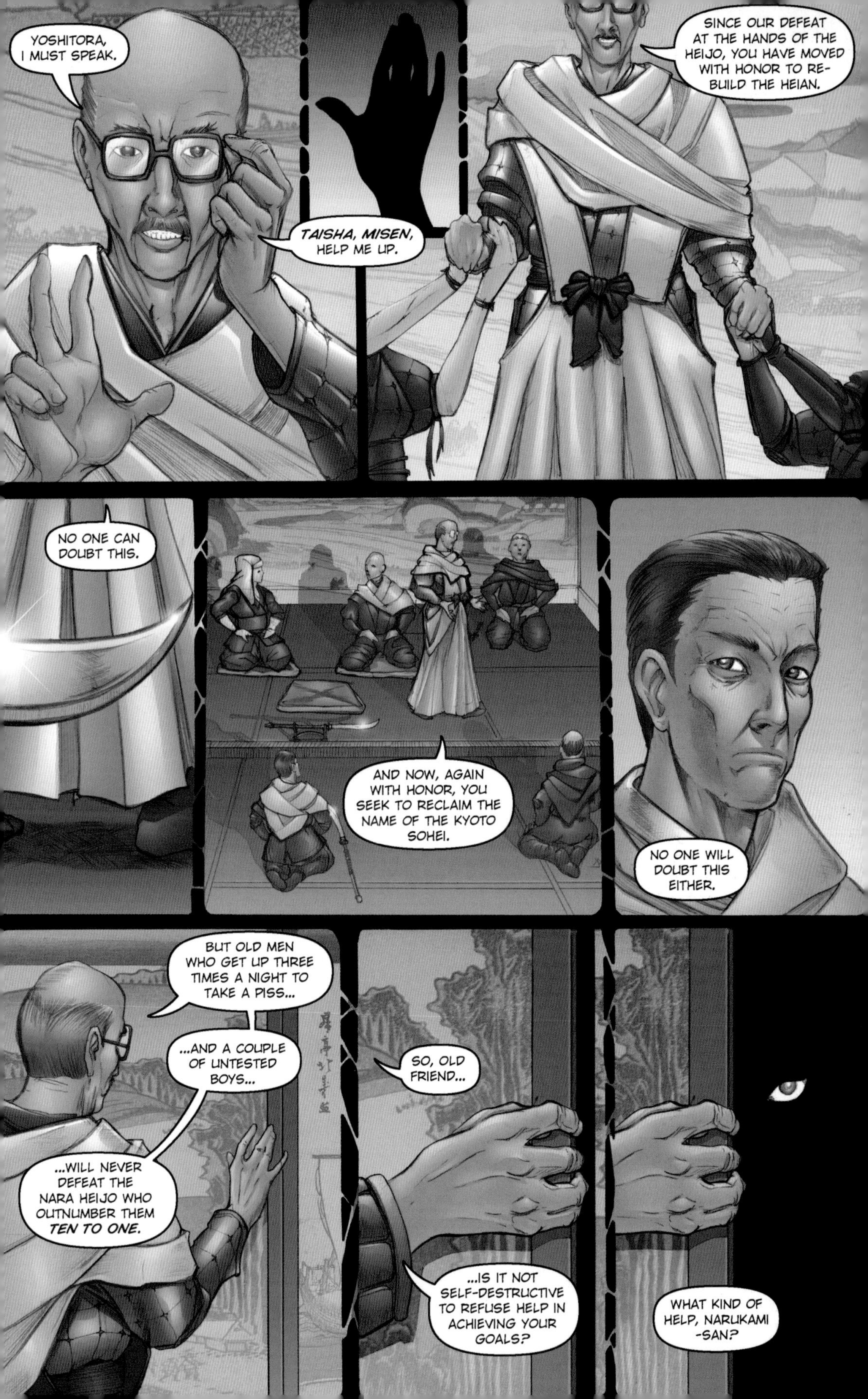
YOSHITORA, I MUST SPEAK.
TAISHA, MISEN, HELP ME UP.
SINCE OUR DEFEAT AT THE HANDS OF THE HEIJO, YOU HAVE MOVED WITH HONOR TO RE-BUILD THE HEIAN.
NO ONE CAN DOUBT THIS.
AND NOW, AGAIN WITH HONOR, YOU SEEK TO RECLAIM THE NAME OF THE KYOTO SOHEI.
NO ONE WILL DOUBT THIS EITHER.
BUT OLD MEN WHO GET UP THREE TIMES A NIGHT TO TAKE A PISS...
...AND A COUPLE OF UNTESTED BOYS...
...WILL NEVER DEFEAT THE NARA HEIJO WHO OUTNUMBER THEM TEN TO ONE.
SO, OLD FRIEND...
...IS IT NOT SELF-DESTRUCTIVE TO REFUSE HELP IN ACHIEVING YOUR GOALS?
WHAT KIND OF HELP, NARUKAMI-SAN?

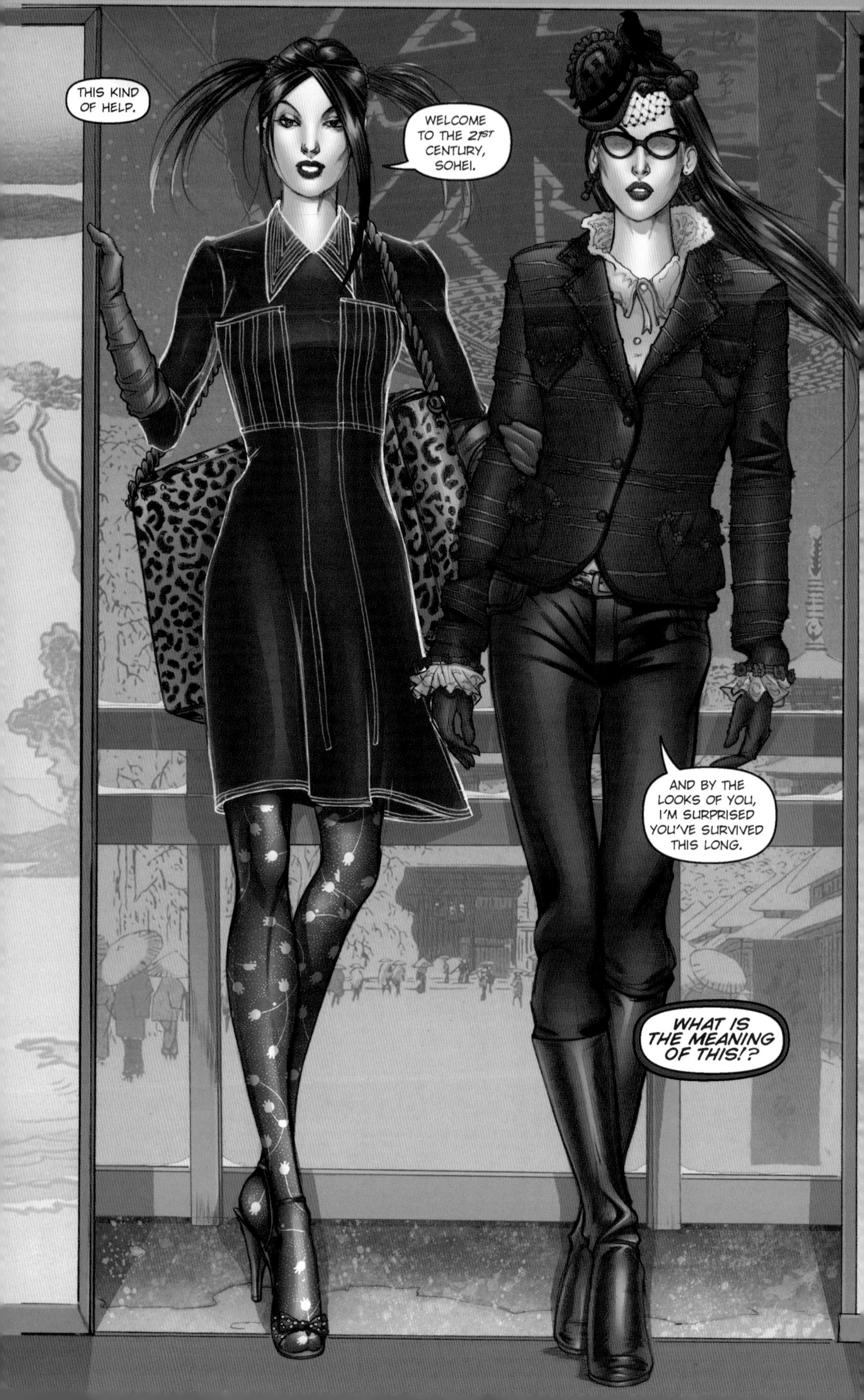
THIS KIND OF HELP.
WELCOME TO THE 21ST CENTURY, SOHEI.
AND BY THE LOOKS OF YOU, I'M SURPRISED YOU'VE SURVIVED THIS LONG.
WHAT IS THE MEANING OF THIS!?

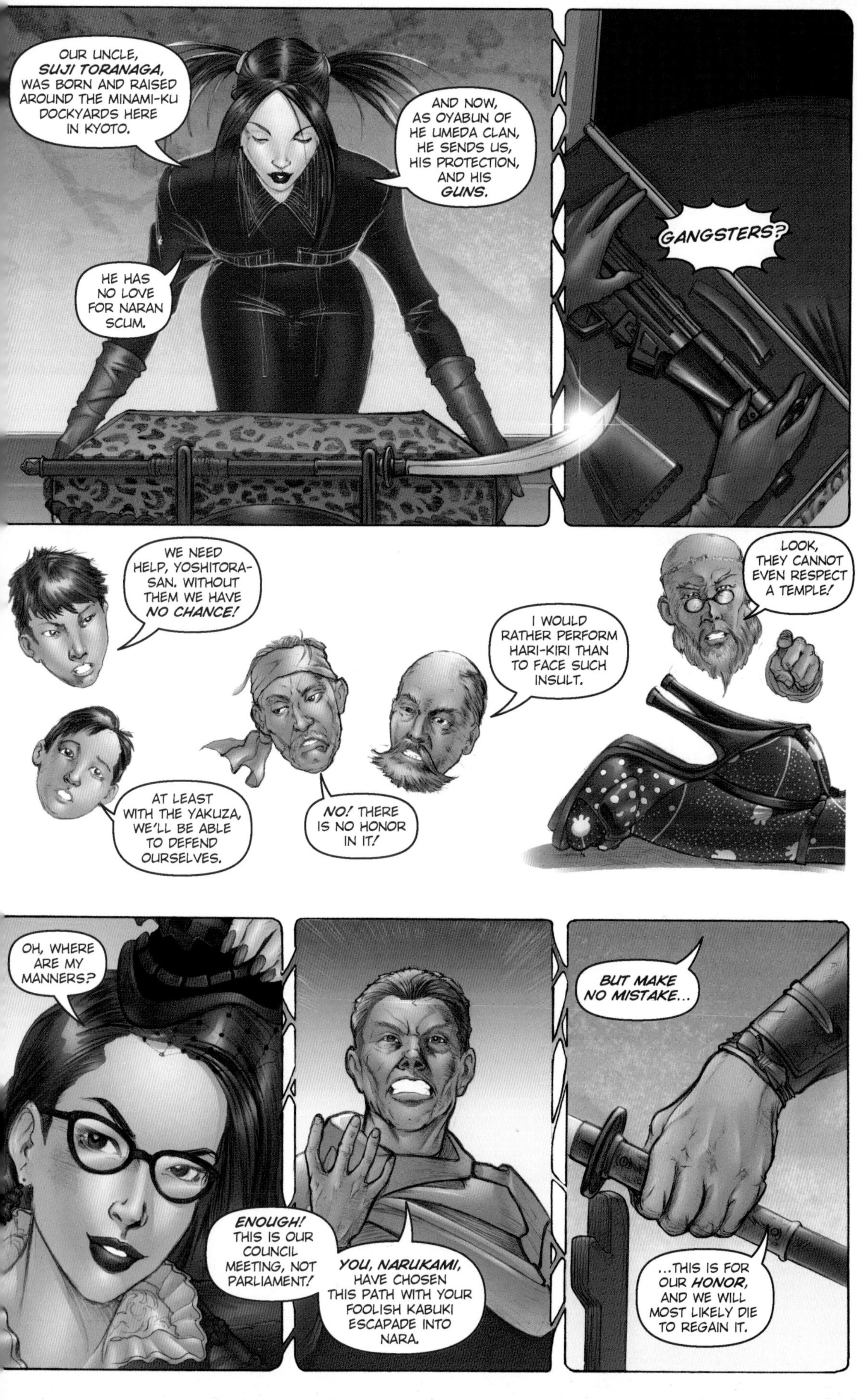

OUR UNCLE, SUJI TORANAGA, WAS BORN AND RAISED AROUND THE MINAMI-KU DOCKYARDS HERE IN KYOTO.
AND NOW, AS OYABUN OF HE UMEDA CLAN, HE SENDS US, HIS PROTECTION, AND HIS GUNS.
HE HAS NO LOVE FOR NARAN SCUM.
GANGSTERS?
WE NEED HELP, YOSHITORA-SAN. WITHOUT THEM WE HAVE NO CHANCE!
AT LEAST WITH THE YAKUZA, WE'LL BE ABLE TO DEFEND OURSELVES.
NO! THERE IS NO HONOR IN IT!
I WOULD RATHER PERFORM HARI-KIRI THAN TO FACE SUCH INSULT.
LOOK, THEY CANNOT EVEN RESPECT A TEMPLE!
OH, WHERE ARE MY MANNERS?
ENOUGH! THIS IS OUR COUNCIL MEETING, NOT PARLIAMENT!
YOU, NARUKAMI, HAVE CHOSEN THIS PATH WITH YOUR FOOLISH KABUKI ESCAPADE INTO NARA.
BUT MAKE NO MISTAKE...
...THIS IS FOR OUR HONOR, AND WE WILL MOST LIKELY DIE TO REGAIN IT.

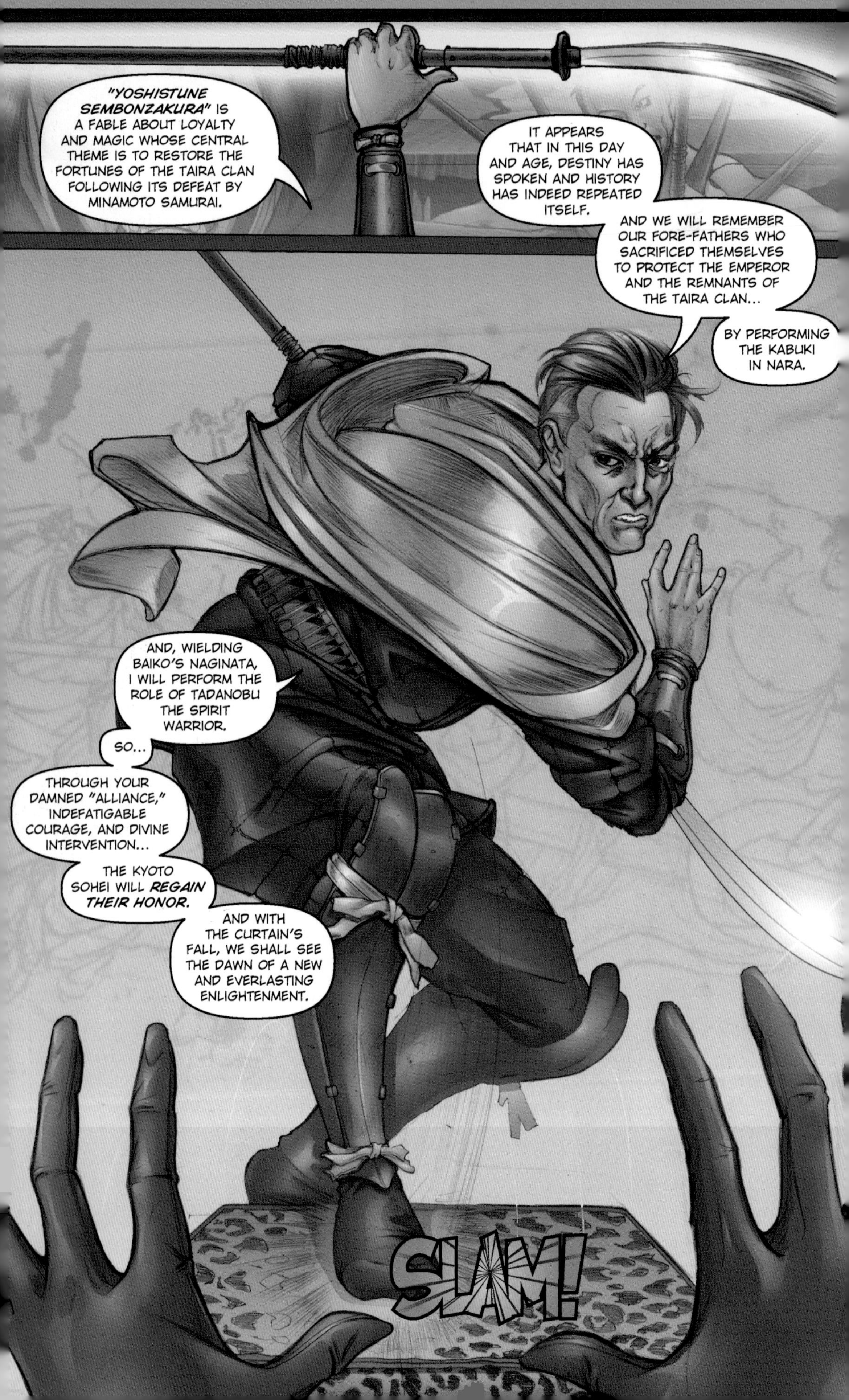
"YOSHISTUNE SEMBONZAKURA" IS A FABLE ABOUT LOYALTY AND MAGIC WHOSE CENTRAL THEME IS TO RESTORE THE FORTUNES OF THE TAIRA CLAN FOLLOWING ITS DEFEAT BY MINAMOTO SAMURAI.
IT APPEARS THAT IN THIS DAY AND AGE, DESTINY HAS SPOKEN AND HISTORY HAS INDEED REPEATED ITSELF.
AND WE WILL REMEMBER OUR FORE-FATHERS WHO SACRIFICED THEMSELVES TO PROTECT THE EMPEROR AND THE REMNANTS OF THE TAIRA CLAN...
BY PERFORMING THE KABUKI IN NARA.
AND, WIELDING BAIKO'S NAGINATA, I WILL PERFORM THE ROLE OF TADANOBU THE SPIRIT WARRIOR.
SO...
THROUGH YOUR DAMNED "ALLIANCE," INDEFATIGABLE COURAGE, AND DIVINE INTERVENTION...
THE KYOTO SOHEI WILL ***REGAIN THEIR HONOR.***
AND WITH THE CURTAIN'S FALL, WE SHALL SEE THE DAWN OF A NEW AND EVERLASTING ENLIGHTENMENT.
SLAM!

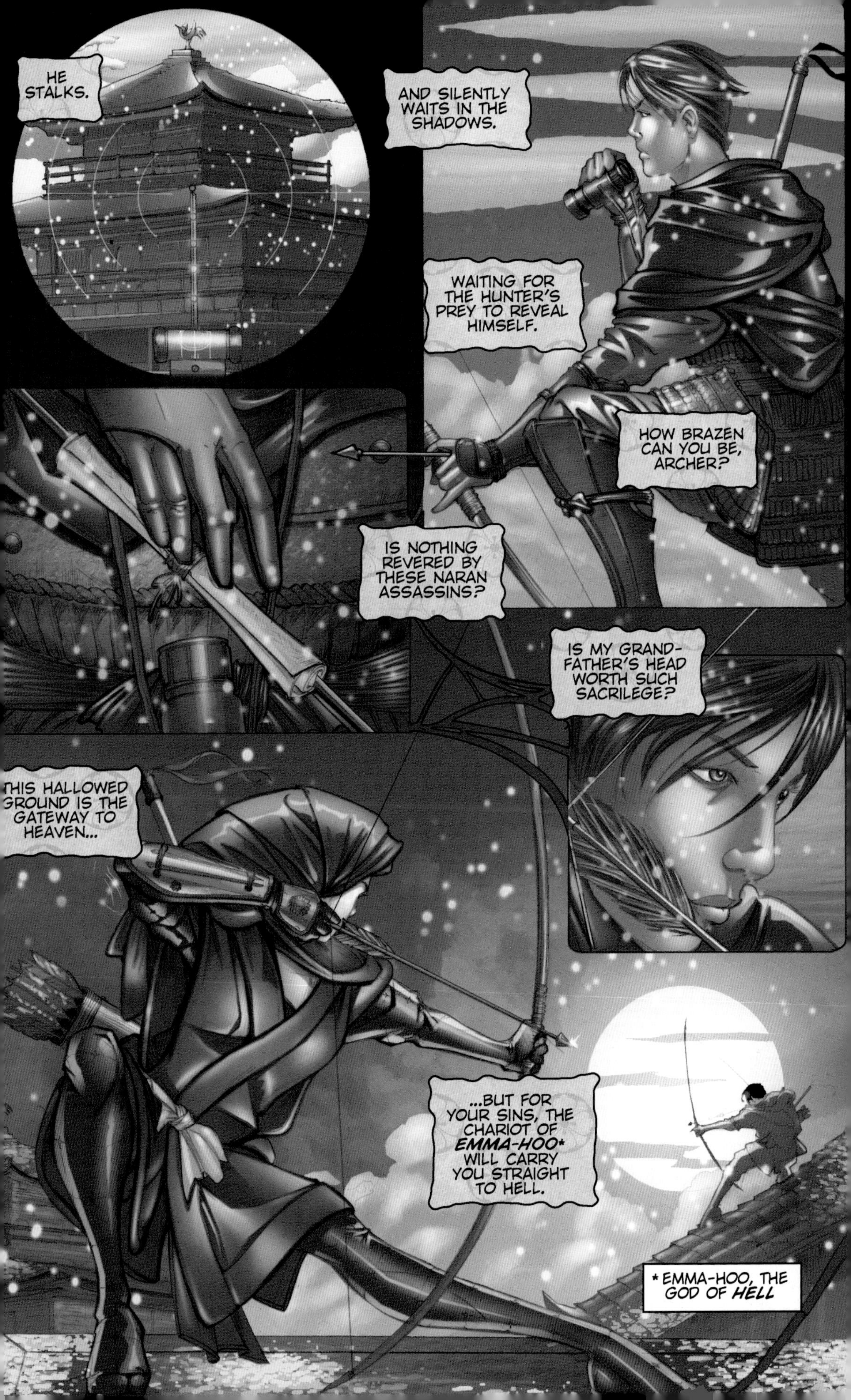
HE STALKS.
AND SILENTLY WAITS IN THE SHADOWS.
WAITING FOR THE HUNTER'S PREY TO REVEAL HIMSELF.
HOW BRAZEN CAN YOU BE, ARCHER?
IS NOTHING REVERED BY THESE NARAN ASSASSINS?
IS MY GRAND-FATHER'S HEAD WORTH SUCH SACRILEGE?
THIS HALLOWED GROUND IS THE GATEWAY TO HEAVEN...
...BUT FOR YOUR SINS, THE CHARIOT OF ***EMMA-HOO**** WILL CARRY YOU STRAIGHT TO HELL.
* EMMA-HOO, THE GOD OF ***HELL***

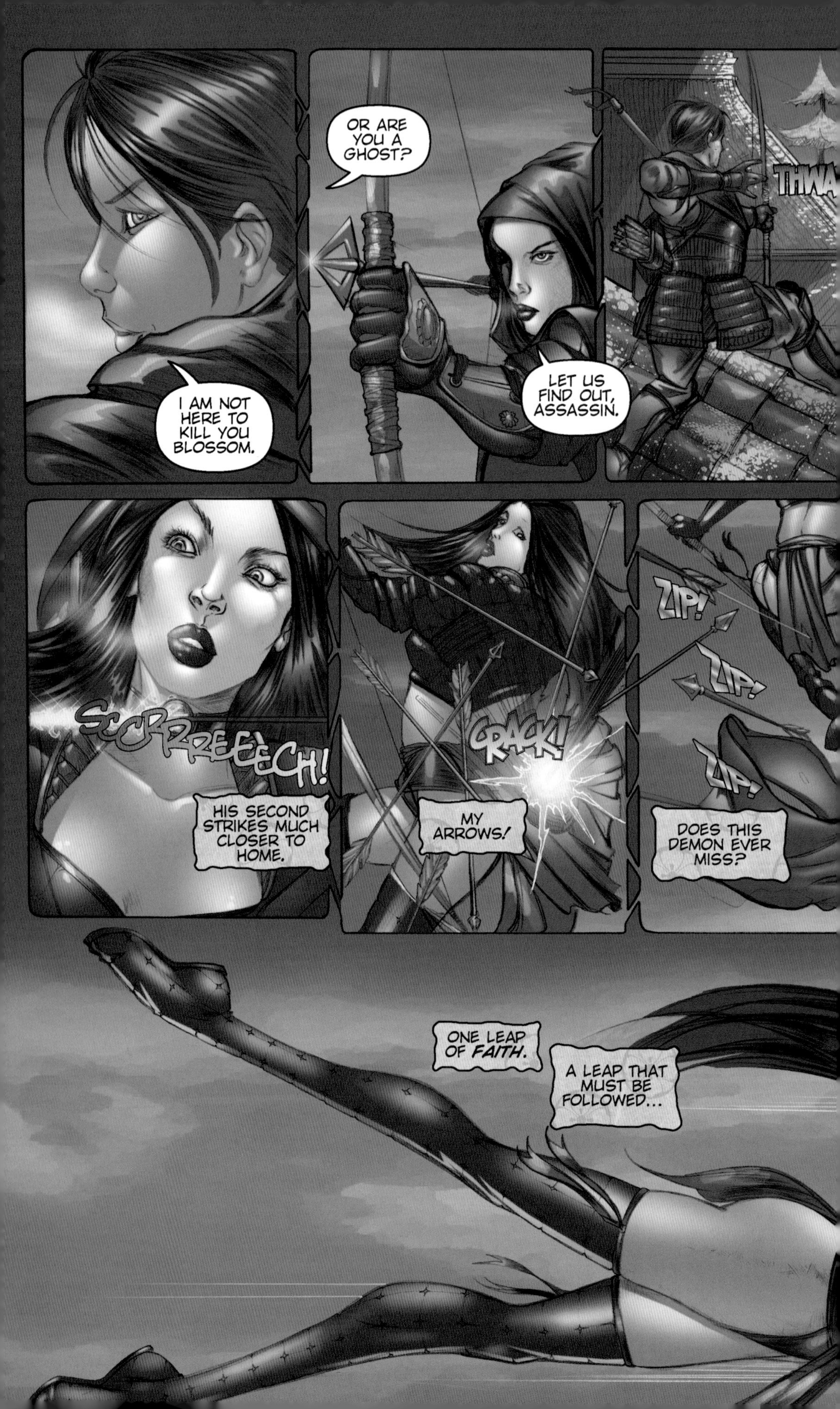
I AM NOT HERE TO KILL YOU BLOSSOM.
OR ARE YOU A GHOST?
LET US FIND OUT, ASSASSIN.
THWA
SCCRRREEEECH!
HIS SECOND STRIKES MUCH CLOSER TO HOME.
CRACK!
MY ARROWS!
ZIP!
ZIP!
ZIP!
DOES THIS DEMON EVER MISS?
ONE LEAP OF *FAITH*.
A LEAP THAT MUST BE FOLLOWED...

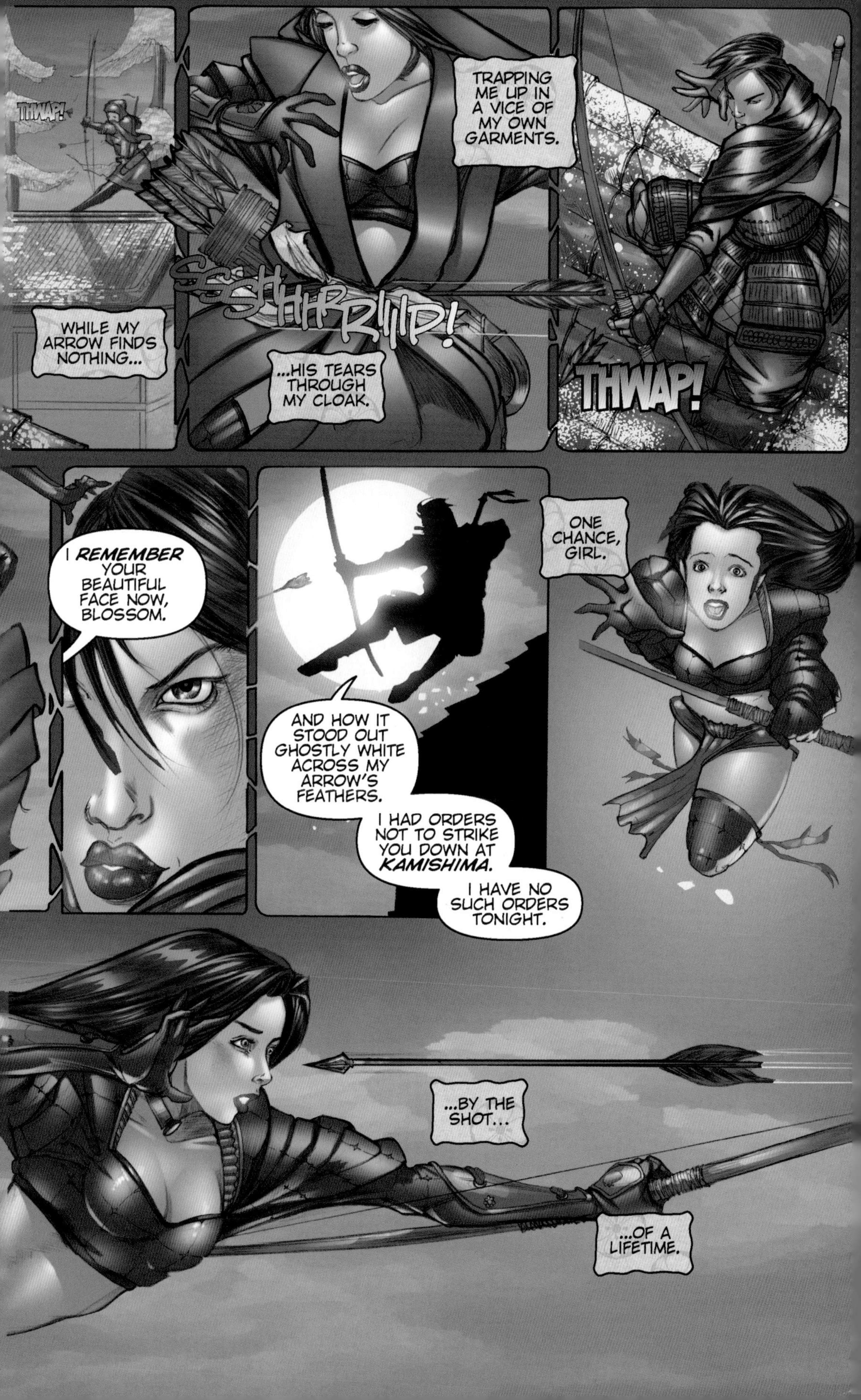
THWAP!
WHILE MY ARROW FINDS NOTHING...
TRAPPING ME UP IN A VICE OF MY OWN GARMENTS.
SSSHHRRIIIP!
...HIS TEARS THROUGH MY CLOAK.
THWAP!
I *REMEMBER* YOUR BEAUTIFUL FACE NOW, BLOSSOM.
AND HOW IT STOOD OUT GHOSTLY WHITE ACROSS MY ARROW'S FEATHERS.
I HAD ORDERS NOT TO STRIKE YOU DOWN AT *KAMISHIMA.*
I HAVE NO SUCH ORDERS TONIGHT.
ONE CHANCE, GIRL.
...BY THE SHOT...
...OF A LIFETIME.

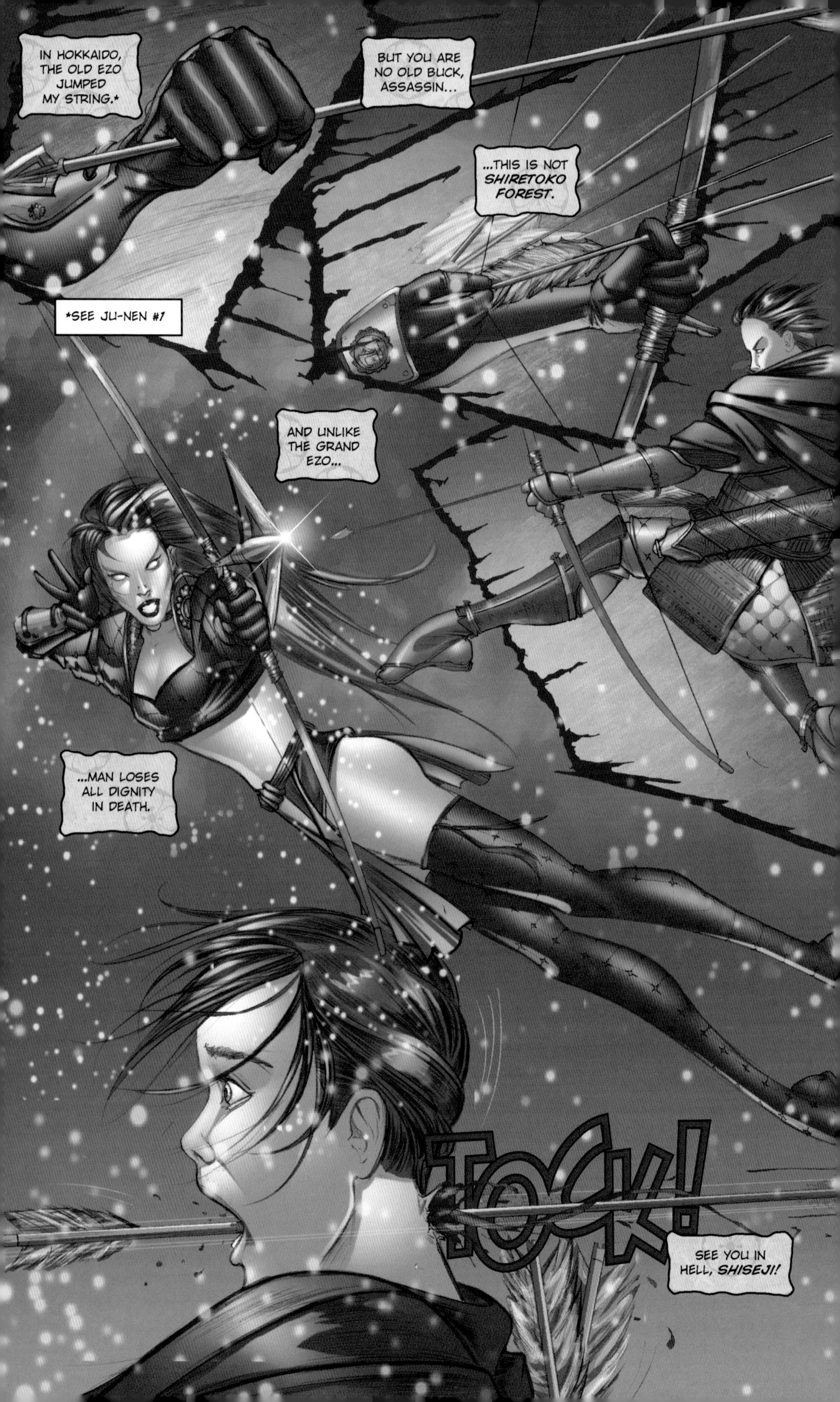
IN HOKKAIDO, THE OLD EZO JUMPED MY STRING.*
BUT YOU ARE NO OLD BUCK, ASSASSIN...
...THIS IS NOT SHIRETOKO FOREST.
*SEE JU-NEN #1
AND UNLIKE THE GRAND EZO...
...MAN LOSES ALL DIGNITY IN DEATH.
TOCK!
SEE YOU IN HELL, SHISEJI!

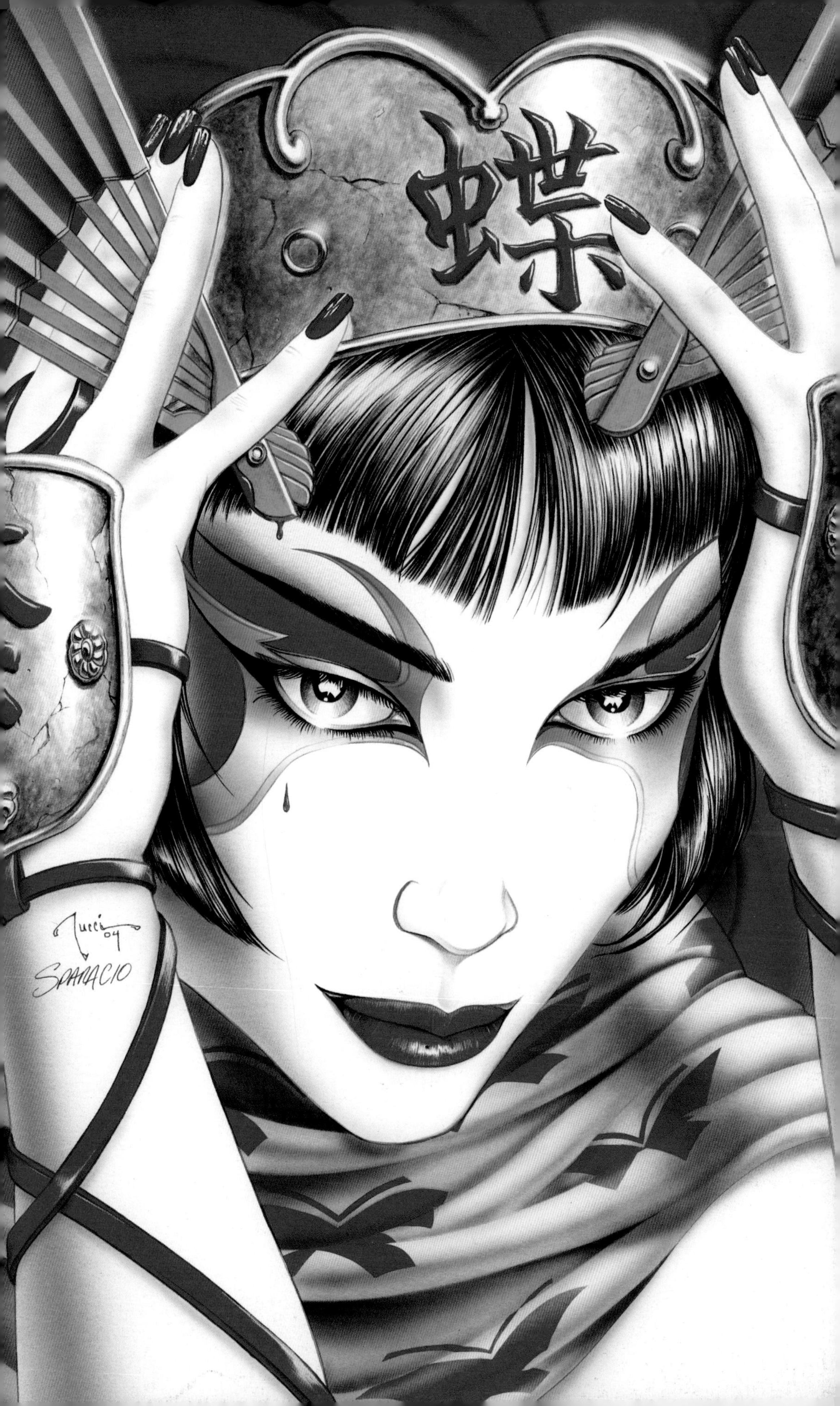
蝶
SPARACIO

STORY, SCRIPT, AND ILLUSTRATION
Billy Tucci

SCRIPT
J.C. Vaughn

COLORS
Brett R. Smith

COLOR FLATS
John Wilson

LETTERING
Marshall Dillon

ART SCANNING AND CLEANUP
Kristen Purdy and Mike Kenzine

COVER
Billy Tucci and Mark Sparacio

ORIGINAL FASHIONS
Anna Sui

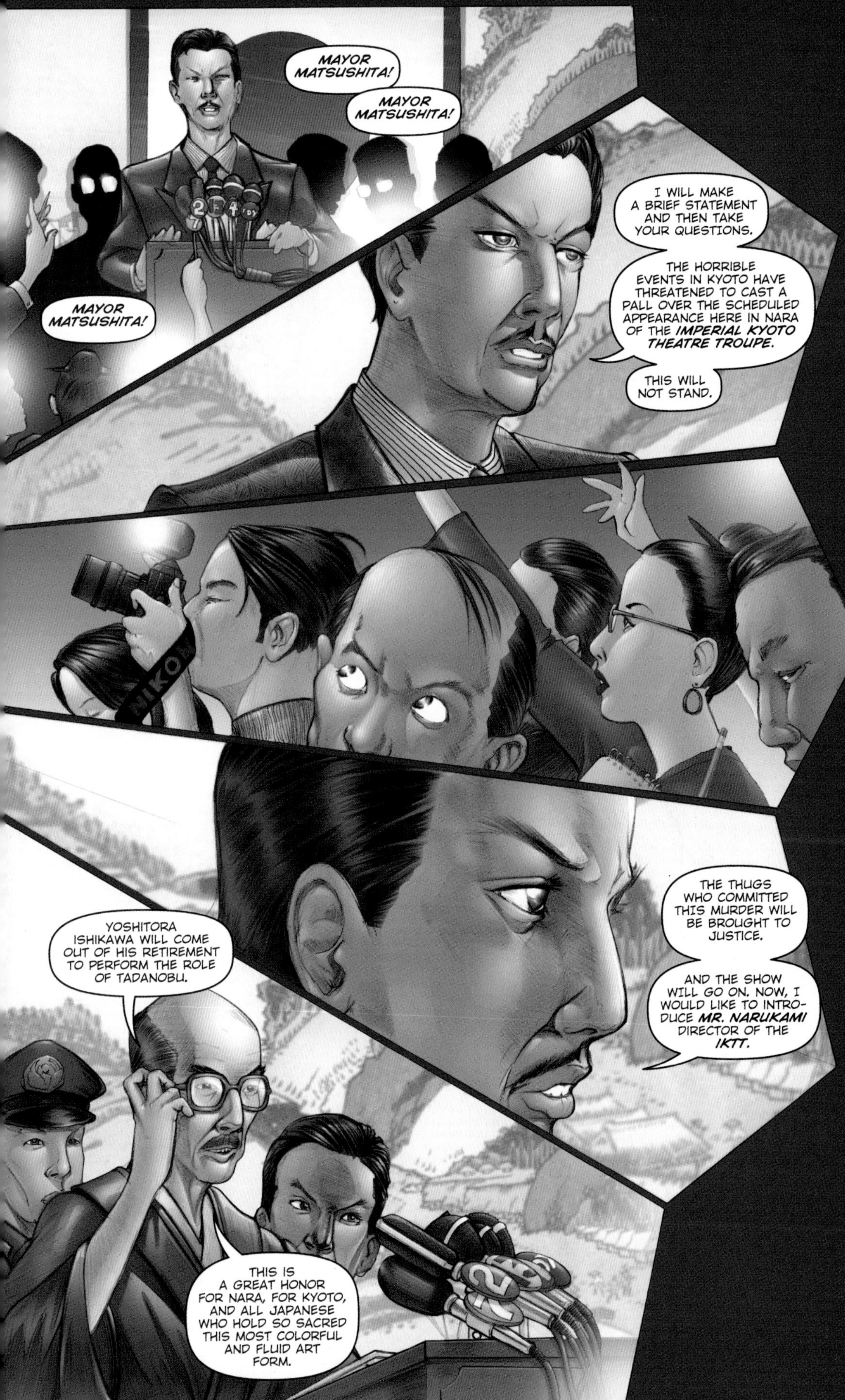

MAYOR MATSUSHITA!
MAYOR MATSUSHITA!
MAYOR MATSUSHITA!
I WILL MAKE A BRIEF STATEMENT AND THEN TAKE YOUR QUESTIONS.
THE HORRIBLE EVENTS IN KYOTO HAVE THREATENED TO CAST A PALL OVER THE SCHEDULED APPEARANCE HERE IN NARA OF THE *IMPERIAL KYOTO THEATRE TROUPE*.
THIS WILL NOT STAND.
THE THUGS WHO COMMITTED THIS MURDER WILL BE BROUGHT TO JUSTICE.
AND THE SHOW WILL GO ON. NOW, I WOULD LIKE TO INTRO-DUCE *MR. NARUKAMI* DIRECTOR OF THE *IKTT*.
YOSHITORA ISHIKAWA WILL COME OUT OF HIS RETIREMENT TO PERFORM THE ROLE OF TADANOBU.
THIS IS A GREAT HONOR FOR NARA, FOR KYOTO, AND ALL JAPANESE WHO HOLD SO SACRED THIS MOST COLORFUL AND FLUID ART FORM.

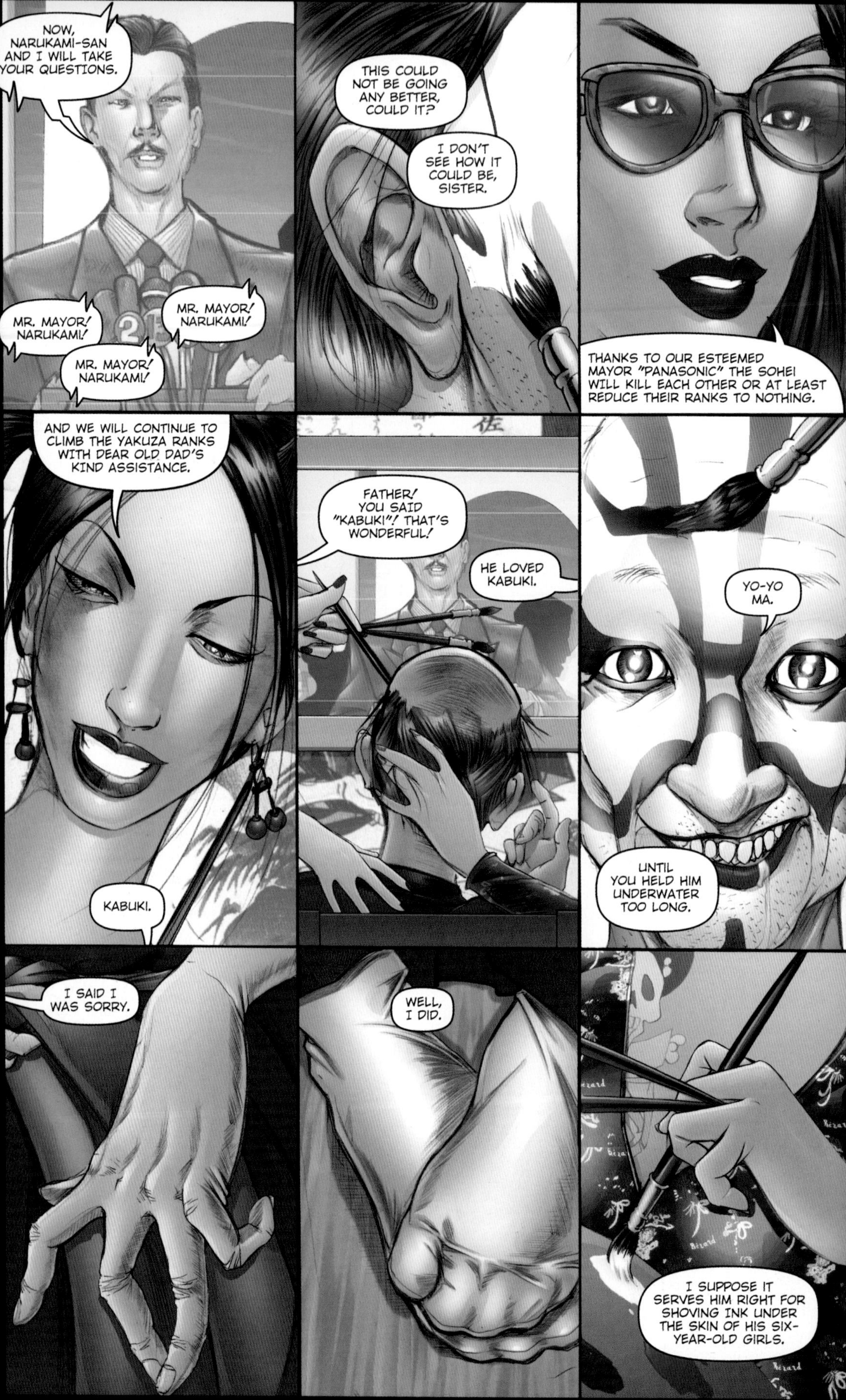
NOW, NARUKAMI-SAN AND I WILL TAKE YOUR QUESTIONS.
MR. MAYOR! NARUKAMI!
MR. MAYOR! NARUKAMI!
MR. MAYOR! NARUKAMI!
THIS COULD NOT BE GOING ANY BETTER, COULD IT?
I DON'T SEE HOW IT COULD BE, SISTER.
THANKS TO OUR ESTEEMED MAYOR "PANASONIC" THE SOHEI WILL KILL EACH OTHER OR AT LEAST REDUCE THEIR RANKS TO NOTHING.
AND WE WILL CONTINUE TO CLIMB THE YAKUZA RANKS WITH DEAR OLD DAD'S KIND ASSISTANCE.
KABUKI.
FATHER! YOU SAID "KABUKI"! THAT'S WONDERFUL!
HE LOVED KABUKI.
YO-YO MA.
UNTIL YOU HELD HIM UNDERWATER TOO LONG.
I SAID I WAS SORRY.
WELL, I DID.
I SUPPOSE IT SERVES HIM RIGHT FOR SHOVING INK UNDER THE SKIN OF HIS SIX-YEAR-OLD GIRLS.

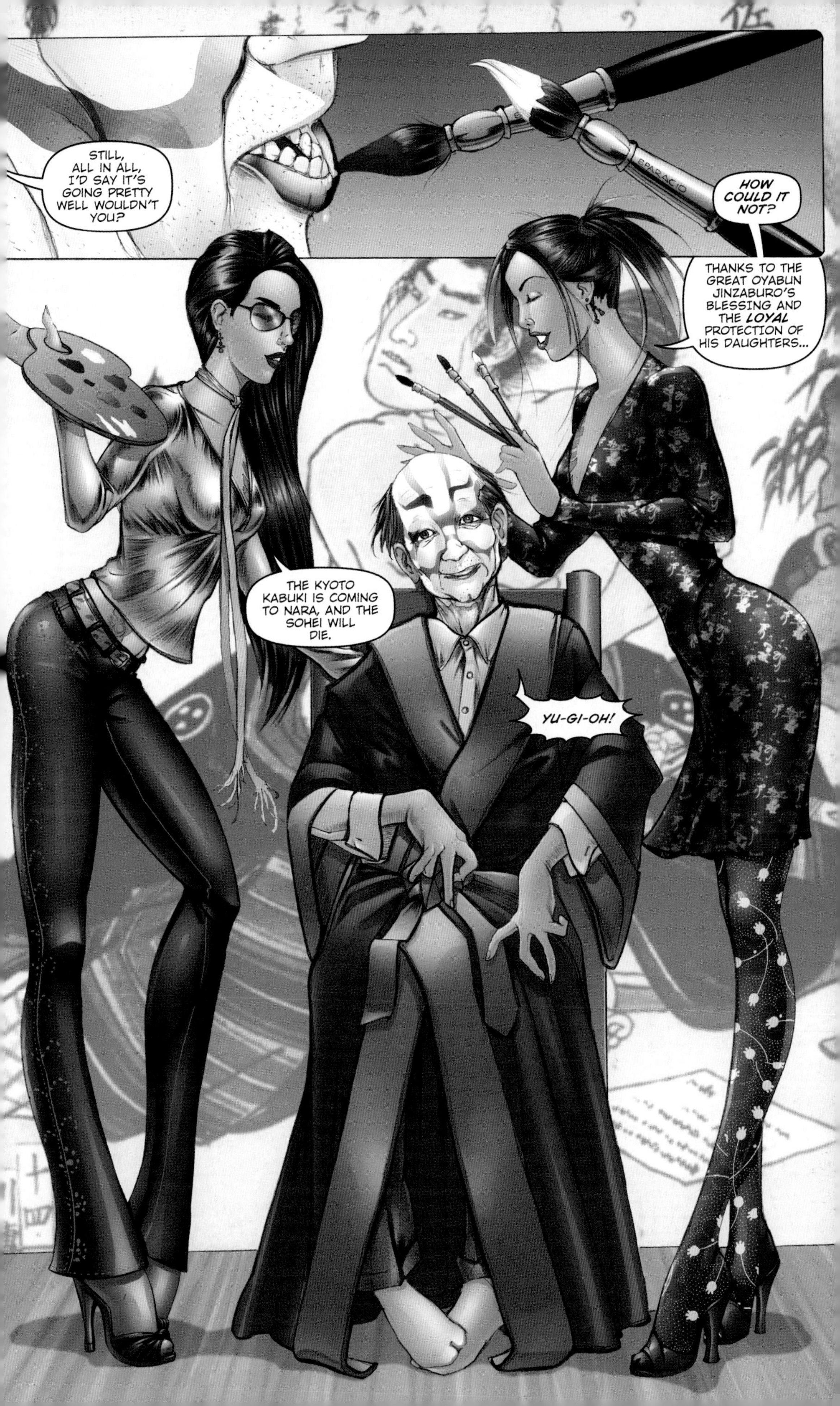
STILL, ALL IN ALL, I'D SAY IT'S GOING PRETTY WELL WOULDN'T YOU?
HOW COULD IT NOT?
THANKS TO THE GREAT OYABUN JINZABURO'S BLESSING AND THE ***LOYAL*** PROTECTION OF HIS DAUGHTERS...
THE KYOTO KABUKI IS COMING TO NARA, AND THE SOHEI WILL DIE.
YU-GI-OH!

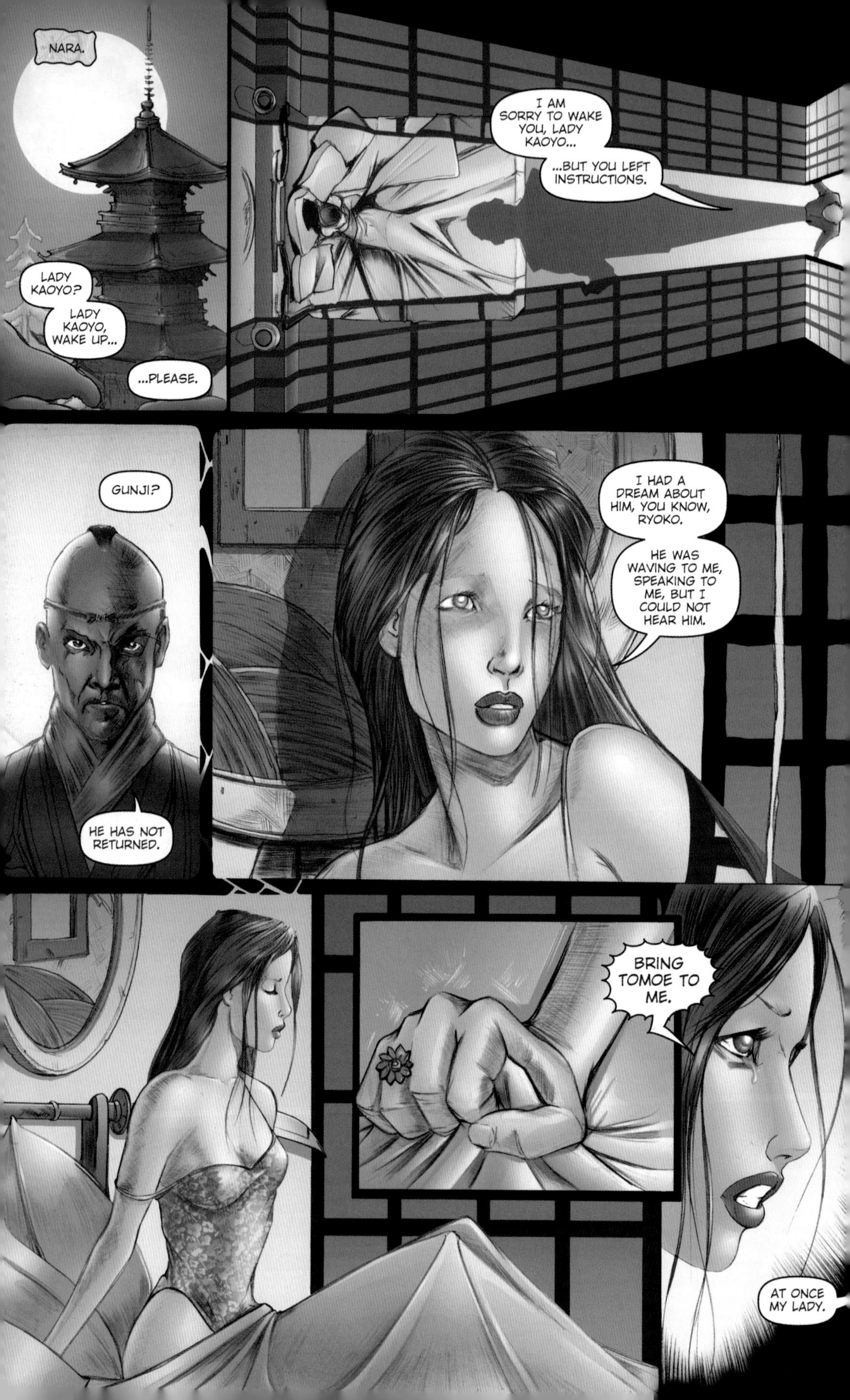
NARA.
LADY KAOYO?
LADY KAOYO, WAKE UP...
...PLEASE.
I AM SORRY TO WAKE YOU, LADY KAOYO...
...BUT YOU LEFT INSTRUCTIONS.
GUNJI?
HE HAS NOT RETURNED.
I HAD A DREAM ABOUT HIM, YOU KNOW, RYOKO.
HE WAS WAVING TO ME, SPEAKING TO ME, BUT I COULD NOT HEAR HIM.
BRING TOMOE TO ME.
AT ONCE MY LADY.

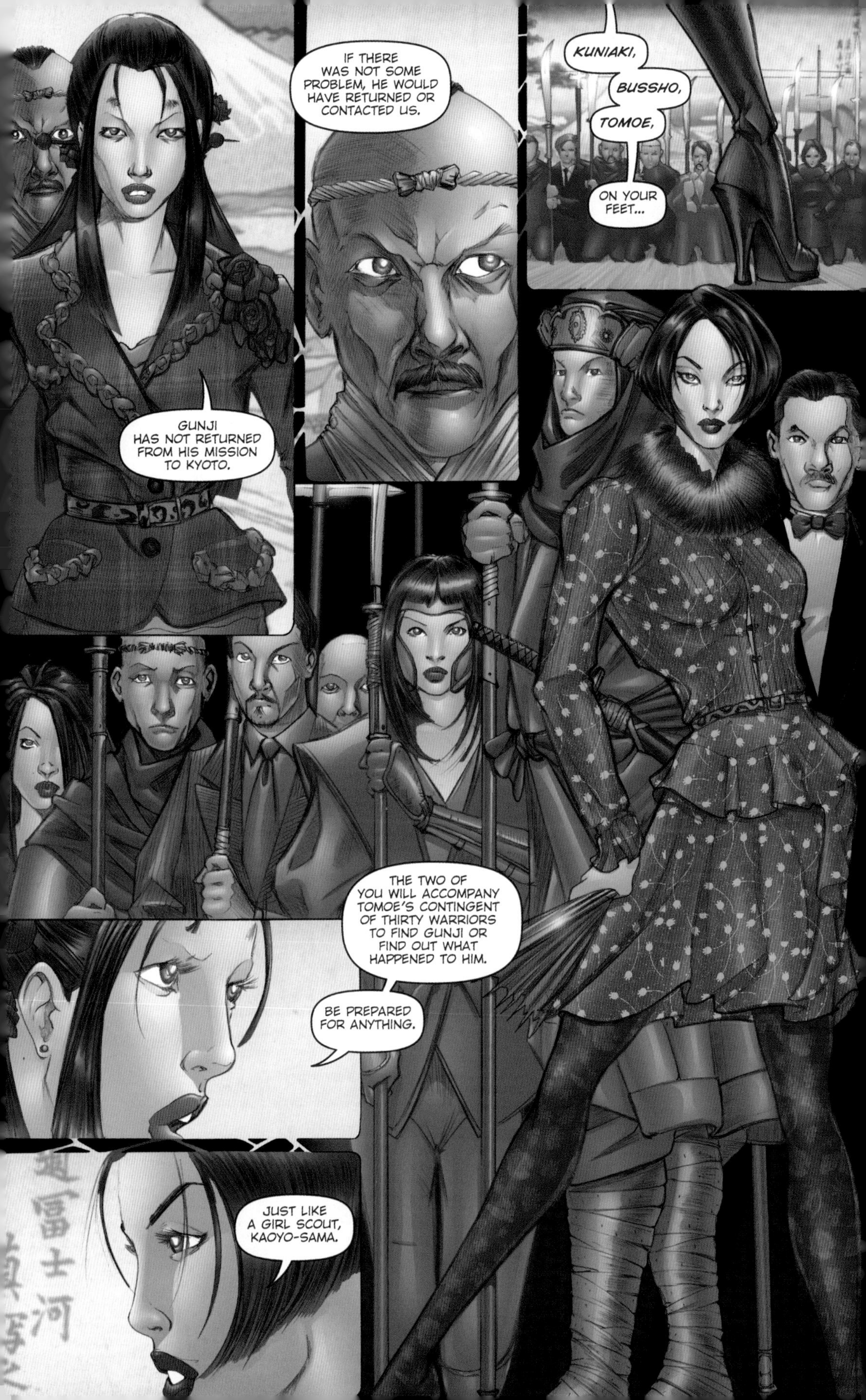
GUNJI HAS NOT RETURNED FROM HIS MISSION TO KYOTO.
IF THERE WAS NOT SOME PROBLEM, HE WOULD HAVE RETURNED OR CONTACTED US.
KUNIAKI,
BUSSHO,
TOMOE,
ON YOUR FEET...
THE TWO OF YOU WILL ACCOMPANY TOMOE'S CONTINGENT OF THIRTY WARRIORS TO FIND GUNJI OR FIND OUT WHAT HAPPENED TO HIM.
BE PREPARED FOR ANYTHING.
JUST LIKE A GIRL SCOUT, KAOYO-SAMA.

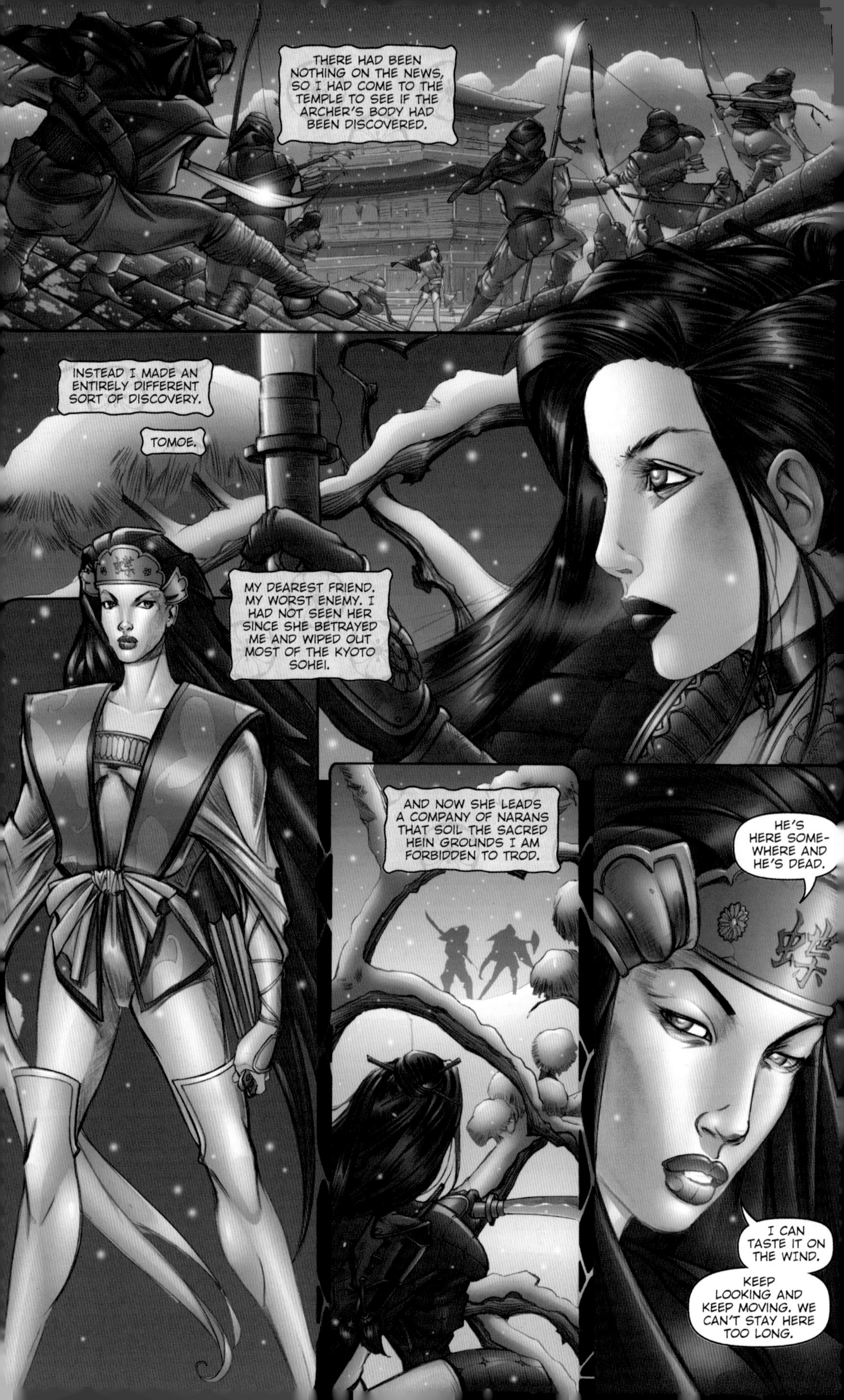
THERE HAD BEEN NOTHING ON THE NEWS, SO I HAD COME TO THE TEMPLE TO SEE IF THE ARCHER'S BODY HAD BEEN DISCOVERED.
INSTEAD I MADE AN ENTIRELY DIFFERENT SORT OF DISCOVERY.
TOMOE.
MY DEAREST FRIEND. MY WORST ENEMY. I HAD NOT SEEN HER SINCE SHE BETRAYED ME AND WIPED OUT MOST OF THE KYOTO SOHEI.
AND NOW SHE LEADS A COMPANY OF NARANS THAT SOIL THE SACRED HEIN GROUNDS I AM FORBIDDEN TO TROD.
HE'S HERE SOMEWHERE AND HE'S DEAD.
I CAN TASTE IT ON THE WIND.
KEEP LOOKING AND KEEP MOVING. WE CAN'T STAY HERE TOO LONG.

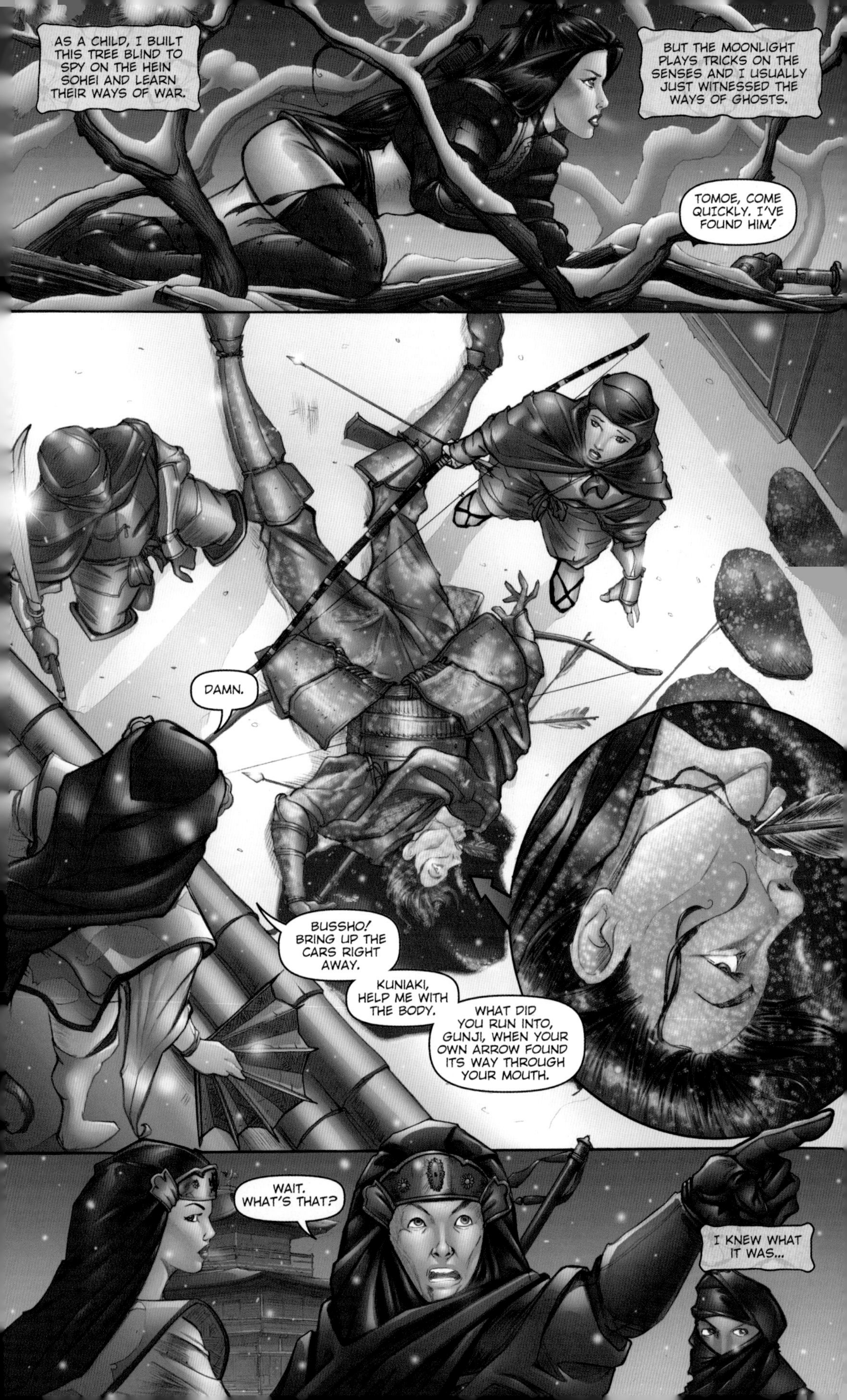
AS A CHILD, I BUILT THIS TREE BLIND TO SPY ON THE HEIN SOHEI AND LEARN THEIR WAYS OF WAR.
BUT THE MOONLIGHT PLAYS TRICKS ON THE SENSES AND I USUALLY JUST WITNESSED THE WAYS OF GHOSTS.
TOMOE, COME QUICKLY. I'VE FOUND HIM!
DAMN.
BUSSHO! BRING UP THE CARS RIGHT AWAY.
KUNIAKI, HELP ME WITH THE BODY.
WHAT DID YOU RUN INTO, GUNJI, WHEN YOUR OWN ARROW FOUND ITS WAY THROUGH YOUR MOUTH.
WAIT. WHAT'S THAT?
I KNEW WHAT IT WAS...

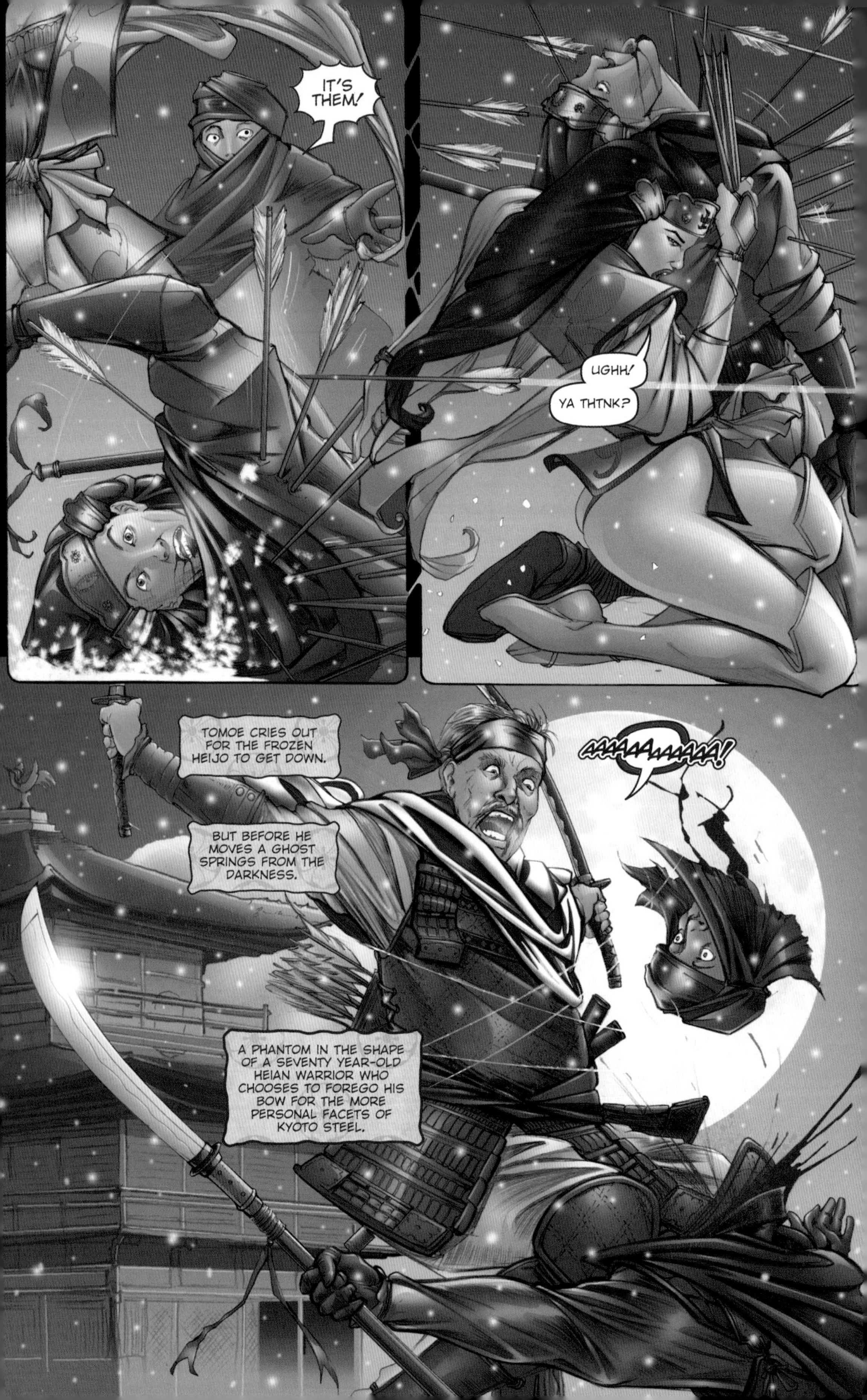
IT'S THEM!
UGHH!
YA THTNK?
TOMOE CRIES OUT FOR THE FROZEN HEIJO TO GET DOWN.
BUT BEFORE HE MOVES A GHOST SPRINGS FROM THE DARKNESS.
AAAAAAAAAAAA!
A PHANTOM IN THE SHAPE OF A SEVENTY YEAR-OLD HEIAN WARRIOR WHO CHOOSES TO FOREGO HIS BOW FOR THE MORE PERSONAL FACETS OF KYOTO STEEL.

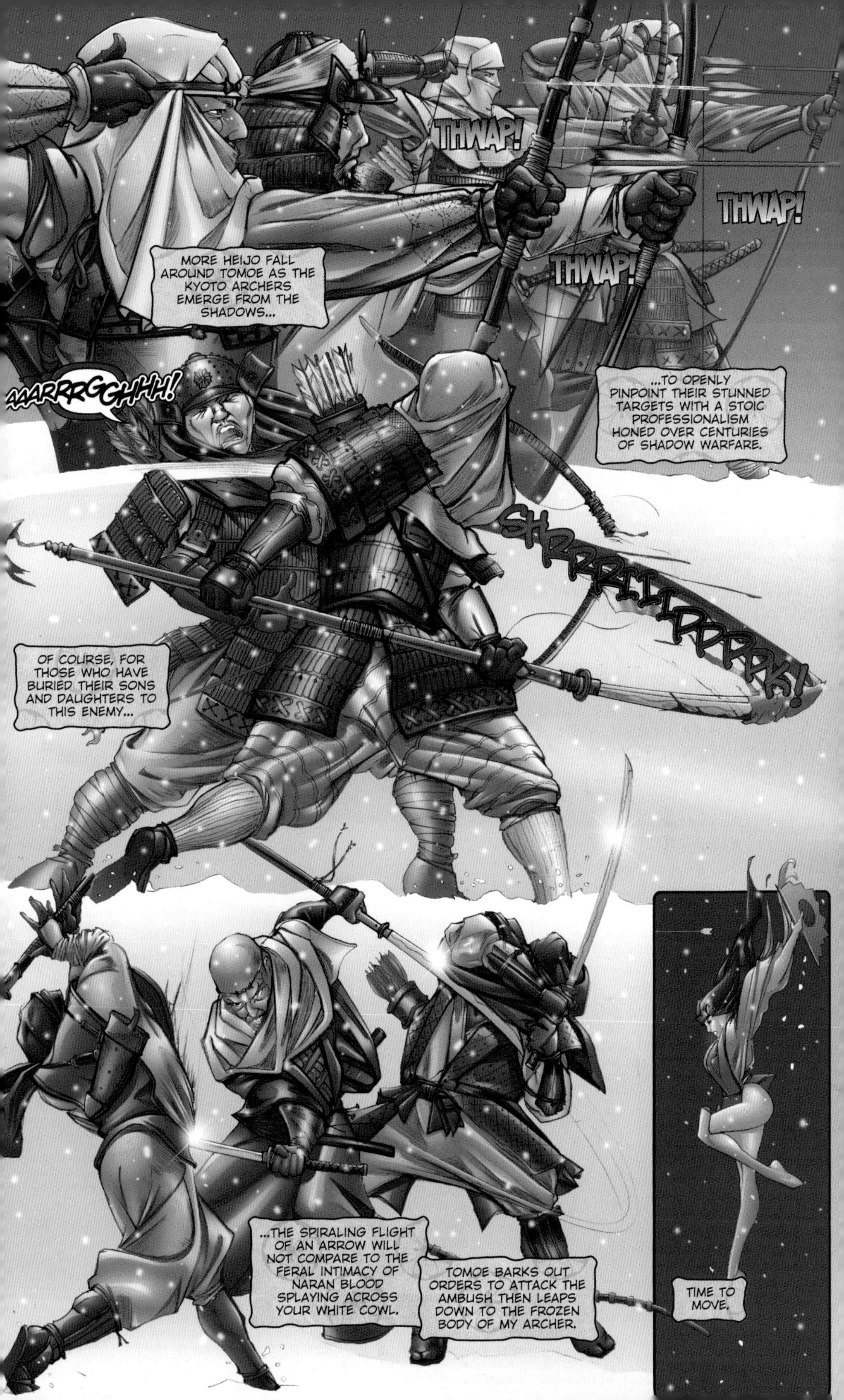
THWAP!
THWAP!
THWAP!
MORE HEIJO FALL AROUND TOMOE AS THE KYOTO ARCHERS EMERGE FROM THE SHADOWS...
...TO OPENLY PINPOINT THEIR STUNNED TARGETS WITH A STOIC PROFESSIONALISM HONED OVER CENTURIES OF SHADOW WARFARE.
AAARRRGGHHH!
SHRRRIIIDDDDK!
OF COURSE, FOR THOSE WHO HAVE BURIED THEIR SONS AND DAUGHTERS TO THIS ENEMY...
...THE SPIRALING FLIGHT OF AN ARROW WILL NOT COMPARE TO THE FERAL INTIMACY OF NARAN BLOOD SPLAYING ACROSS YOUR WHITE COWL.
TOMOE BARKS OUT ORDERS TO ATTACK THE AMBUSH THEN LEAPS DOWN TO THE FROZEN BODY OF MY ARCHER.
TIME TO MOVE.

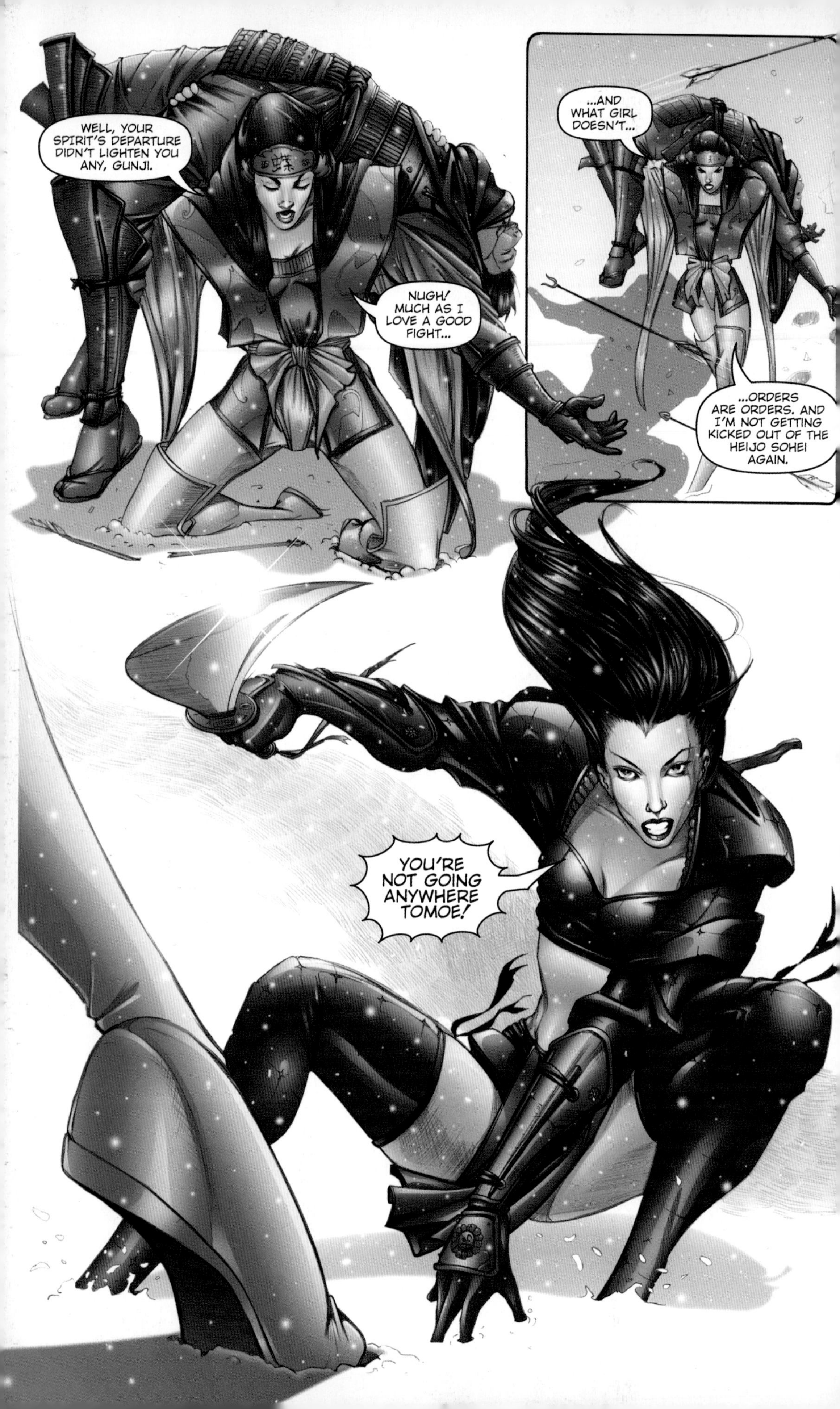
WELL, YOUR SPIRIT'S DEPARTURE DIDN'T LIGHTEN YOU ANY, GUNJI.
NUGH! MUCH AS I LOVE A GOOD FIGHT...
...AND WHAT GIRL DOESN'T...
...ORDERS ARE ORDERS. AND I'M NOT GETTING KICKED OUT OF THE HEIJO SOHEI AGAIN.
YOU'RE NOT GOING ANYWHERE TOMOE!

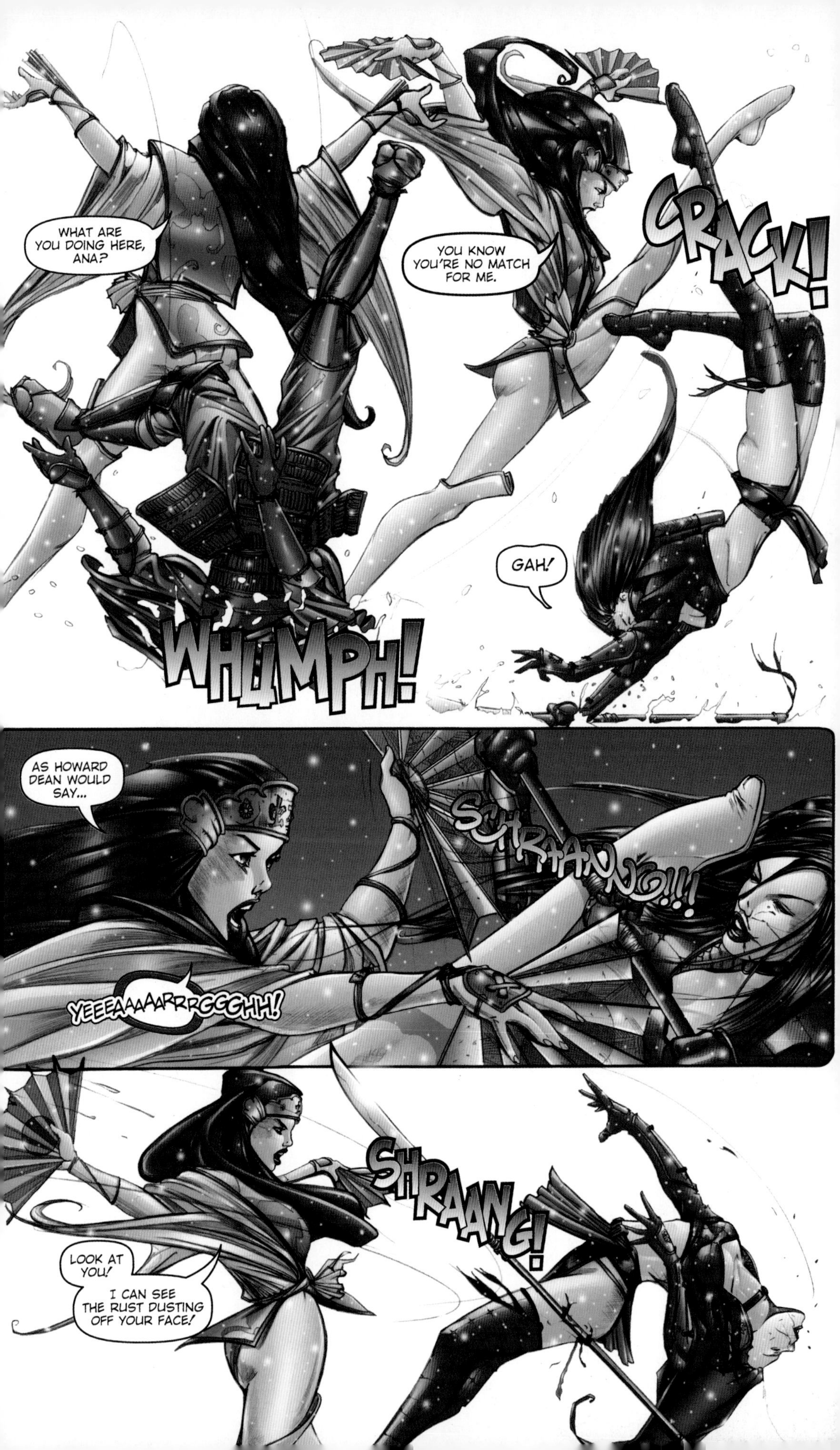
WHAT ARE YOU DOING HERE, ANA?
YOU KNOW YOU'RE NO MATCH FOR ME.
CRACK!
GAH!
WHUMPH!
AS HOWARD DEAN WOULD SAY...
SCHRAANNG!!!
YEEEAAAARRRGGHH!
SHRAANG!
LOOK AT YOU!
I CAN SEE THE RUST DUSTING OFF YOUR FACE!

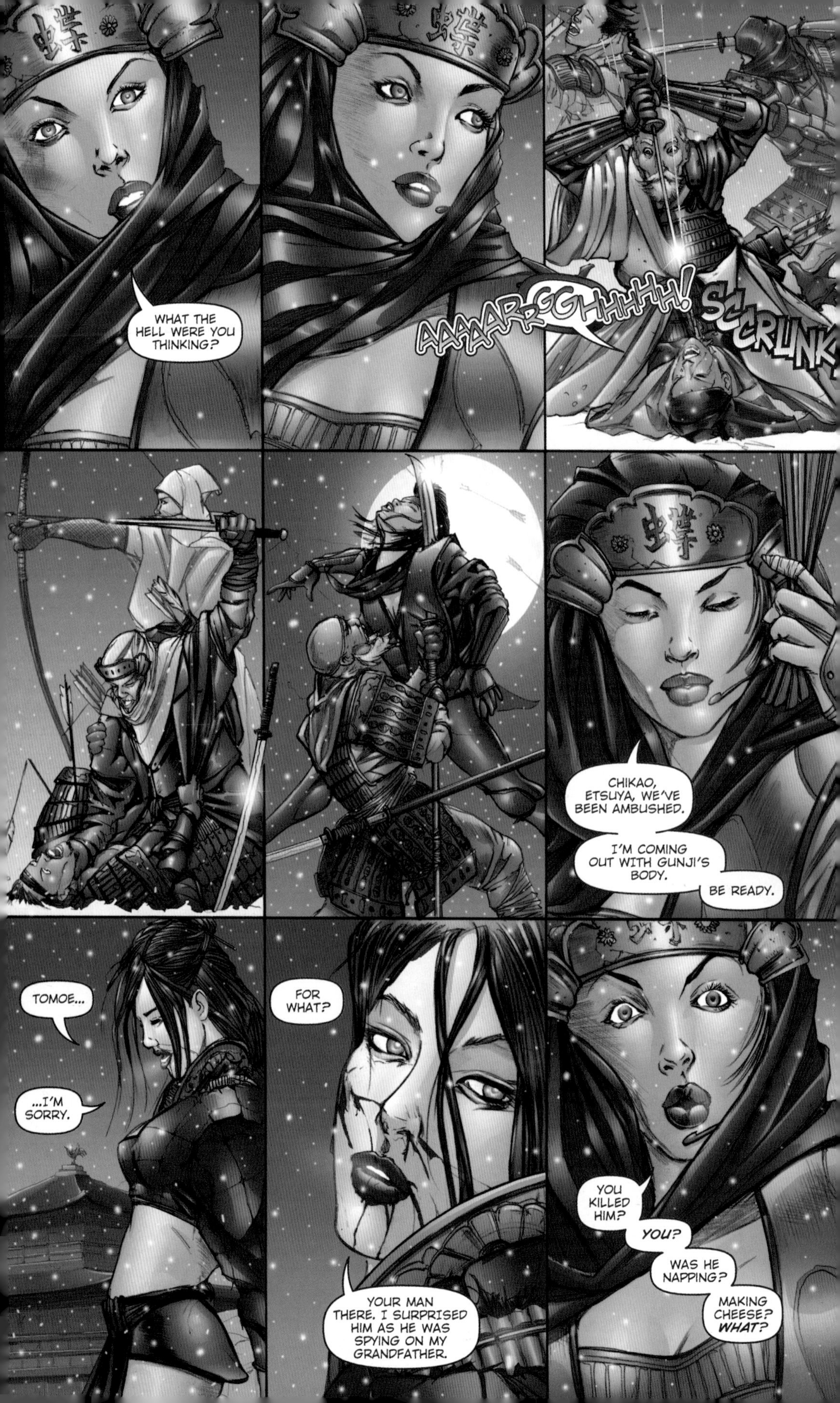
WHAT THE HELL WERE YOU THINKING?
AAAAARRGGHHHHH!
SCCRUNK
CHIKAO, ETSUYA, WE'VE BEEN AMBUSHED.
I'M COMING OUT WITH GUNJI'S BODY.
BE READY.
TOMOE...
...I'M SORRY.
FOR WHAT?
YOUR MAN THERE. I SURPRISED HIM AS HE WAS SPYING ON MY GRANDFATHER.
YOU KILLED HIM?
YOU?
WAS HE NAPPING?
MAKING CHEESE? ***WHAT?***

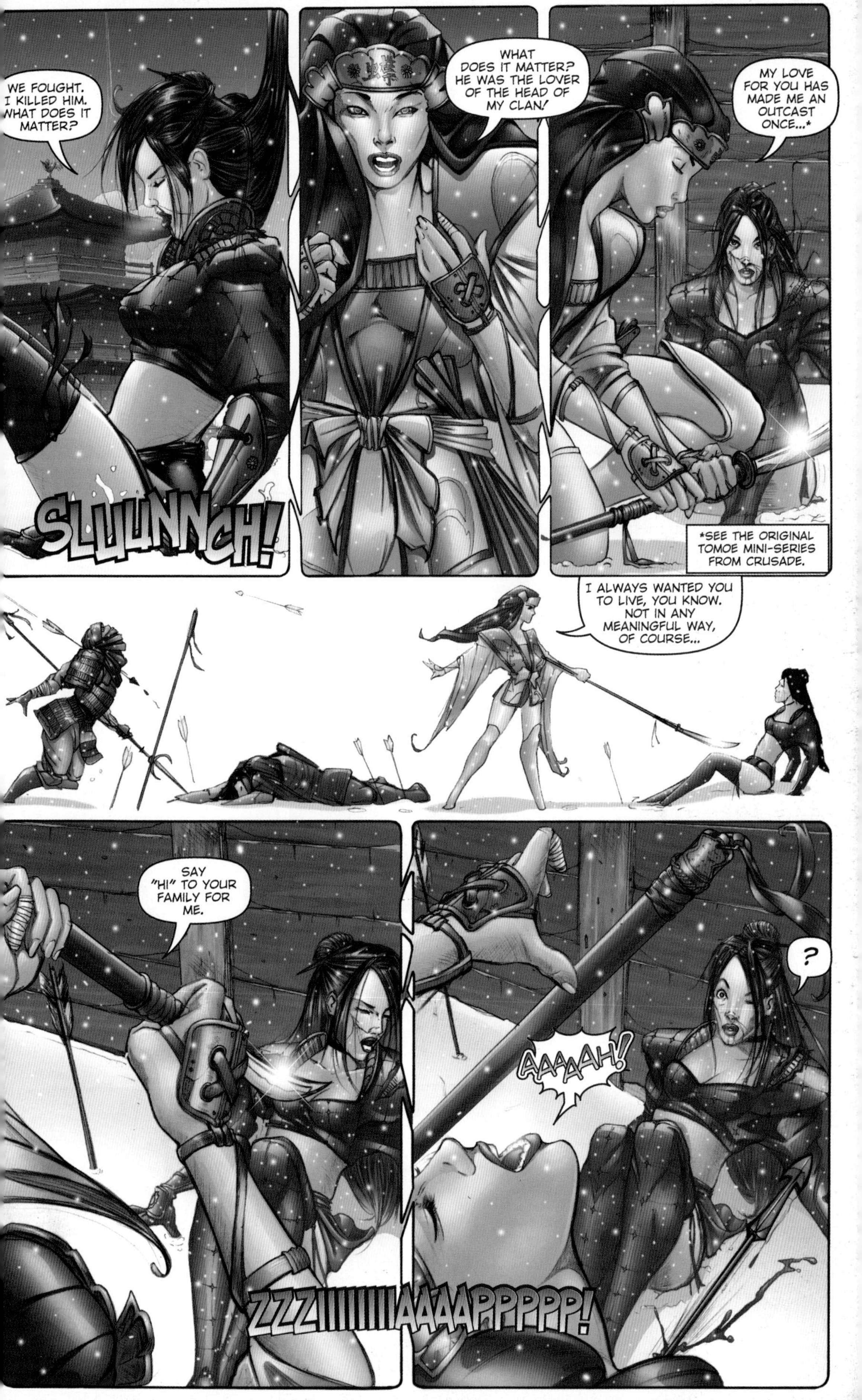
WE FOUGHT. I KILLED HIM. WHAT DOES IT MATTER?
SLUUNNCH!
WHAT DOES IT MATTER? HE WAS THE LOVER OF THE HEAD OF MY CLAN!
MY LOVE FOR YOU HAS MADE ME AN OUTCAST ONCE...*
*SEE THE ORIGINAL TOMOE MINI-SERIES FROM CRUSADE.
I ALWAYS WANTED YOU TO LIVE, YOU KNOW. NOT IN ANY MEANINGFUL WAY, OF COURSE...
SAY "HI" TO YOUR FAMILY FOR ME.
AAAAAH!
?
ZZZIIIIIIIIAAAAPPPPPP!

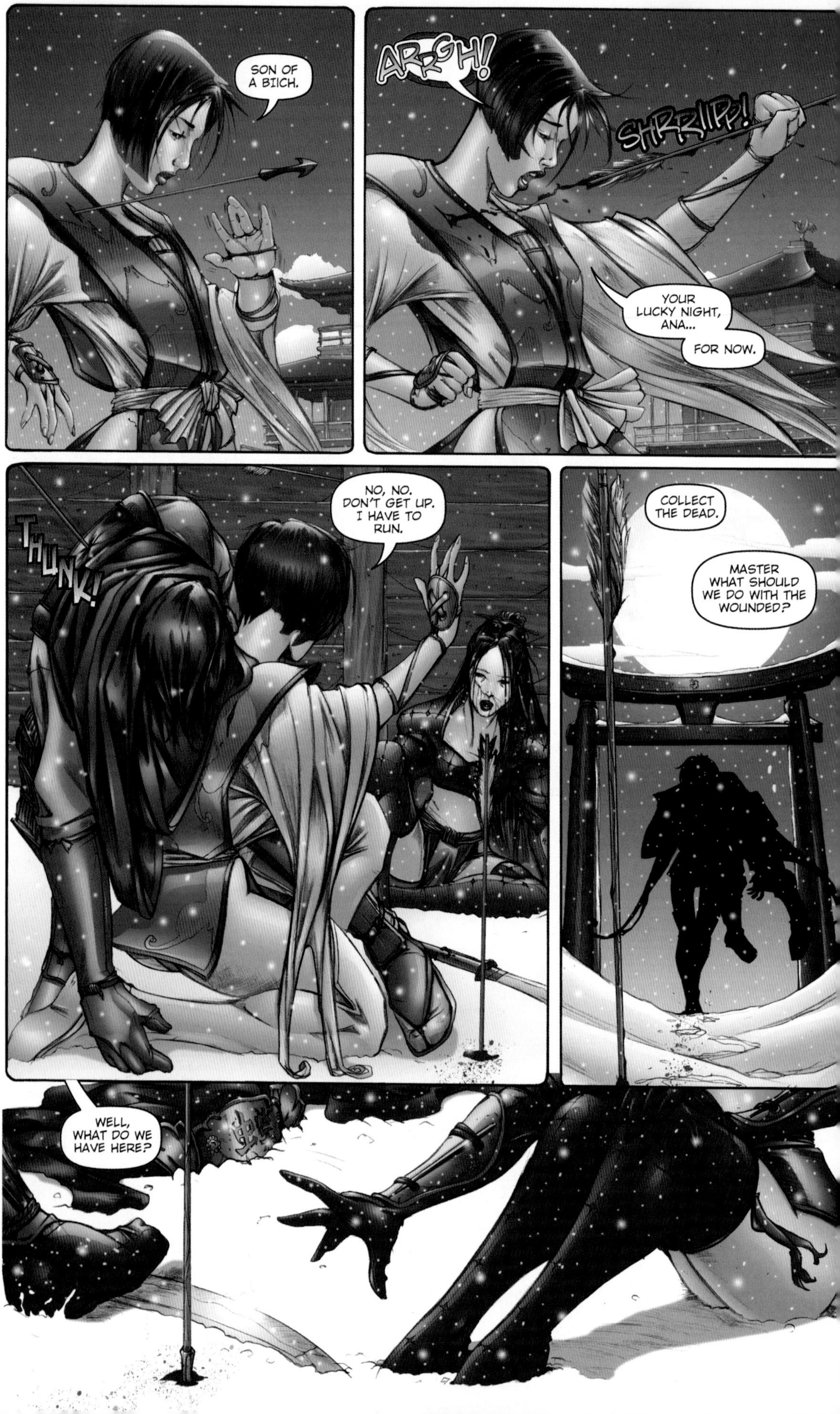
SON OF A BIICH.
ARRGH!
SHRRIIPP!
YOUR LUCKY NIGHT, ANA...
FOR NOW.
THUNK!
NO, NO. DON'T GET UP. I HAVE TO RUN.
COLLECT THE DEAD.
MASTER WHAT SHOULD WE DO WITH THE WOUNDED?
WELL, WHAT DO WE HAVE HERE?

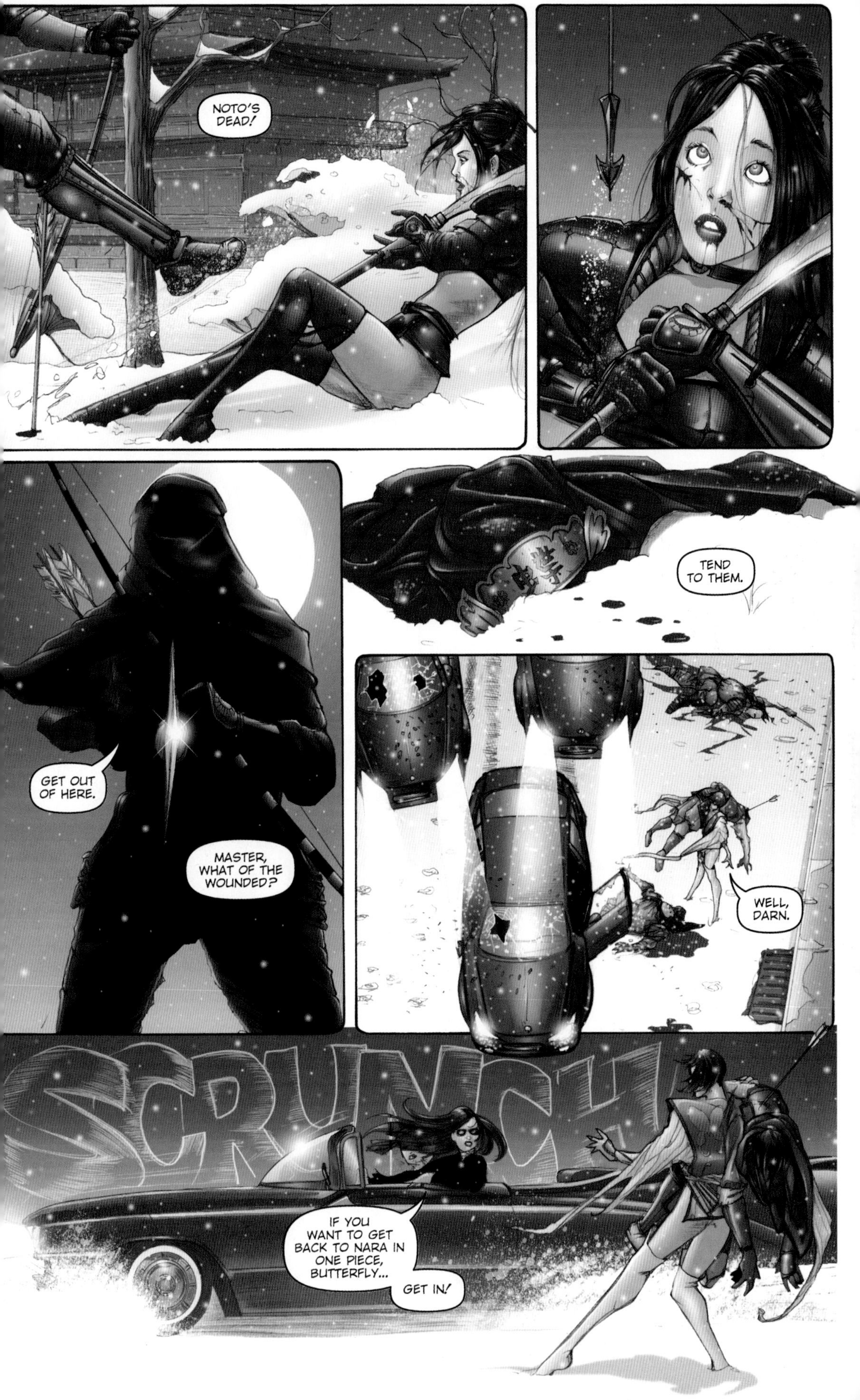
NOTO'S DEAD!
GET OUT OF HERE.
MASTER, WHAT OF THE WOUNDED?
TEND TO THEM.
WELL, DARN.
SCRUNCH
IF YOU WANT TO GET BACK TO NARA IN ONE PIECE, BUTTERFLY...
GET IN!

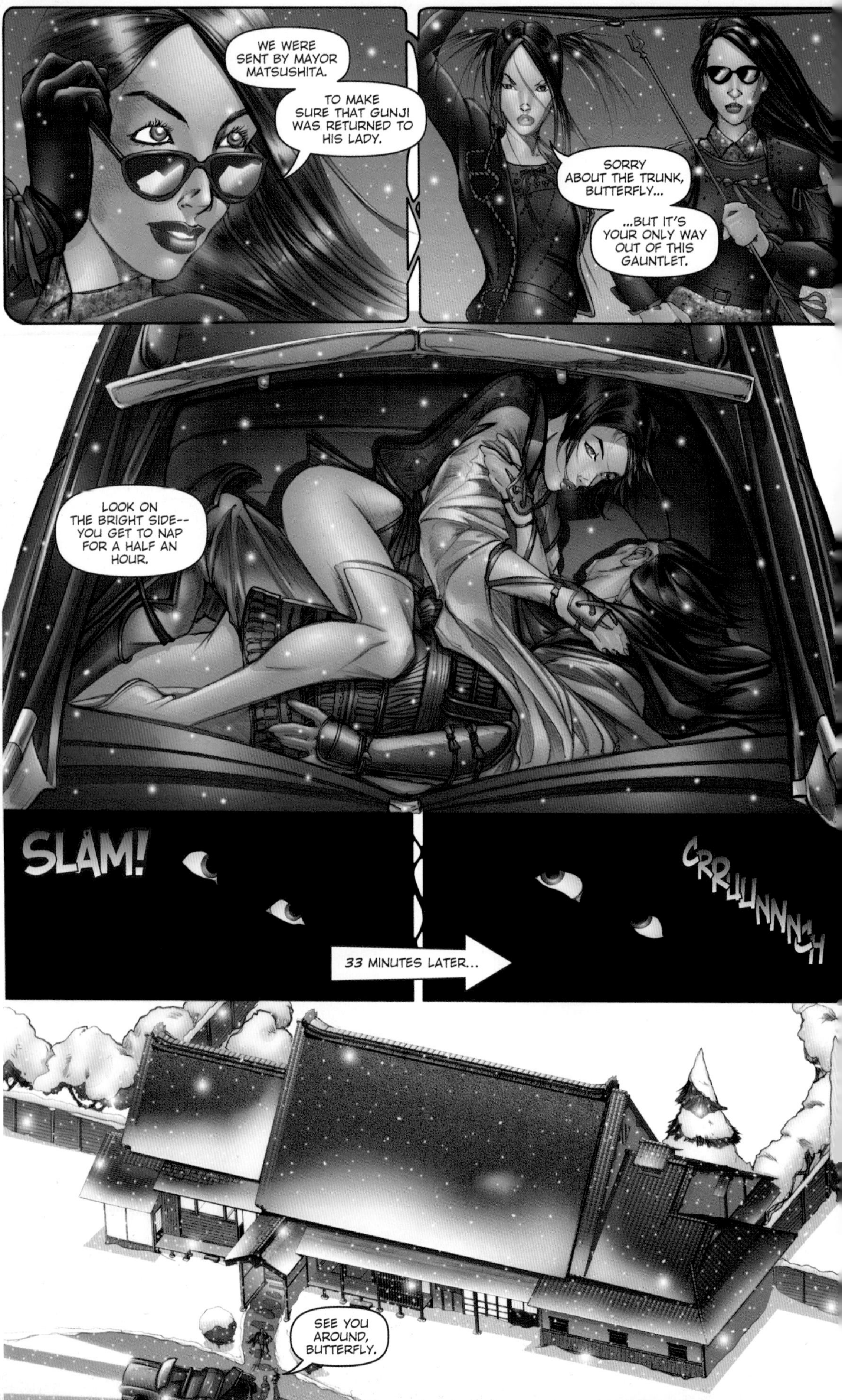
WE WERE SENT BY MAYOR MATSUSHITA.
TO MAKE SURE THAT GUNJI WAS RETURNED TO HIS LADY.
SORRY ABOUT THE TRUNK, BUTTERFLY...
...BUT IT'S YOUR ONLY WAY OUT OF THIS GAUNTLET.
LOOK ON THE BRIGHT SIDE--YOU GET TO NAP FOR A HALF AN HOUR.
SLAM!
33 MINUTES LATER...
CRRUUNNNCH
SEE YOU AROUND, BUTTERFLY.

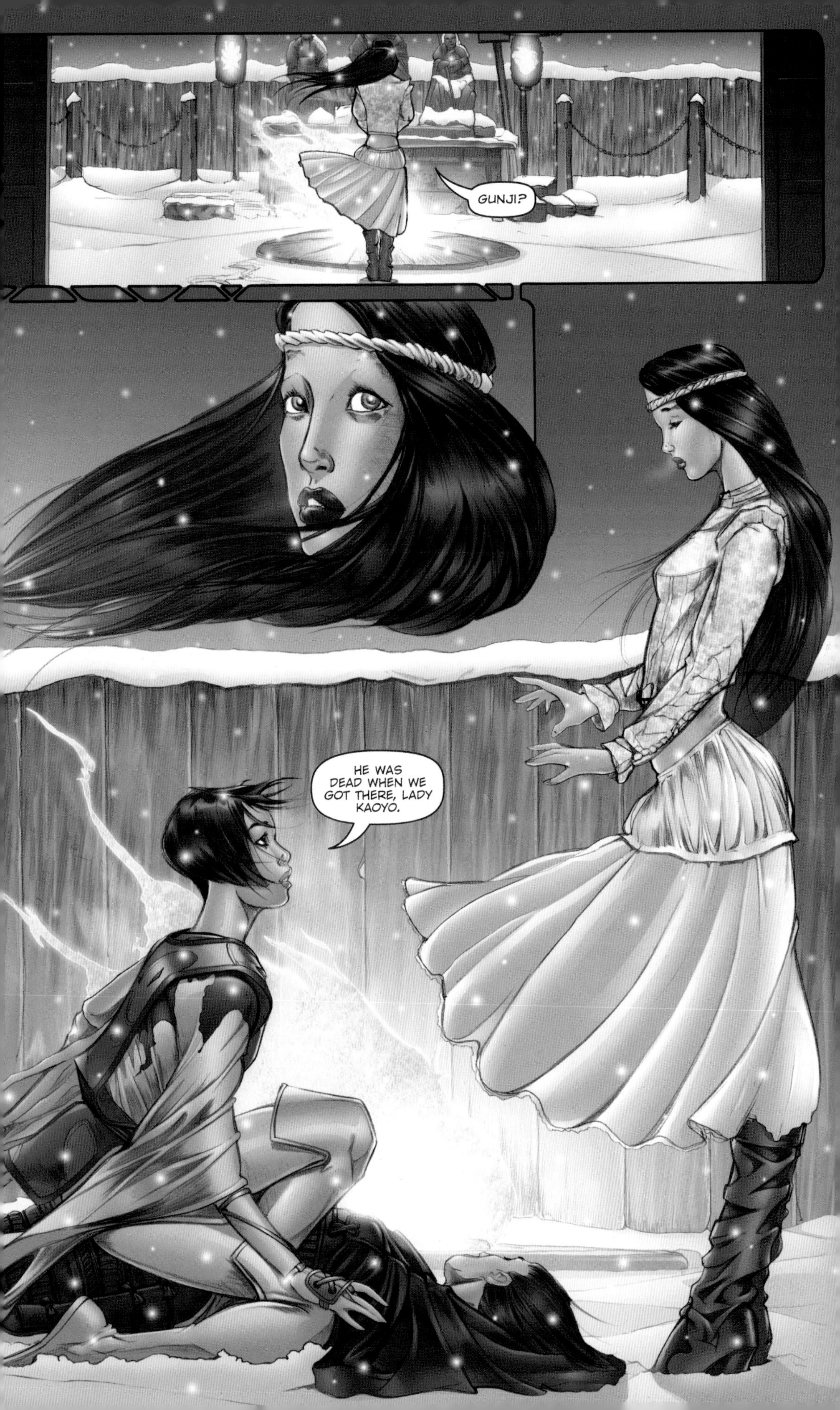
GUNJI?
HE WAS DEAD WHEN WE GOT THERE, LADY KAOYO.

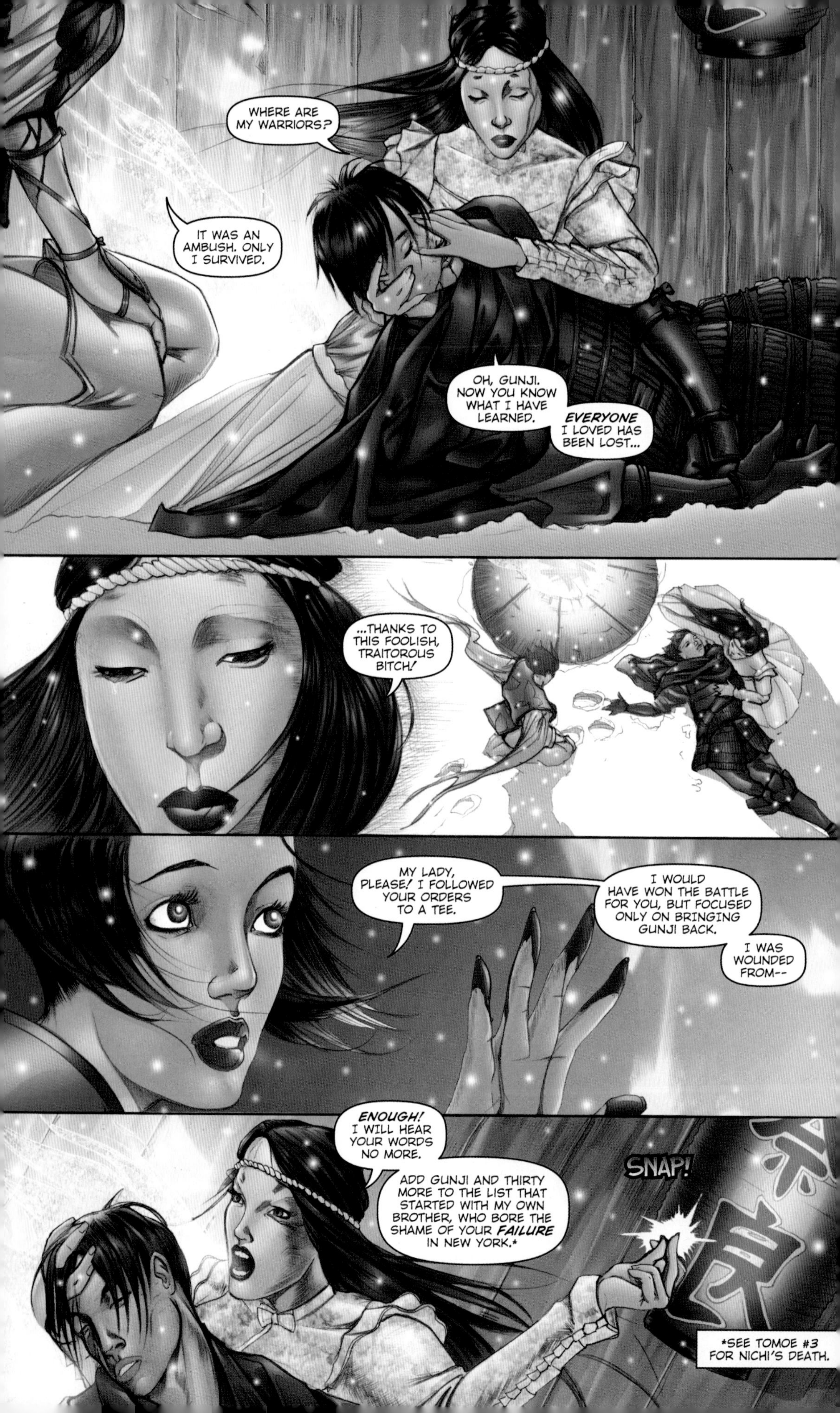
WHERE ARE MY WARRIORS?
IT WAS AN AMBUSH. ONLY I SURVIVED.
OH, GUNJI. NOW YOU KNOW WHAT I HAVE LEARNED.
EVERYONE I LOVED HAS BEEN LOST...
...THANKS TO THIS FOOLISH, TRAITOROUS BITCH!
MY LADY, PLEASE! I FOLLOWED YOUR ORDERS TO A TEE.
I WOULD HAVE WON THE BATTLE FOR YOU, BUT FOCUSED ONLY ON BRINGING GUNJI BACK.
I WAS WOUNDED FROM--
ENOUGH! I WILL HEAR YOUR WORDS NO MORE.
ADD GUNJI AND THIRTY MORE TO THE LIST THAT STARTED WITH MY OWN BROTHER, WHO BORE THE SHAME OF YOUR *FAILURE* IN NEW YORK.*
SNAP!
*SEE TOMOE #3 FOR NICHI'S DEATH.

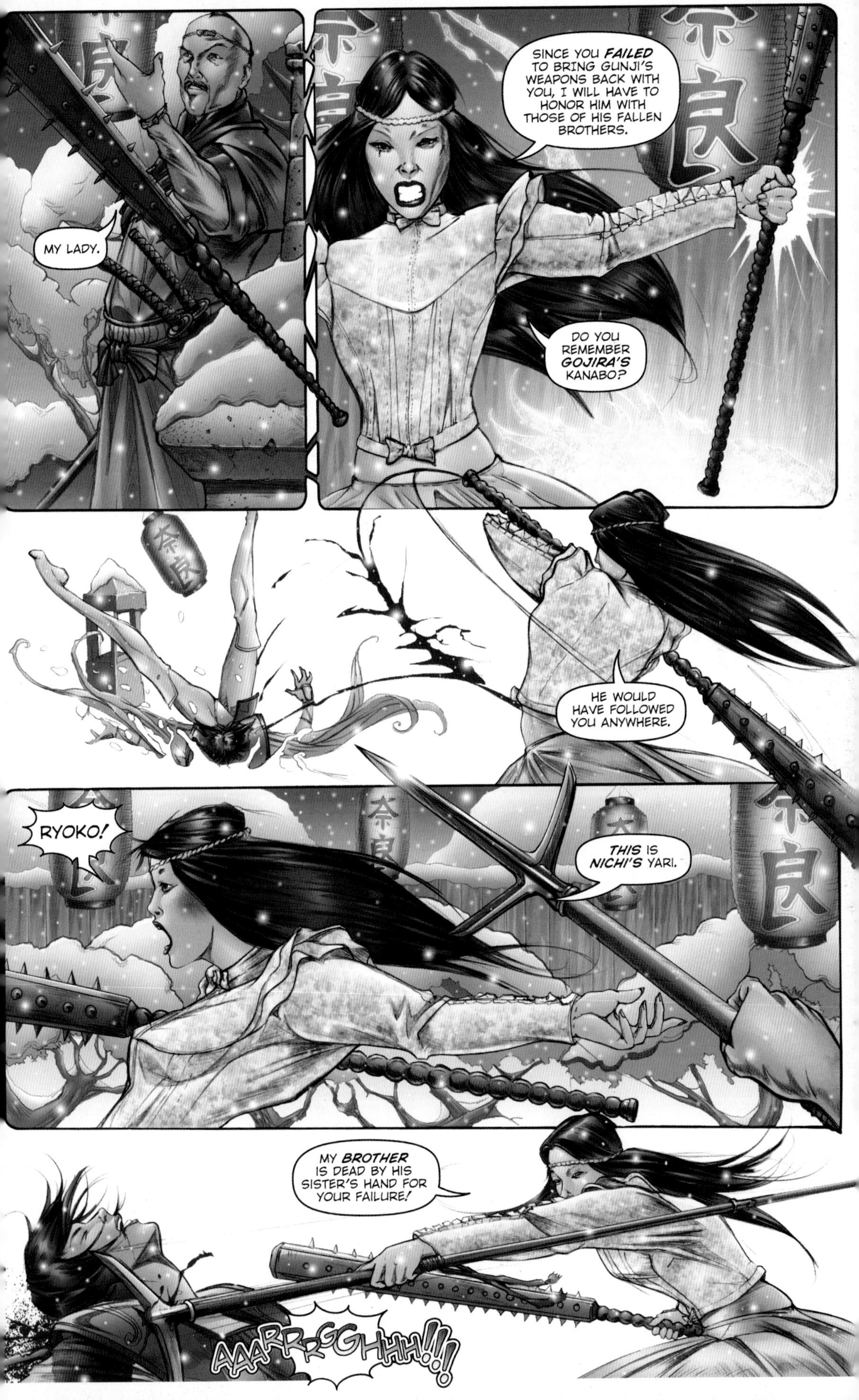

MY LADY.
SINCE YOU FAILED TO BRING GUNJI'S WEAPONS BACK WITH YOU, I WILL HAVE TO HONOR HIM WITH THOSE OF HIS FALLEN BROTHERS.
DO YOU REMEMBER GOJIRA'S KANABO?
HE WOULD HAVE FOLLOWED YOU ANYWHERE.
RYOKO!
THIS IS NICHI'S YARI.
MY BROTHER IS DEAD BY HIS SISTER'S HAND FOR YOUR FAILURE!
AAARRRGHHH!!!

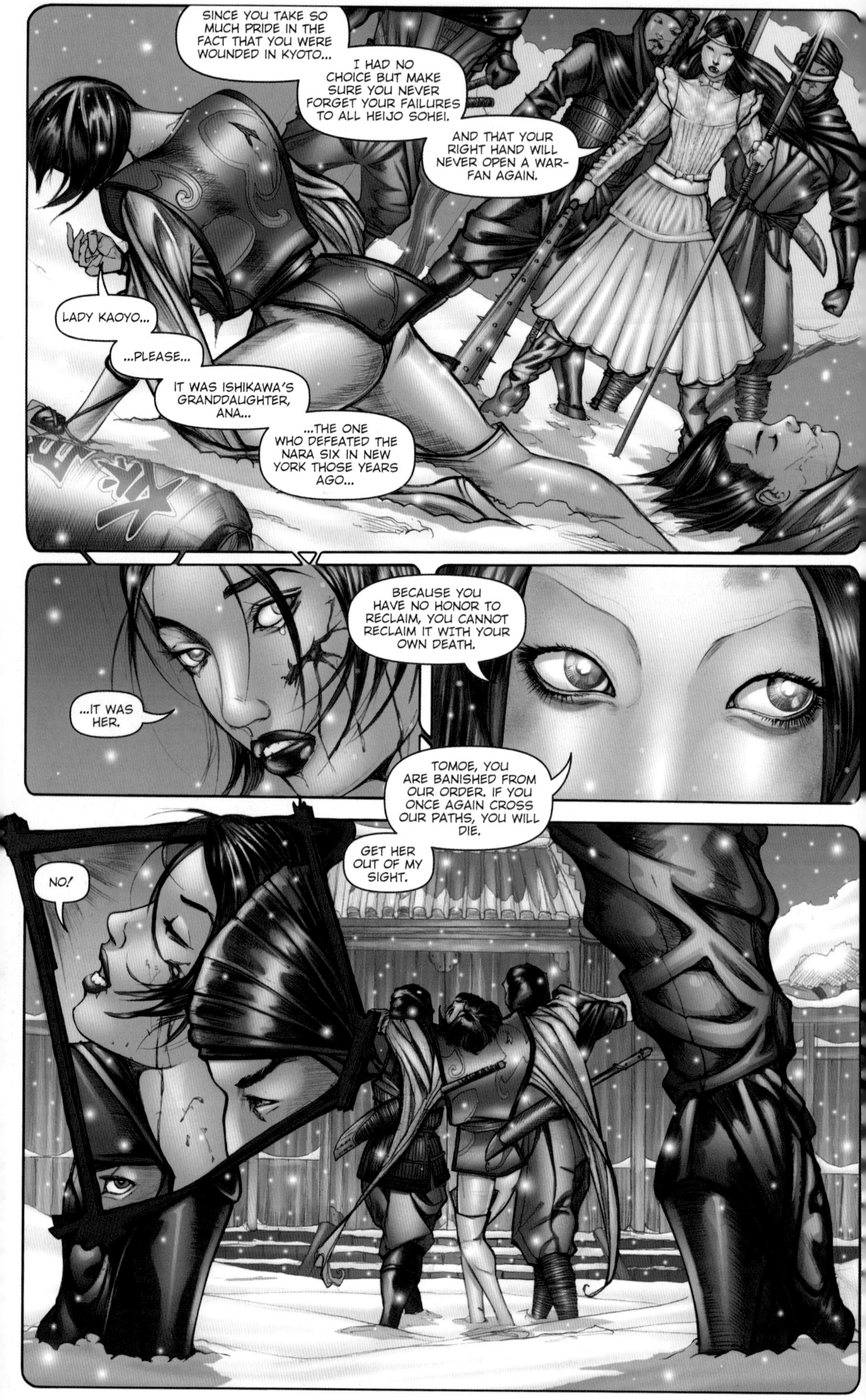

SINCE YOU TAKE SO MUCH PRIDE IN THE FACT THAT YOU WERE WOUNDED IN KYOTO...
I HAD NO CHOICE BUT MAKE SURE YOU NEVER FORGET YOUR FAILURES TO ALL HEIJO SOHEI.
AND THAT YOUR RIGHT HAND WILL NEVER OPEN A WAR-FAN AGAIN.
LADY KAOYO...
...PLEASE...
IT WAS ISHIKAWA'S GRANDDAUGHTER, ANA...
...THE ONE WHO DEFEATED THE NARA SIX IN NEW YORK THOSE YEARS AGO...
...IT WAS HER.
BECAUSE YOU HAVE NO HONOR TO RECLAIM, YOU CANNOT RECLAIM IT WITH YOUR OWN DEATH.
TOMOE, YOU ARE BANISHED FROM OUR ORDER. IF YOU ONCE AGAIN CROSS OUR PATHS, YOU WILL DIE.
NO!
GET HER OUT OF MY SIGHT.

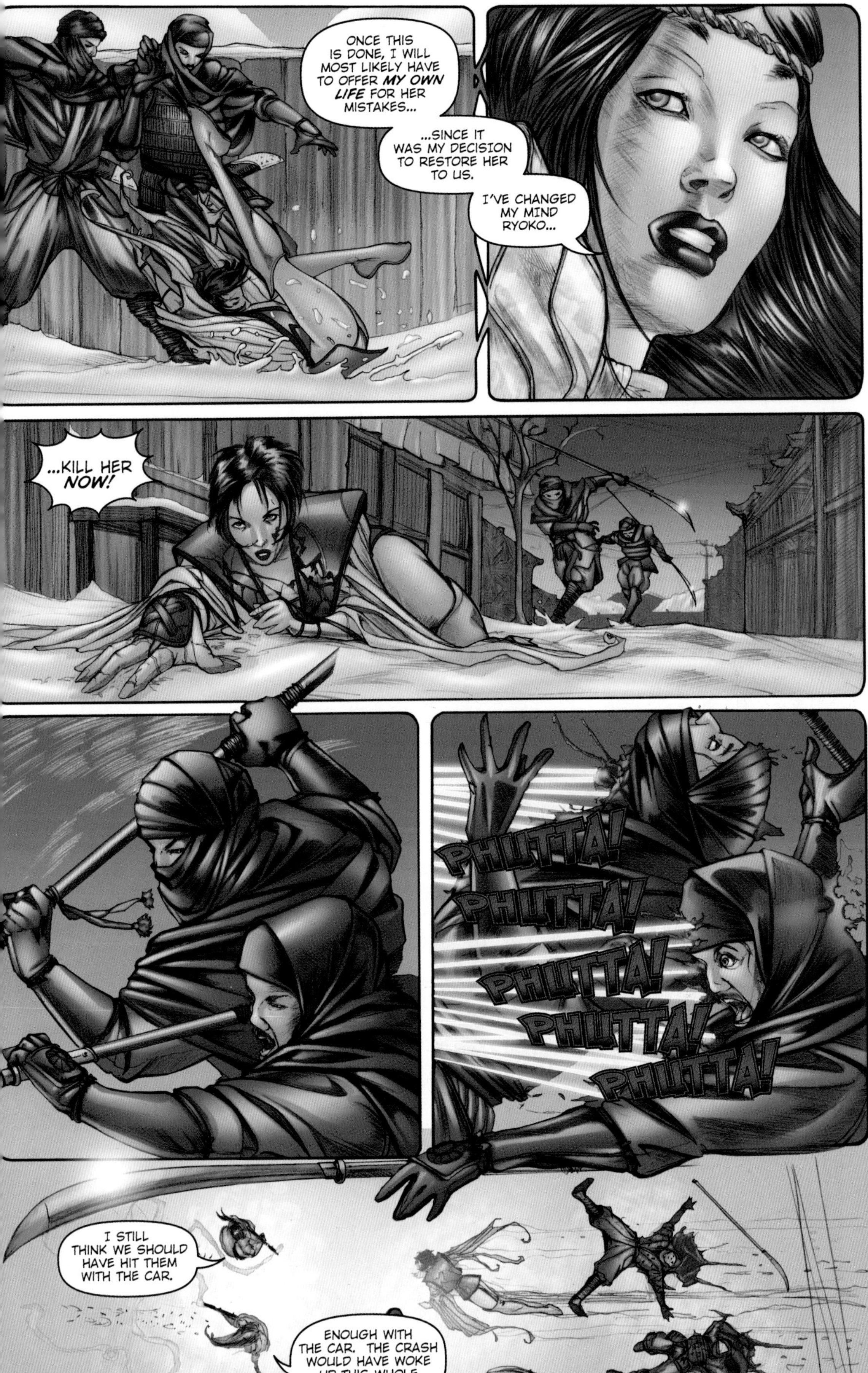
ONCE THIS IS DONE, I WILL MOST LIKELY HAVE TO OFFER MY OWN LIFE FOR HER MISTAKES...
...SINCE IT WAS MY DECISION TO RESTORE HER TO US.
I'VE CHANGED MY MIND RYOKO...
...KILL HER NOW!
PHUTTA!
PHUTTA!
PHUTTA!
PHUTTA!
PHUTTA!
I STILL THINK WE SHOULD HAVE HIT THEM WITH THE CAR.
ENOUGH WITH THE CAR. THE CRASH WOULD HAVE WOKE UP THIS WHOLE DAMN TOWN.

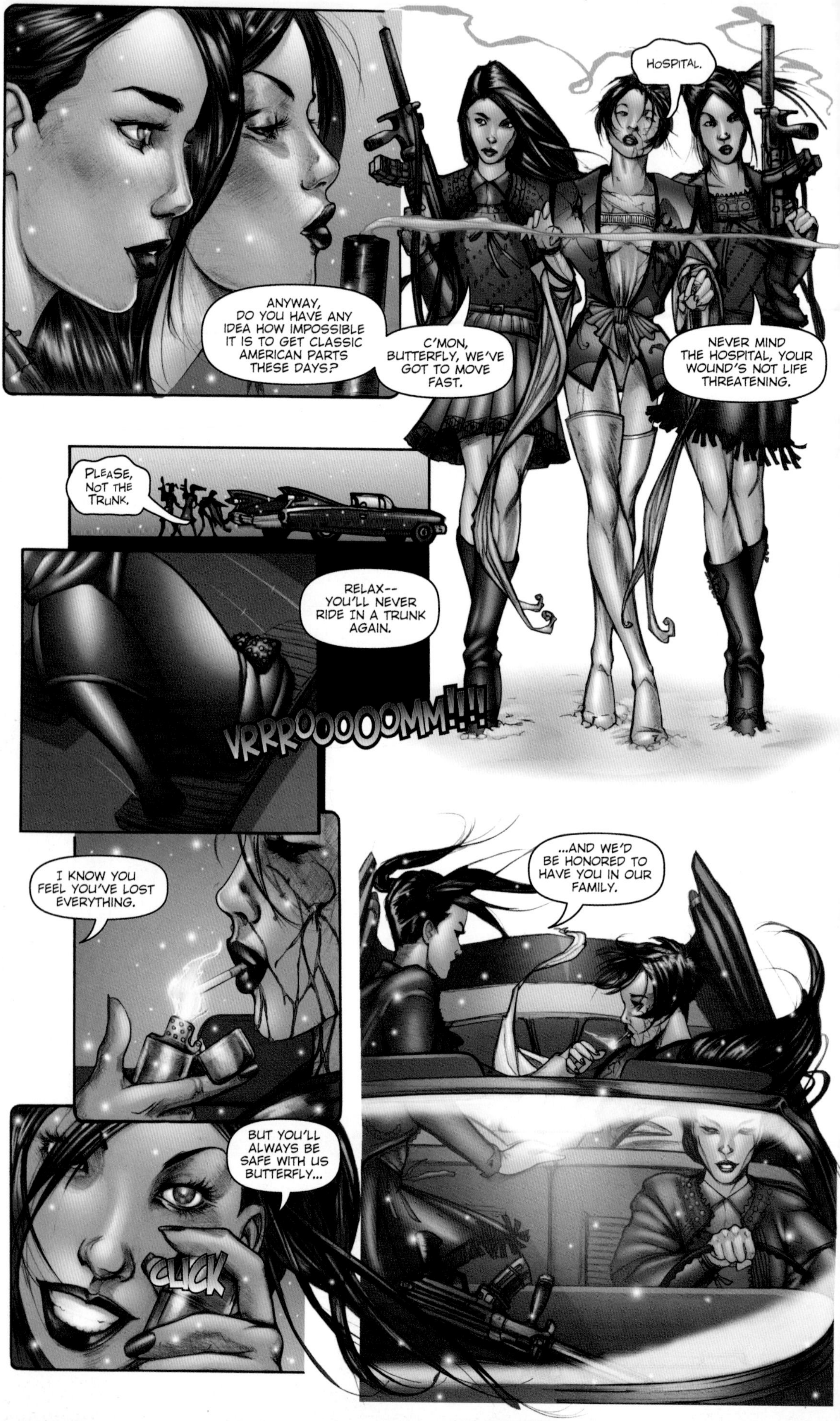

ANYWAY, DO YOU HAVE ANY IDEA HOW IMPOSSIBLE IT IS TO GET CLASSIC AMERICAN PARTS THESE DAYS?
C'MON, BUTTERFLY, WE'VE GOT TO MOVE FAST.
HOSPITAL.
NEVER MIND THE HOSPITAL, YOUR WOUND'S NOT LIFE THREATENING.
PLEASE, NOT THE TRUNK.
RELAX-- YOU'LL NEVER RIDE IN A TRUNK AGAIN.
VRRROOOOOOMM!!!!
I KNOW YOU FEEL YOU'VE LOST EVERYTHING.
BUT YOU'LL ALWAYS BE SAFE WITH US BUTTERFLY...
CLICK
...AND WE'D BE HONORED TO HAVE YOU IN OUR FAMILY.

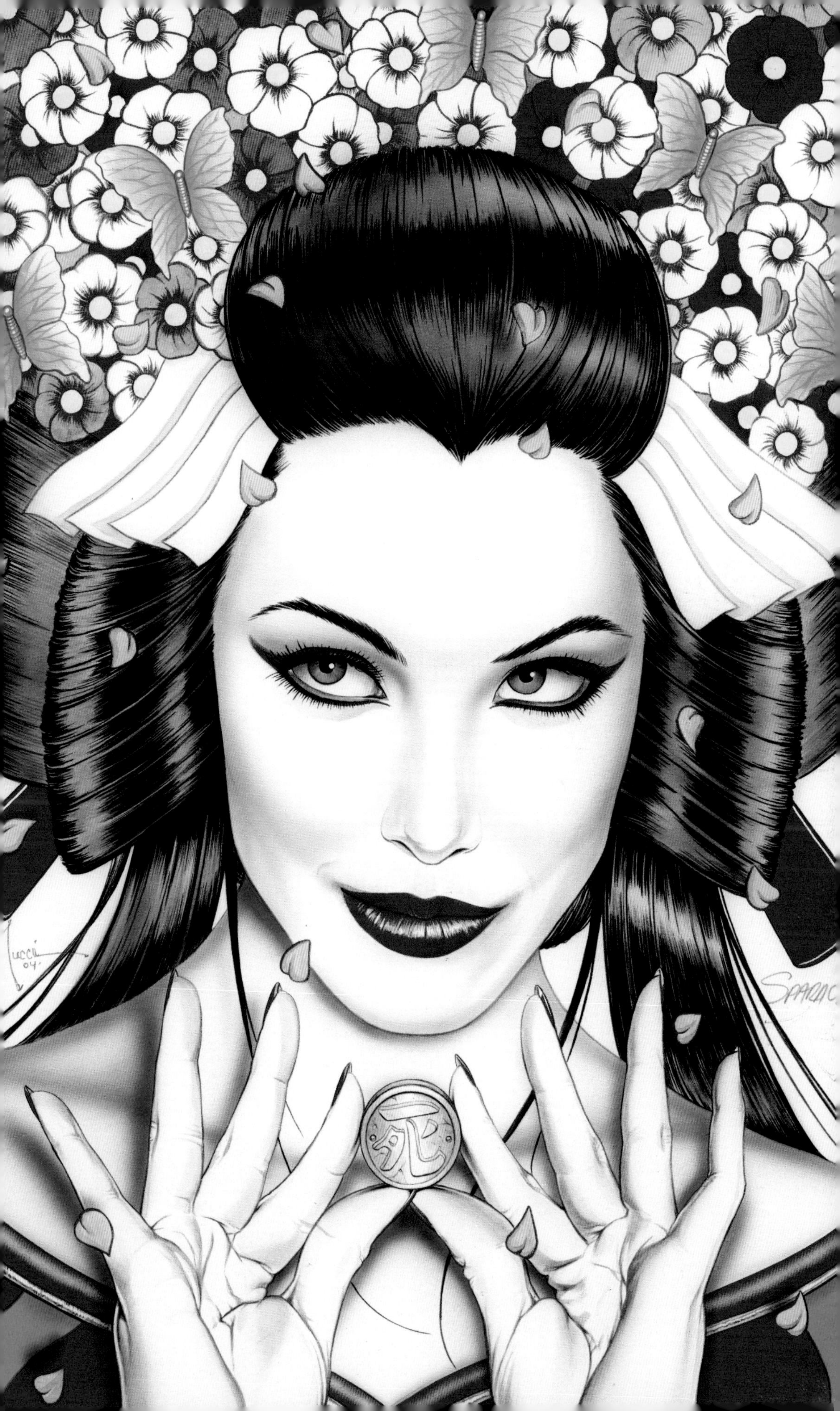

STORY, SCRIPT, AND ILLUSTRATION
Billy Tucci

SCRIPT
J.C. Vaughn

COLORS
**Myrton Belwry, Anna Polonsky,
Wilson Ramos, and Jamie Schaub**

LETTERING
Marshall Dillon

ART SCANNING AND CLEANUP
Mike Kenzine

COVER
Billy Tucci and Mark Sparacio

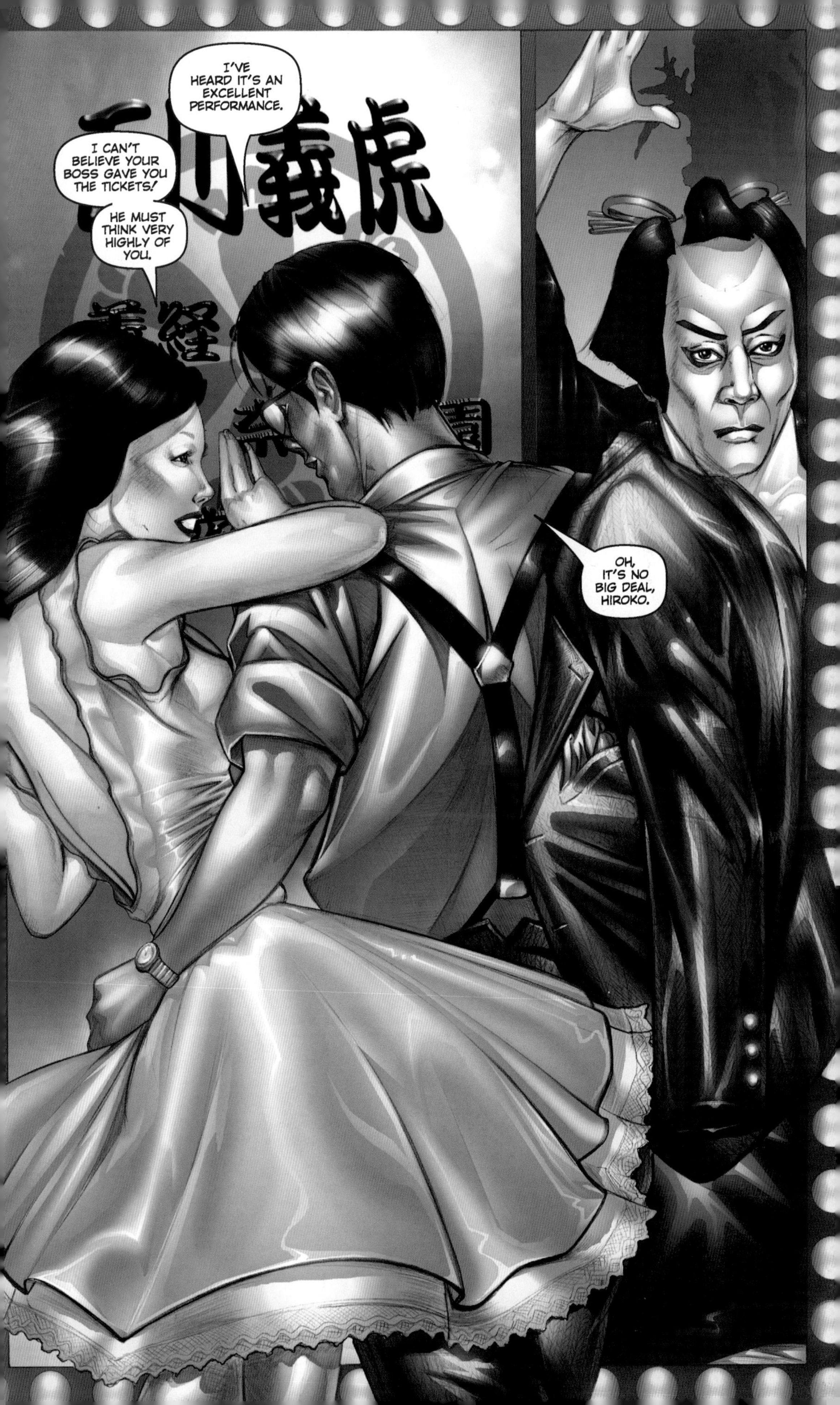
I'VE HEARD IT'S AN EXCELLENT PERFORMANCE.
I CAN'T BELIEVE YOUR BOSS GAVE YOU THE TICKETS!
HE MUST THINK VERY HIGHLY OF YOU.
OH, IT'S NO BIG DEAL, HIROKO.

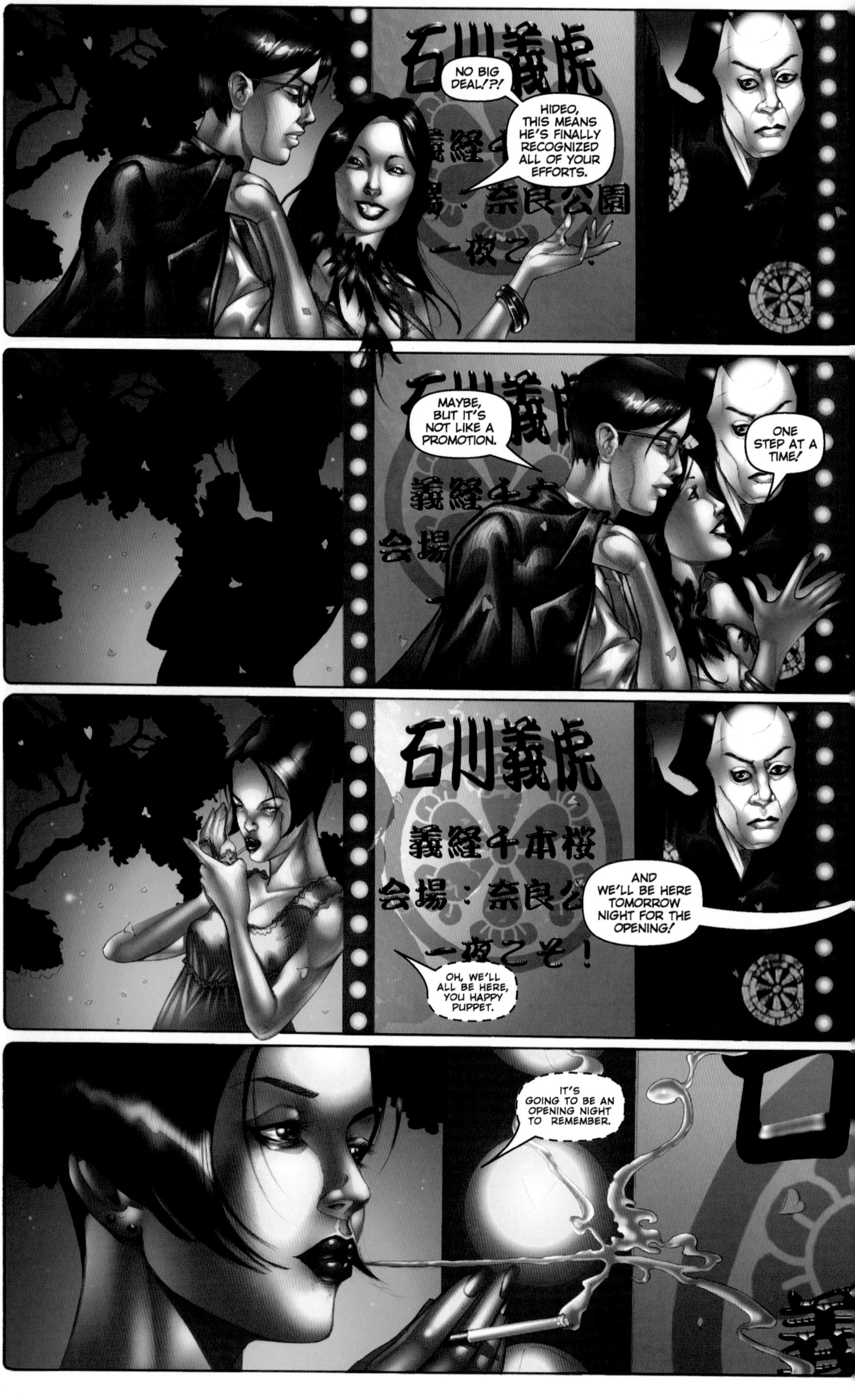
NO BIG DEAL!?!
HIDEO, THIS MEANS HE'S FINALLY RECOGNIZED ALL OF YOUR EFFORTS.
MAYBE, BUT IT'S NOT LIKE A PROMOTION.
ONE STEP AT A TIME!
石川義虎
義経千本桜
会場：奈良公
一夜こそ！
AND WE'LL BE HERE TOMORROW NIGHT FOR THE OPENING!
OH, WE'LL ALL BE HERE, YOU HAPPY PUPPET.
IT'S GOING TO BE AN OPENING NIGHT TO REMEMBER.

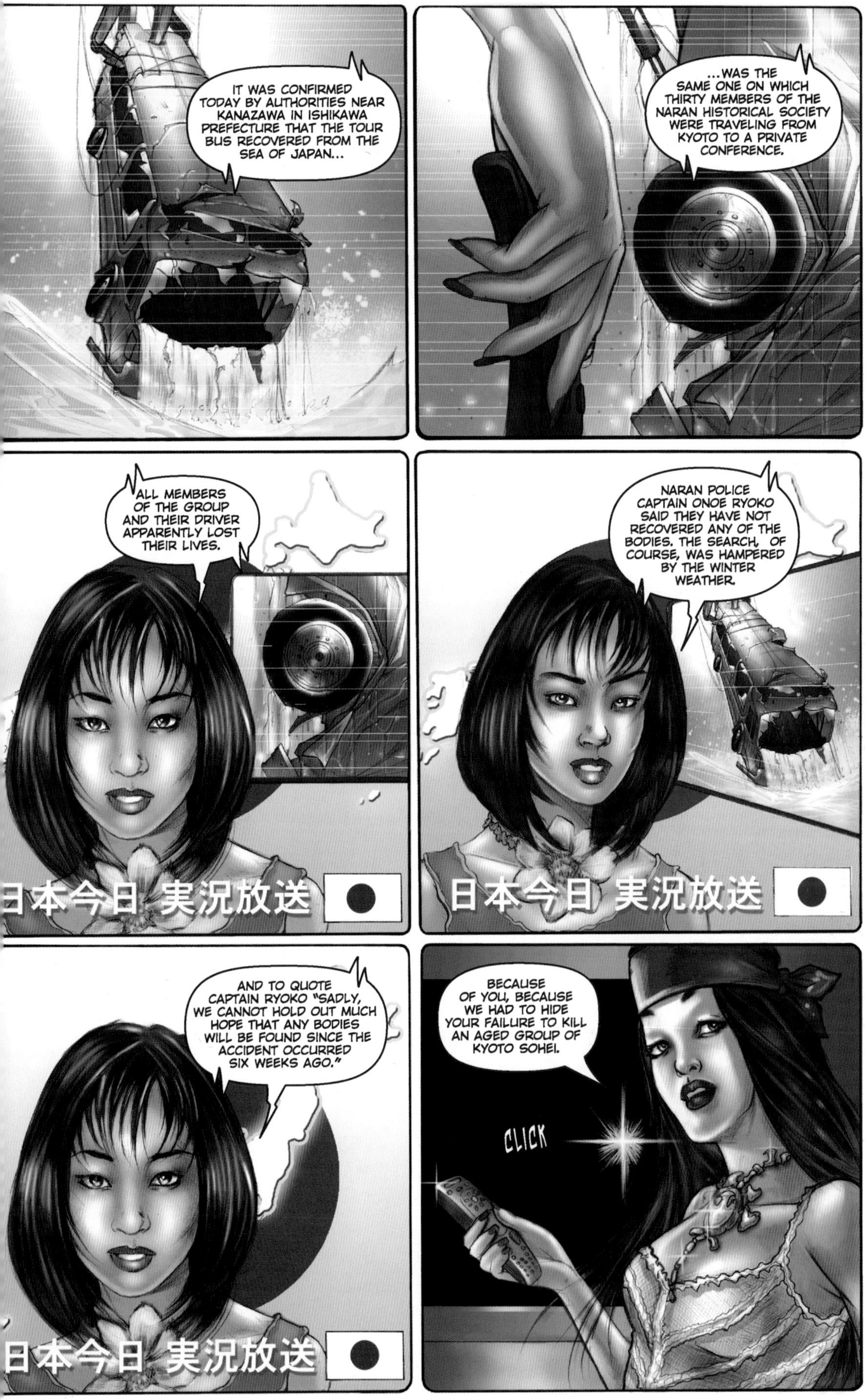
IT WAS CONFIRMED TODAY BY AUTHORITIES NEAR KANAZAWA IN ISHIKAWA PREFECTURE THAT THE TOUR BUS RECOVERED FROM THE SEA OF JAPAN...
...WAS THE SAME ONE ON WHICH THIRTY MEMBERS OF THE NARAN HISTORICAL SOCIETY WERE TRAVELING FROM KYOTO TO A PRIVATE CONFERENCE.
ALL MEMBERS OF THE GROUP AND THEIR DRIVER APPARENTLY LOST THEIR LIVES.
日本今日 実況放送
NARAN POLICE CAPTAIN ONOE RYOKO SAID THEY HAVE NOT RECOVERED ANY OF THE BODIES. THE SEARCH, OF COURSE, WAS HAMPERED BY THE WINTER WEATHER.
日本今日 実況放送
AND TO QUOTE CAPTAIN RYOKO "SADLY, WE CANNOT HOLD OUT MUCH HOPE THAT ANY BODIES WILL BE FOUND SINCE THE ACCIDENT OCCURRED SIX WEEKS AGO."
日本今日 実況放送
BECAUSE OF YOU, BECAUSE WE HAD TO HIDE YOUR FAILURE TO KILL AN AGED GROUP OF KYOTO SOHEI.
CLICK

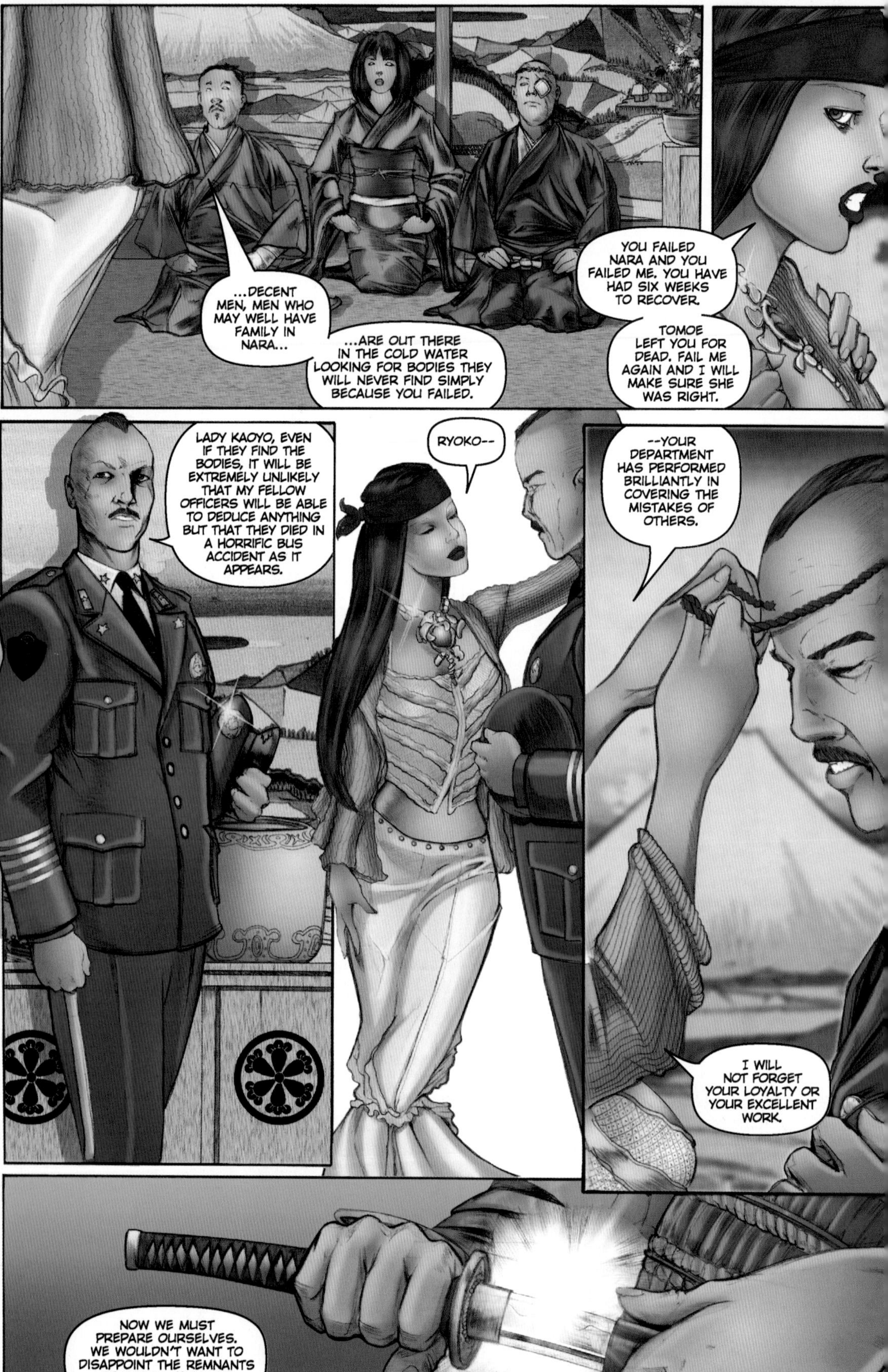
...DECENT MEN, MEN WHO MAY WELL HAVE FAMILY IN NARA...
...ARE OUT THERE IN THE COLD WATER LOOKING FOR BODIES THEY WILL NEVER FIND SIMPLY BECAUSE YOU FAILED.
YOU FAILED NARA AND YOU FAILED ME. YOU HAVE HAD SIX WEEKS TO RECOVER.
TOMOE LEFT YOU FOR DEAD. FAIL ME AGAIN AND I WILL MAKE SURE SHE WAS RIGHT.
LADY KAOYO, EVEN IF THEY FIND THE BODIES, IT WILL BE EXTREMELY UNLIKELY THAT MY FELLOW OFFICERS WILL BE ABLE TO DEDUCE ANYTHING BUT THAT THEY DIED IN A HORRIFIC BUS ACCIDENT AS IT APPEARS.
RYOKO--
--YOUR DEPARTMENT HAS PERFORMED BRILLIANTLY IN COVERING THE MISTAKES OF OTHERS.
I WILL NOT FORGET YOUR LOYALTY OR YOUR EXCELLENT WORK.
NOW WE MUST PREPARE OURSELVES. WE WOULDN'T WANT TO DISAPPOINT THE REMNANTS OF KYOTO. I'M SURE THEY'LL BE READY.

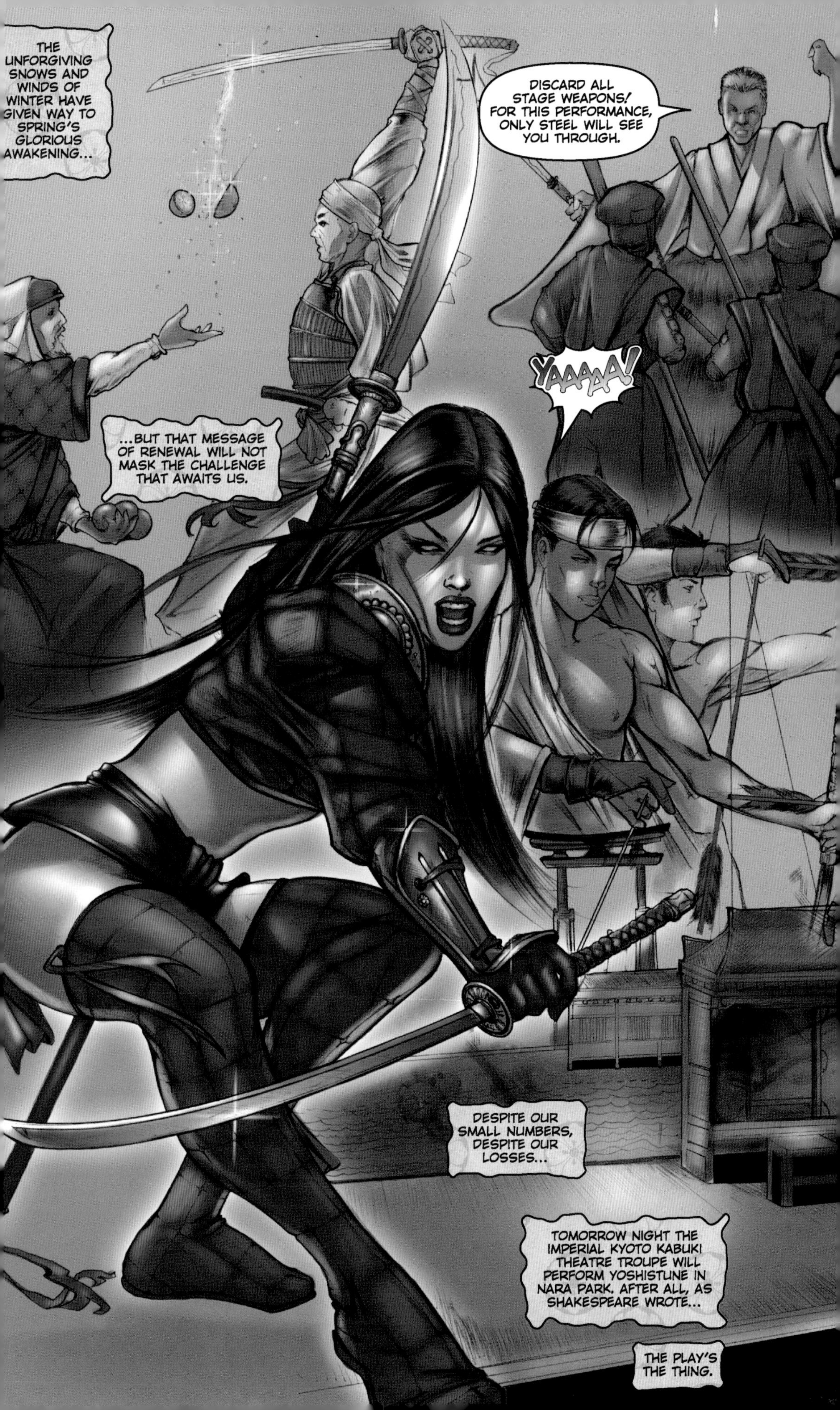
THE UNFORGIVING SNOWS AND WINDS OF WINTER HAVE GIVEN WAY TO SPRING'S GLORIOUS AWAKENING...
DISCARD ALL STAGE WEAPONS! FOR THIS PERFORMANCE, ONLY STEEL WILL SEE YOU THROUGH.
YAAAAA!
...BUT THAT MESSAGE OF RENEWAL WILL NOT MASK THE CHALLENGE THAT AWAITS US.
DESPITE OUR SMALL NUMBERS, DESPITE OUR LOSSES...
TOMORROW NIGHT THE IMPERIAL KYOTO KABUKI THEATRE TROUPE WILL PERFORM YOSHISTUNE IN NARA PARK. AFTER ALL, AS SHAKESPEARE WROTE...
THE PLAY'S THE THING.

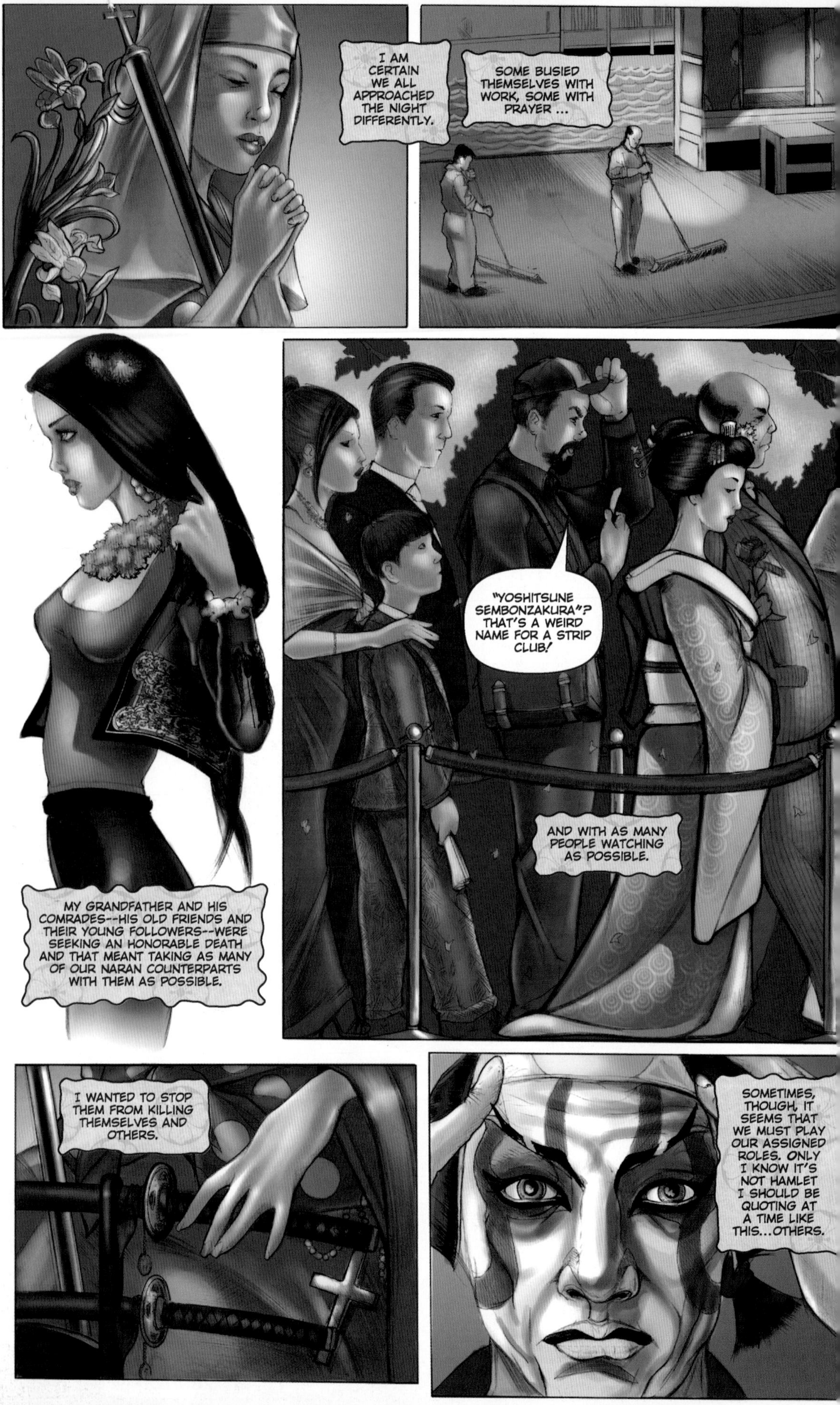
I AM CERTAIN WE ALL APPROACHED THE NIGHT DIFFERENTLY.
SOME BUSIED THEMSELVES WITH WORK, SOME WITH PRAYER ...
MY GRANDFATHER AND HIS COMRADES--HIS OLD FRIENDS AND THEIR YOUNG FOLLOWERS--WERE SEEKING AN HONORABLE DEATH AND THAT MEANT TAKING AS MANY OF OUR NARAN COUNTERPARTS WITH THEM AS POSSIBLE.
"YOSHITSUNE SEMBONZAKURA"? THAT'S A WEIRD NAME FOR A STRIP CLUB!
AND WITH AS MANY PEOPLE WATCHING AS POSSIBLE.
I WANTED TO STOP THEM FROM KILLING THEMSELVES AND OTHERS.
SOMETIMES, THOUGH, IT SEEMS THAT WE MUST PLAY OUR ASSIGNED ROLES. ONLY I KNOW IT'S NOT HAMLET I SHOULD BE QUOTING AT A TIME LIKE THIS...OTHERS.

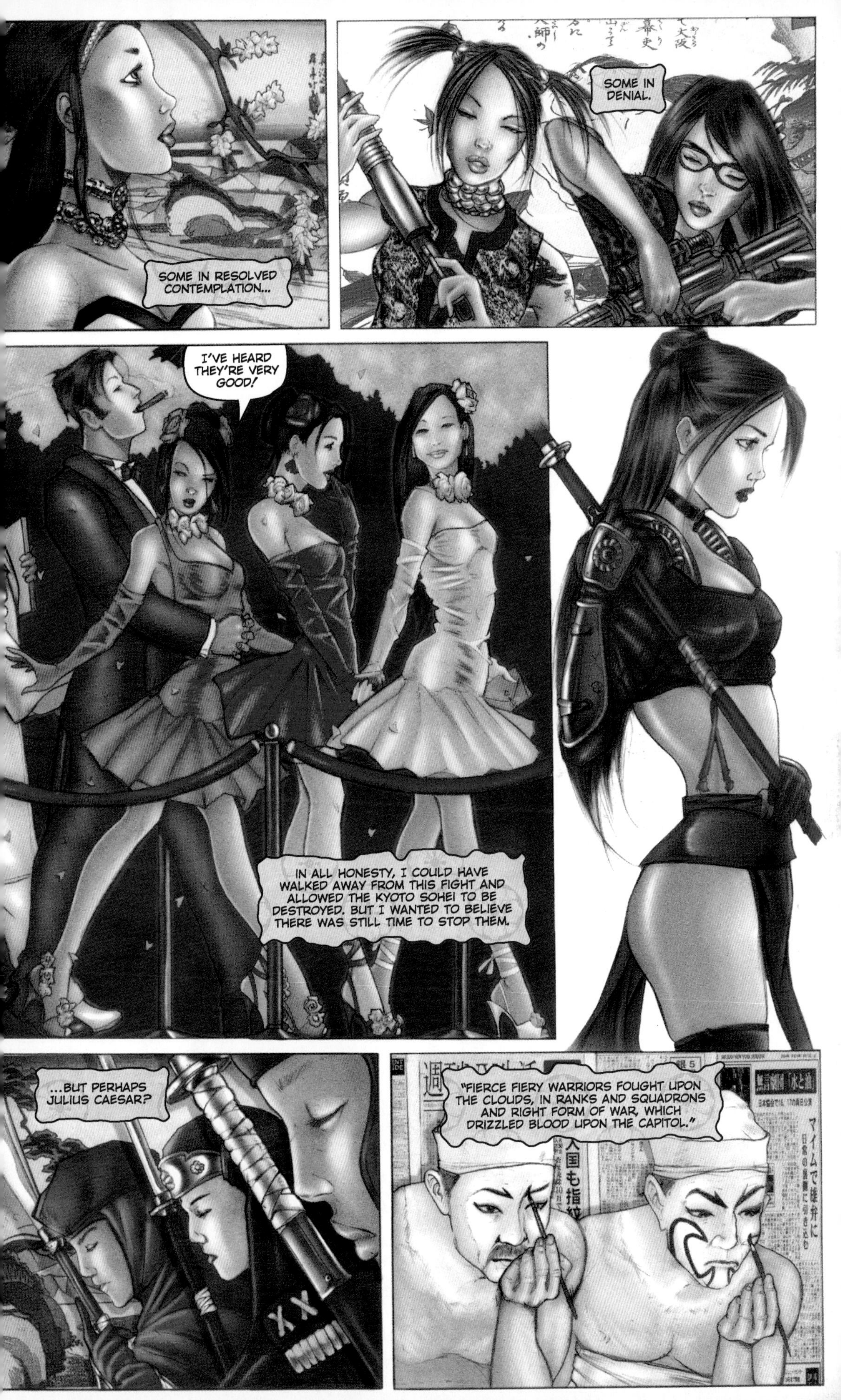
SOME IN RESOLVED CONTEMPLATION...
SOME IN DENIAL.
I'VE HEARD THEY'RE VERY GOOD!
IN ALL HONESTY, I COULD HAVE WALKED AWAY FROM THIS FIGHT AND ALLOWED THE KYOTO SOHEI TO BE DESTROYED. BUT I WANTED TO BELIEVE THERE WAS STILL TIME TO STOP THEM.
...BUT PERHAPS JULIUS CAESAR?
"FIERCE FIERY WARRIORS FOUGHT UPON THE CLOUDS, IN RANKS AND SQUADRONS AND RIGHT FORM OF WAR, WHICH DRIZZLED BLOOD UPON THE CAPITOL."

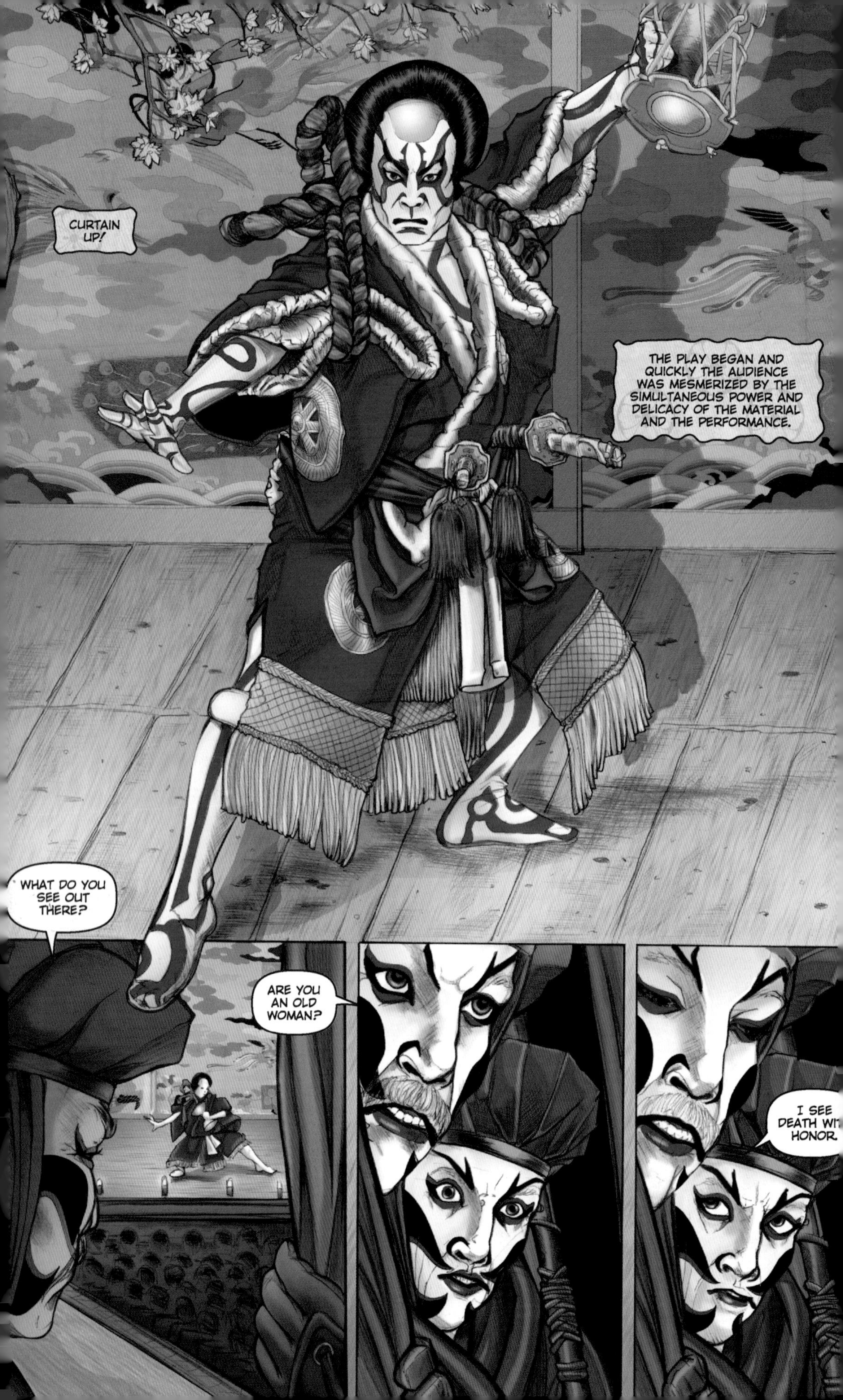
CURTAIN UP!
THE PLAY BEGAN AND QUICKLY THE AUDIENCE WAS MESMERIZED BY THE SIMULTANEOUS POWER AND DELICACY OF THE MATERIAL AND THE PERFORMANCE.
WHAT DO YOU SEE OUT THERE?
ARE YOU AN OLD WOMAN?
I SEE DEATH WIT HONOR

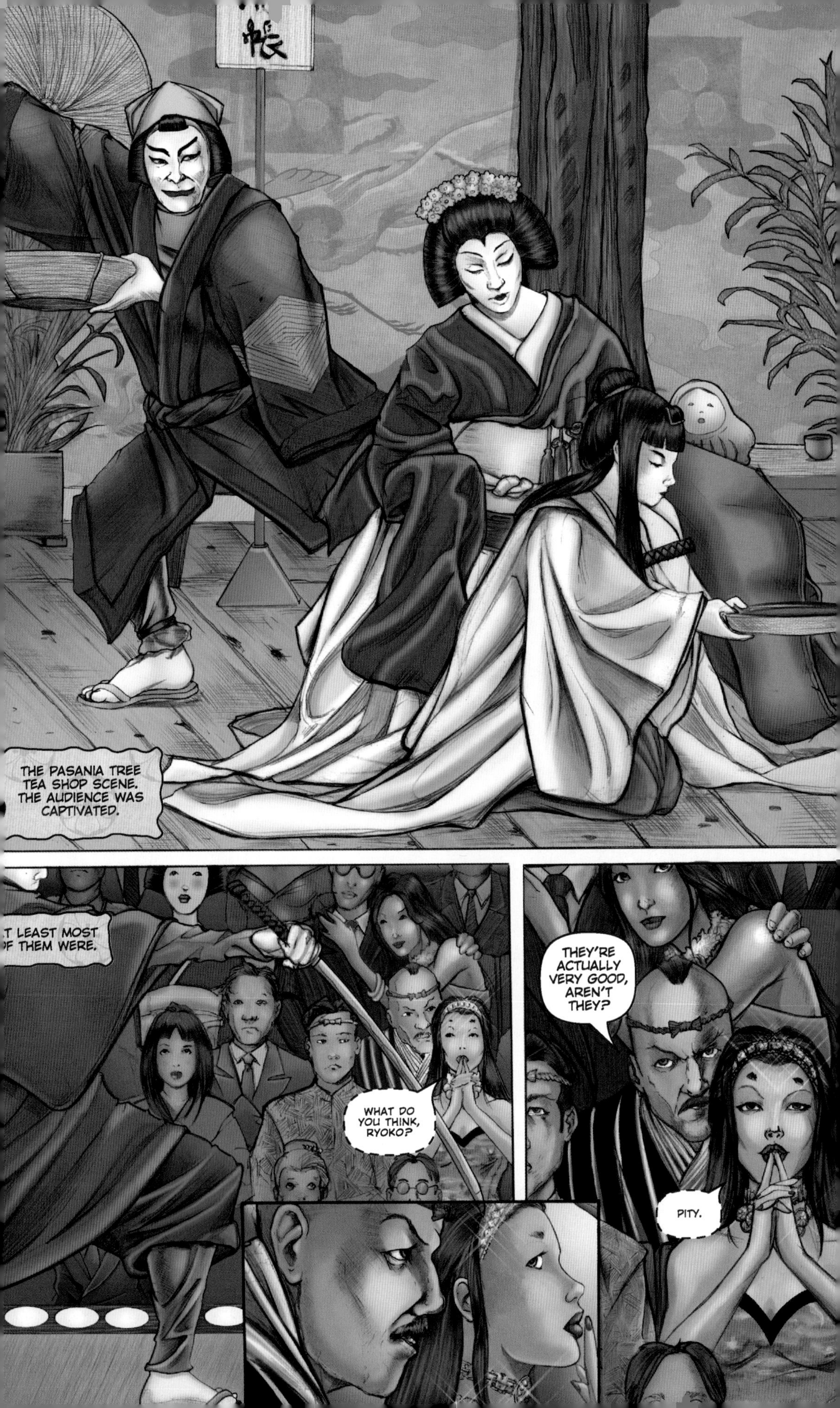
THE PASANIA TREE TEA SHOP SCENE. THE AUDIENCE WAS CAPTIVATED.
T LEAST MOST F THEM WERE.
WHAT DO YOU THINK, RYOKO?
THEY'RE ACTUALLY VERY GOOD, AREN'T THEY?
PITY.

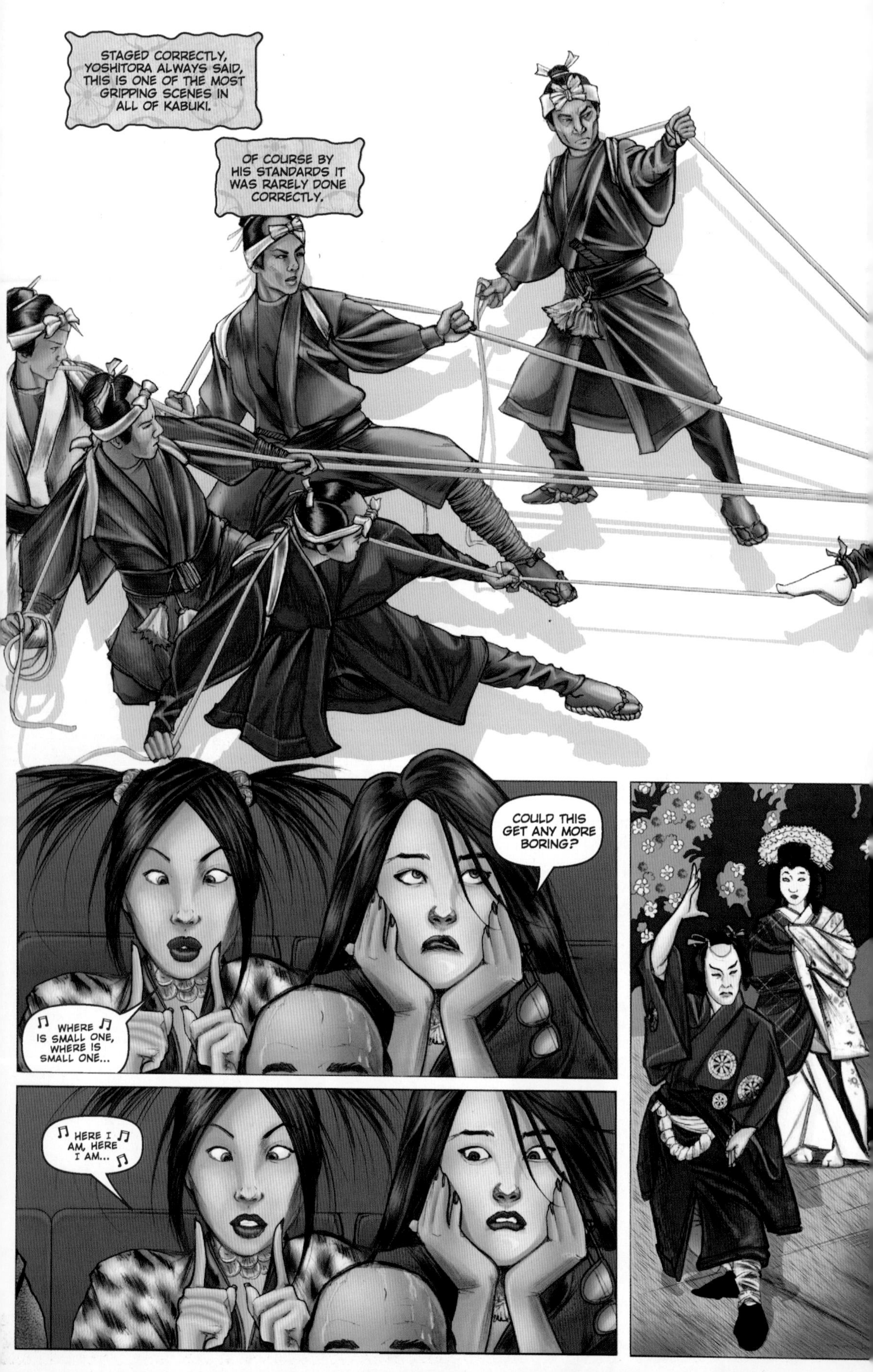
STAGED CORRECTLY, YOSHITORA ALWAYS SAID, THIS IS ONE OF THE MOST GRIPPING SCENES IN ALL OF KABUKI.
OF COURSE BY HIS STANDARDS IT WAS RARELY DONE CORRECTLY.
♫ WHERE ♫ IS SMALL ONE, WHERE IS SMALL ONE...
COULD THIS GET ANY MORE BORING?
♫ HERE I ♫ AM, HERE I AM... ♫

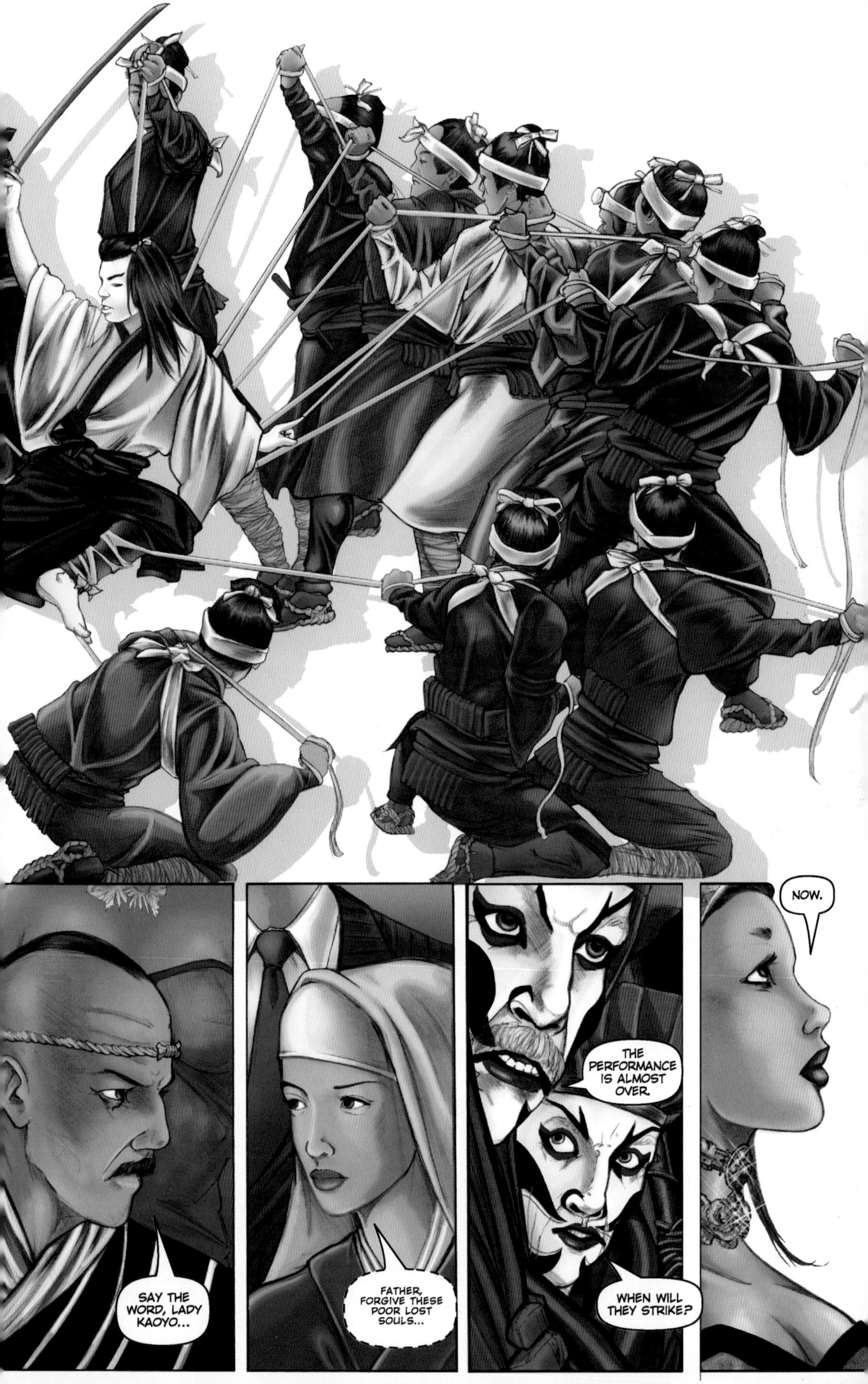
SAY THE WORD, LADY KAOYO...
FATHER, FORGIVE THESE POOR LOST SOULS...
THE PERFORMANCE IS ALMOST OVER.
WHEN WILL THEY STRIKE?
NOW.

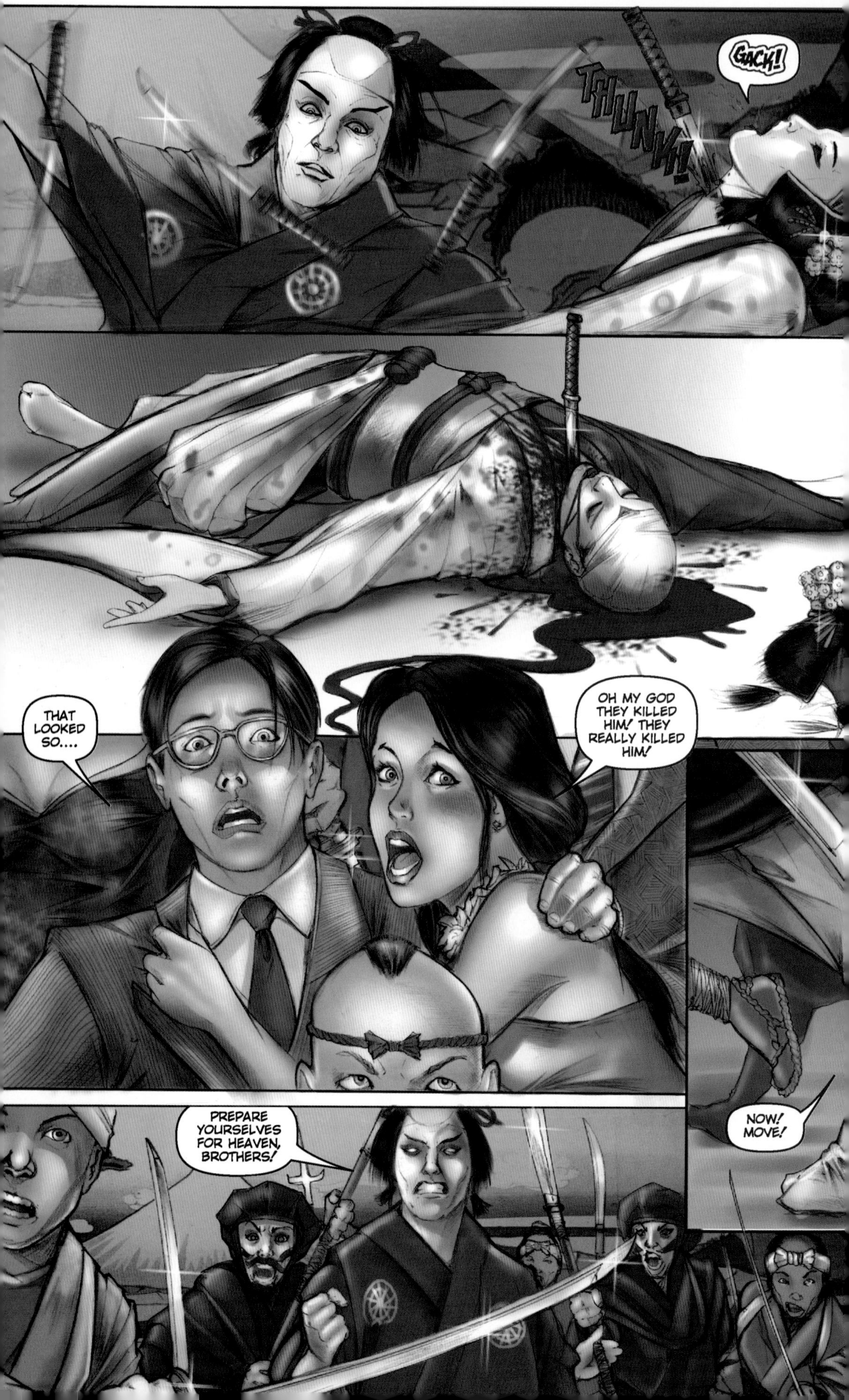
THUNK!
GACK!
THAT LOOKED SO....
OH MY GOD THEY KILLED HIM! THEY REALLY KILLED HIM!
NOW! MOVE!
PREPARE YOURSELVES FOR HEAVEN, BROTHERS!

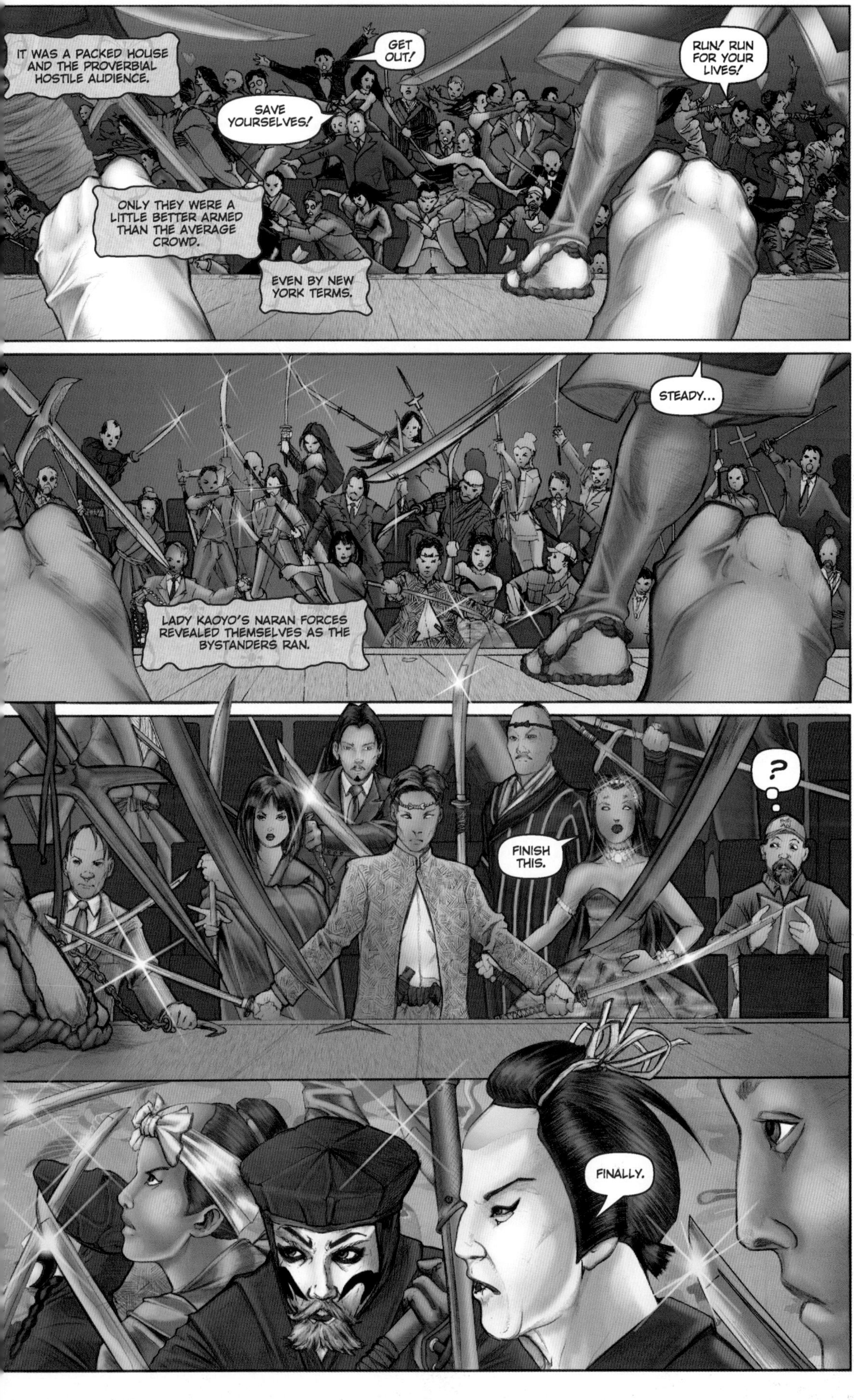

IT WAS A PACKED HOUSE AND THE PROVERBIAL HOSTILE AUDIENCE.
GET OUT!
SAVE YOURSELVES!
RUN! RUN FOR YOUR LIVES!
ONLY THEY WERE A LITTLE BETTER ARMED THAN THE AVERAGE CROWD.
EVEN BY NEW YORK TERMS.
STEADY...
LADY KAOYO'S NARAN FORCES REVEALED THEMSELVES AS THE BYSTANDERS RAN.
FINISH THIS.
?
FINALLY.

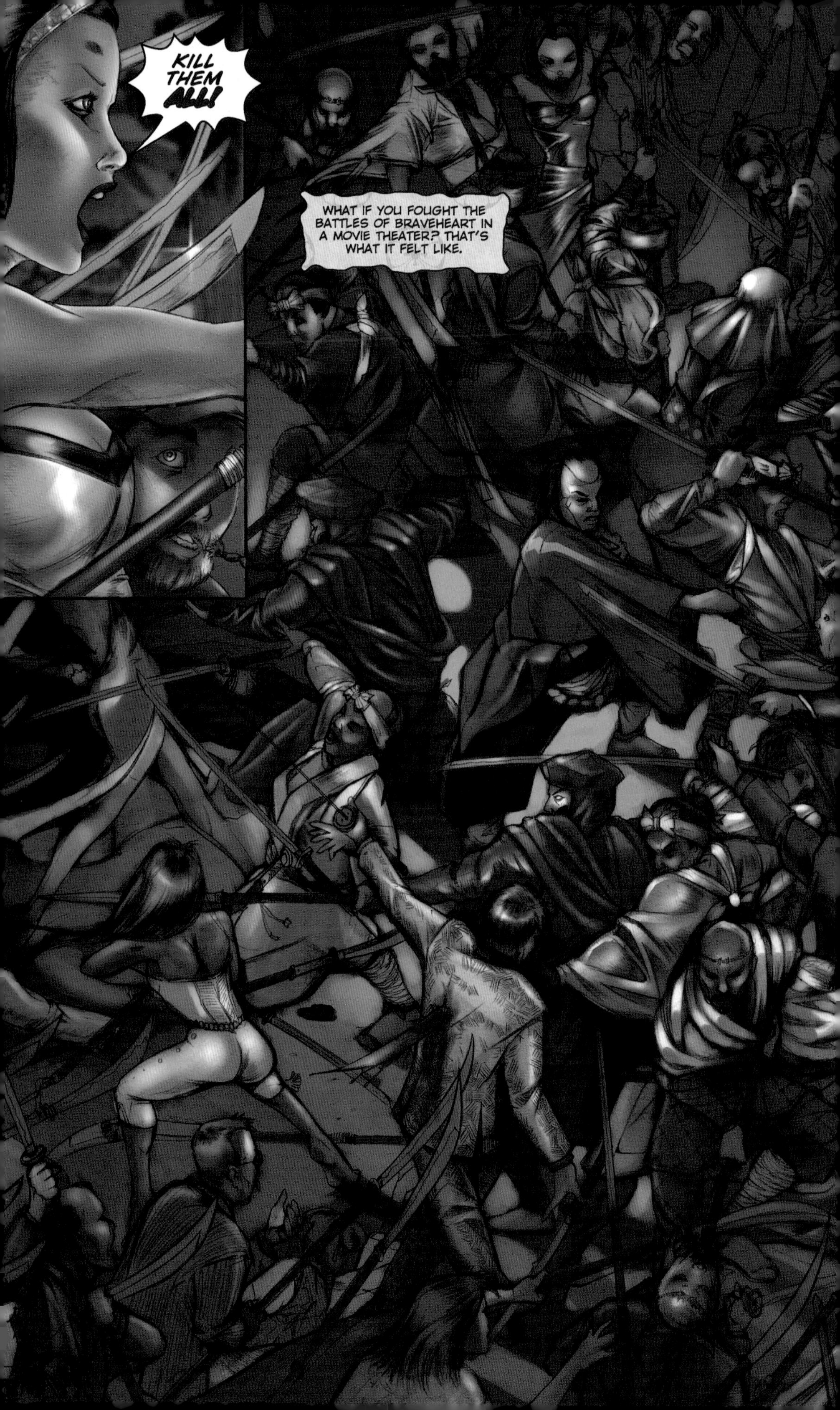
KILL THEM ALL!
WHAT IF YOU FOUGHT THE BATTLES OF BRAVEHEART IN A MOVIE THEATER? THAT'S WHAT IT FELT LIKE.

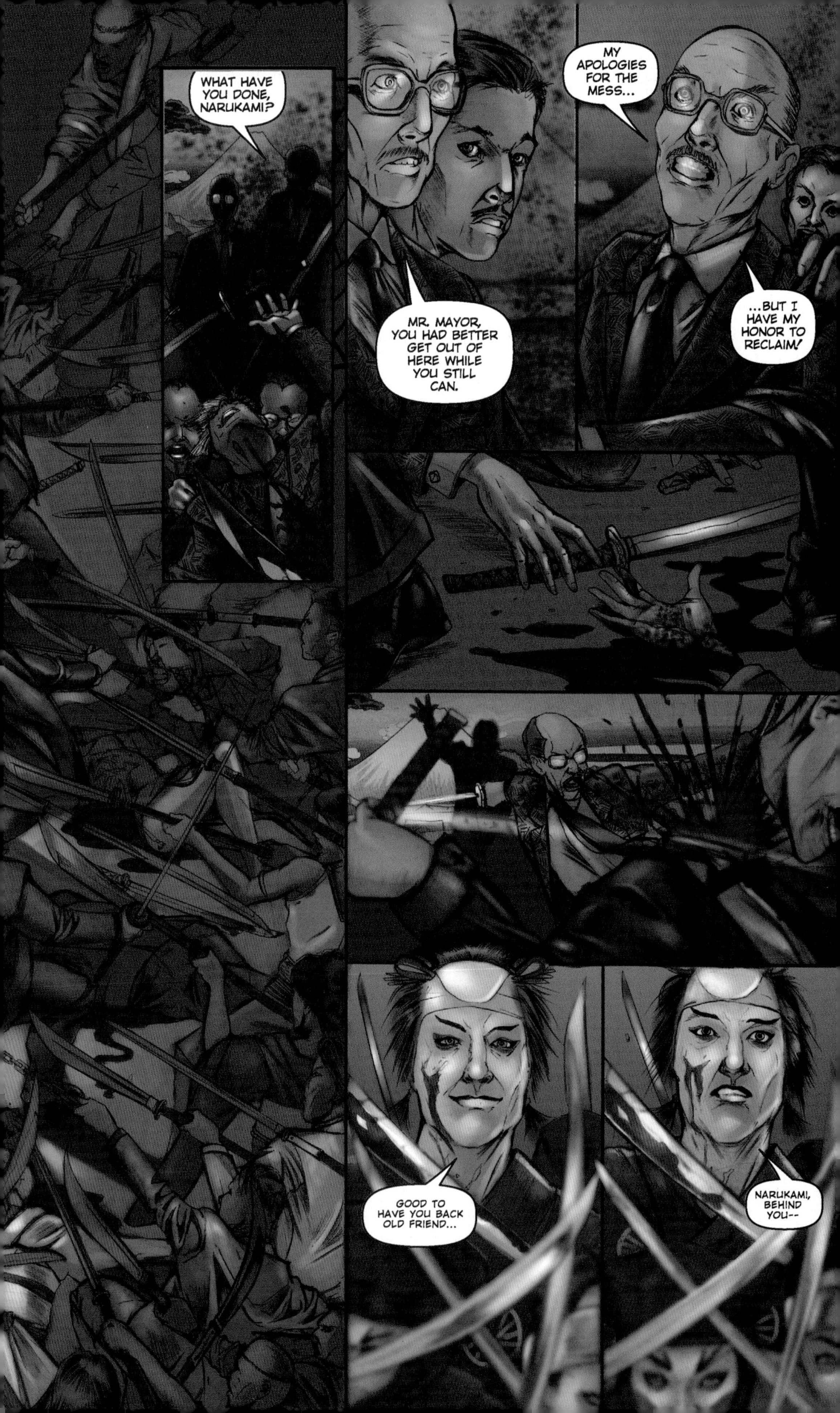
WHAT HAVE YOU DONE, NARUKAMI?
MR. MAYOR, YOU HAD BETTER GET OUT OF HERE WHILE YOU STILL CAN.
MY APOLOGIES FOR THE MESS...
...BUT I HAVE MY HONOR TO RECLAIM!
GOOD TO HAVE YOU BACK OLD FRIEND...
NARUKAMI, BEHIND YOU--

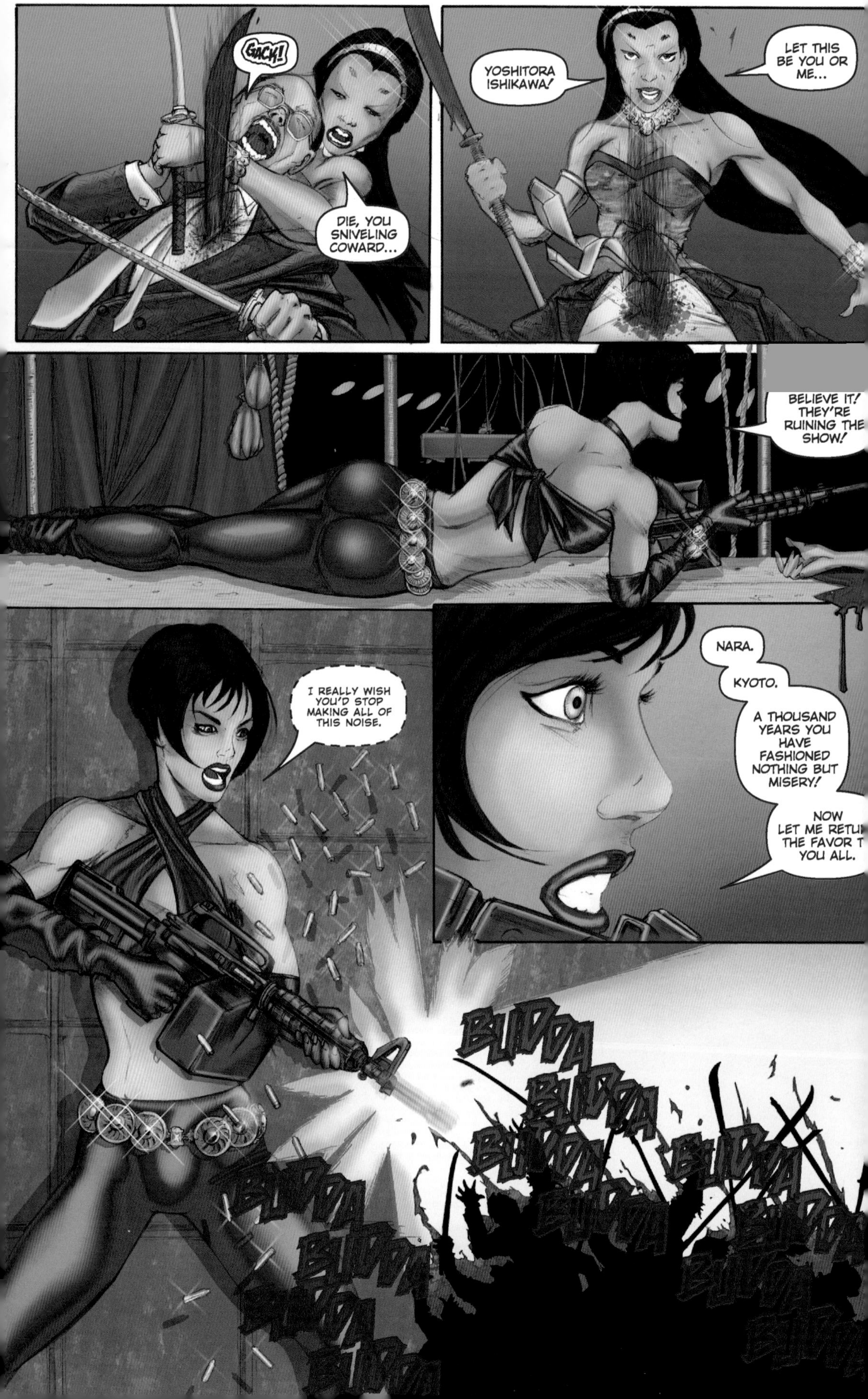
GACK!
DIE, YOU SNIVELING COWARD...
YOSHITORA ISHIKAWA!
LET THIS BE YOU OR ME...
BELIEVE IT! THEY'RE RUINING THE SHOW!
I REALLY WISH YOU'D STOP MAKING ALL OF THIS NOISE.
NARA.
KYOTO.
A THOUSAND YEARS YOU HAVE FASHIONED NOTHING BUT MISERY!
NOW LET ME RETU THE FAVOR T YOU ALL.

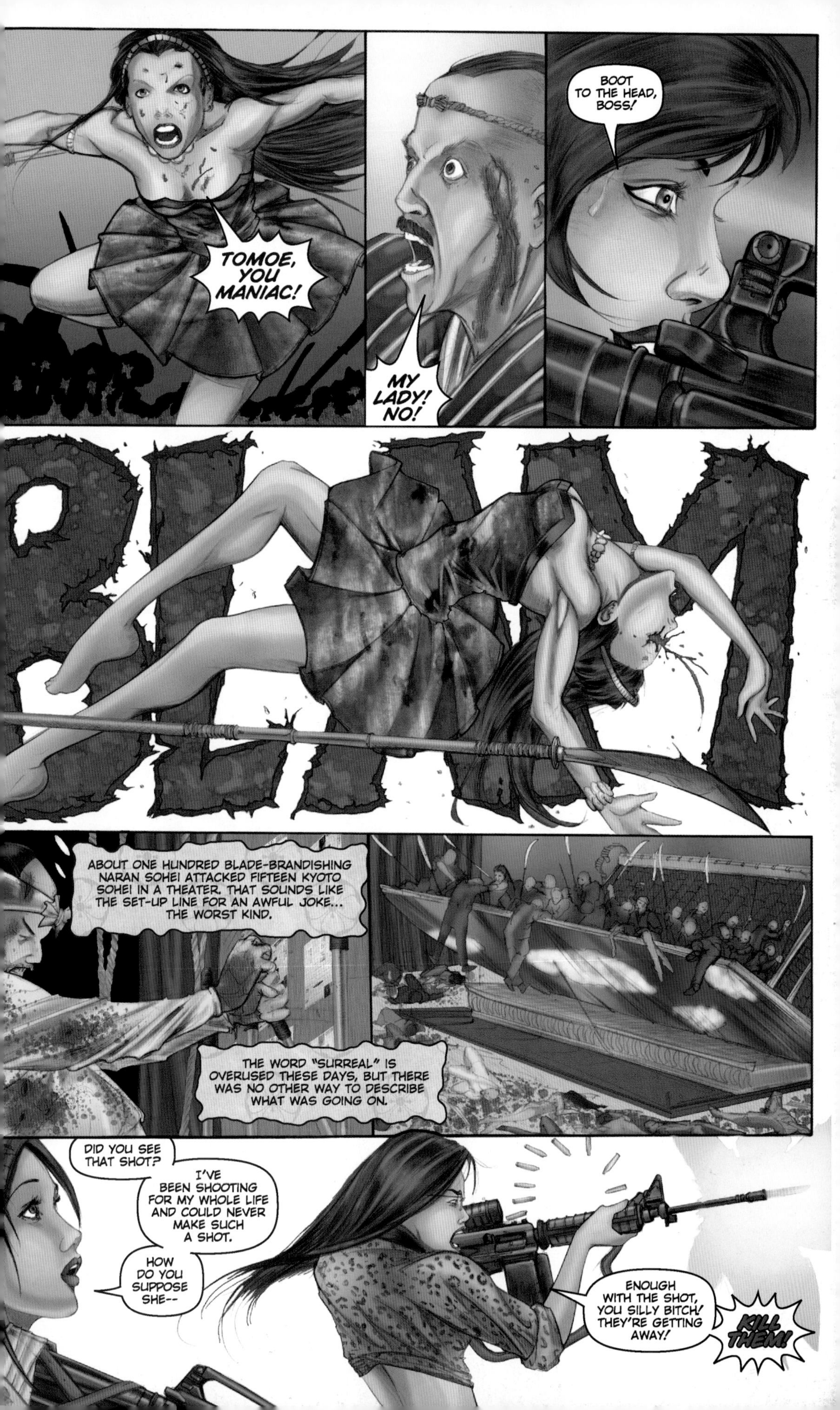
TOMOE, YOU MANIAC!
MY LADY! NO!
BOOT TO THE HEAD, BOSS!
ABOUT ONE HUNDRED BLADE-BRANDISHING NARAN SOHEI ATTACKED FIFTEEN KYOTO SOHEI IN A THEATER. THAT SOUNDS LIKE THE SET-UP LINE FOR AN AWFUL JOKE... THE WORST KIND.
THE WORD "SURREAL" IS OVERUSED THESE DAYS, BUT THERE WAS NO OTHER WAY TO DESCRIBE WHAT WAS GOING ON.
DID YOU SEE THAT SHOT?
I'VE BEEN SHOOTING FOR MY WHOLE LIFE AND COULD NEVER MAKE SUCH A SHOT.
HOW DO YOU SUPPOSE SHE--
ENOUGH WITH THE SHOT, YOU SILLY BITCH! THEY'RE GETTING AWAY!
KILL THEM!

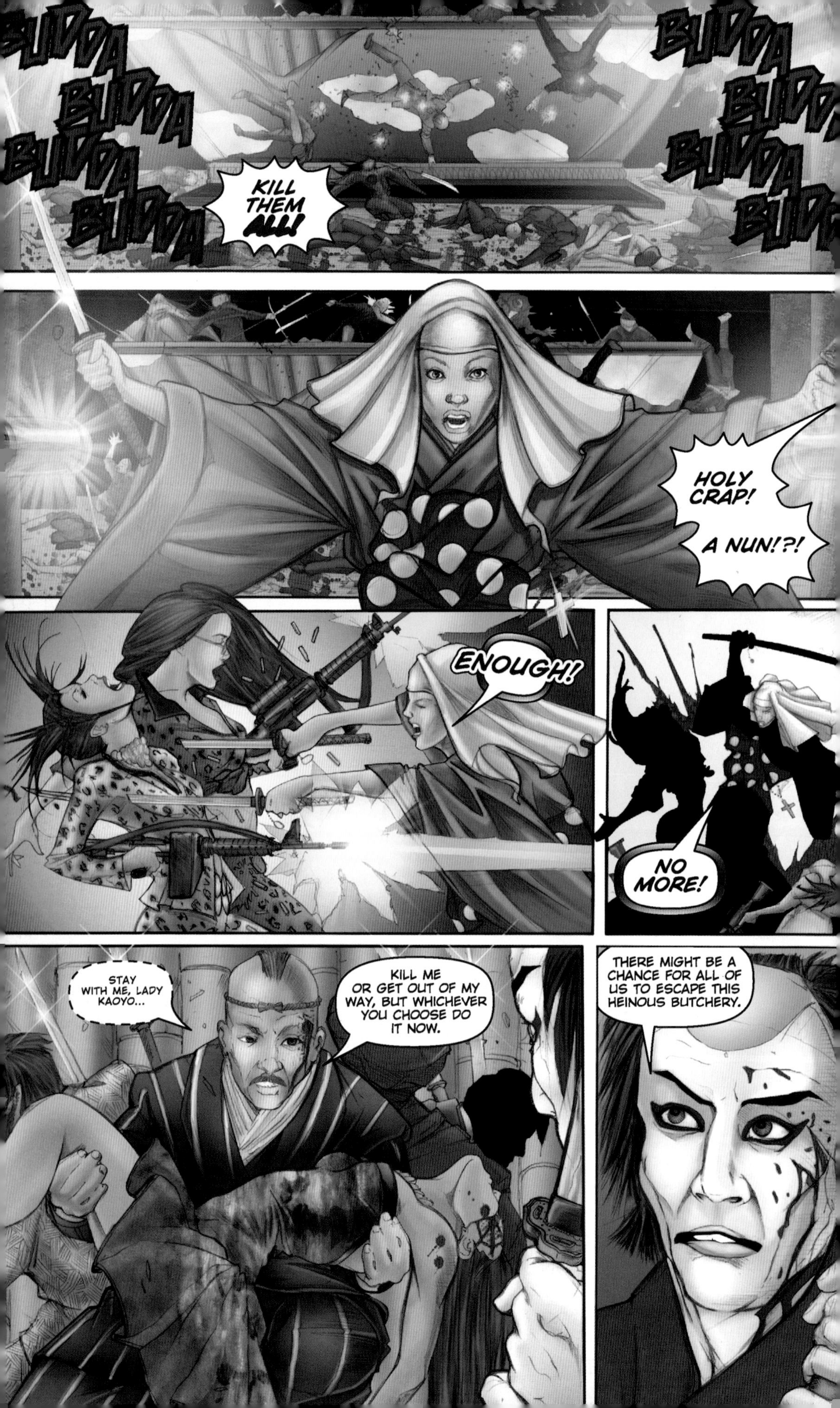
BUDDA BUDDA BUDDA BUDDA
KILL THEM ALL!
BUDDA BUDDA BUDDA BUDDA
HOLY CRAP!
A NUN!?!
ENOUGH!
NO MORE!
STAY WITH ME, LADY KAOYO...
KILL ME OR GET OUT OF MY WAY, BUT WHICHEVER YOU CHOOSE DO IT NOW.
THERE MIGHT BE A CHANCE FOR ALL OF US TO ESCAPE THIS HEINOUS BUTCHERY.

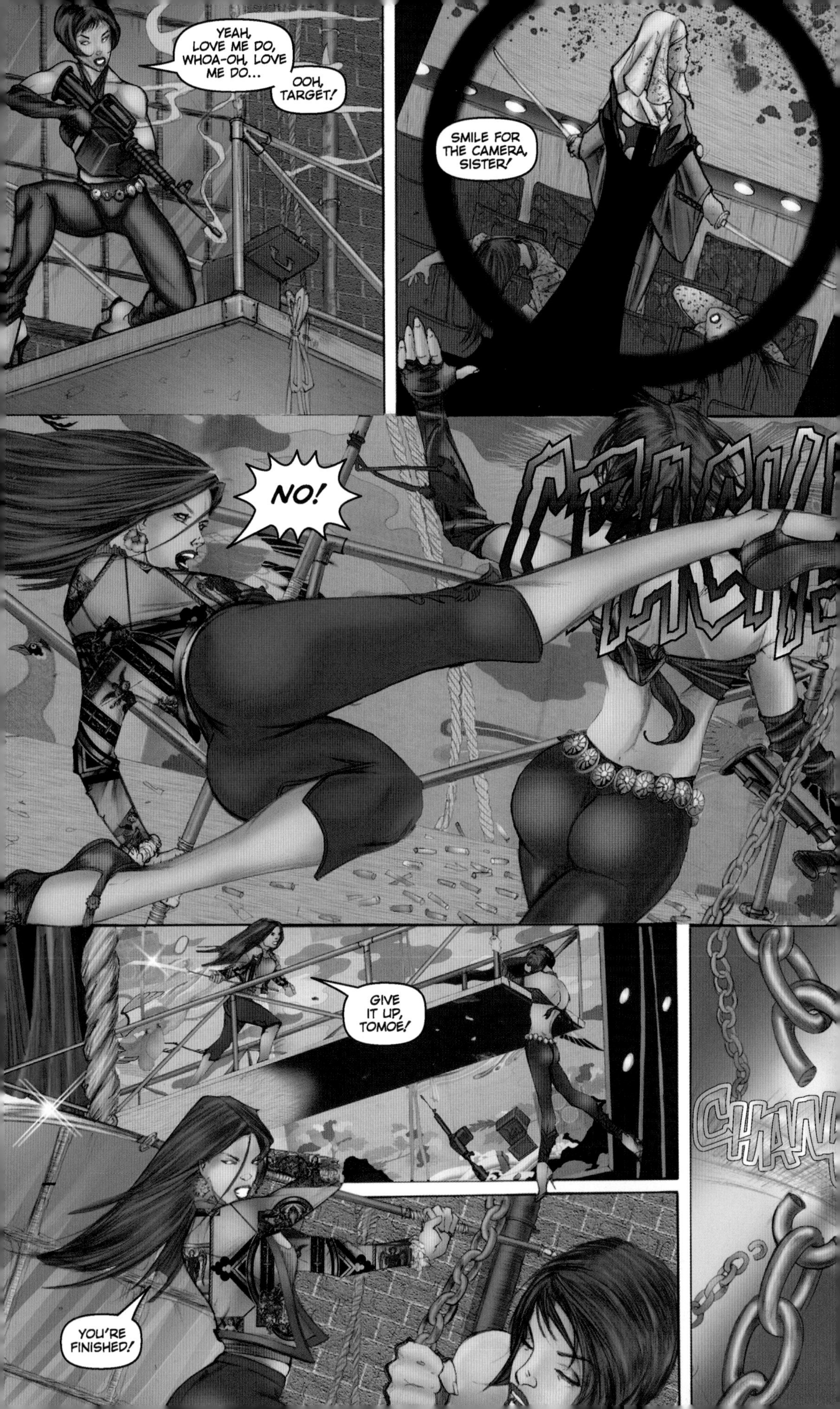
YEAH, LOVE ME DO, WHOA-OH, LOVE ME DO...
OOH, TARGET!
SMILE FOR THE CAMERA, SISTER!
NO!
GIVE IT UP, TOMOE!
YOU'RE FINISHED!

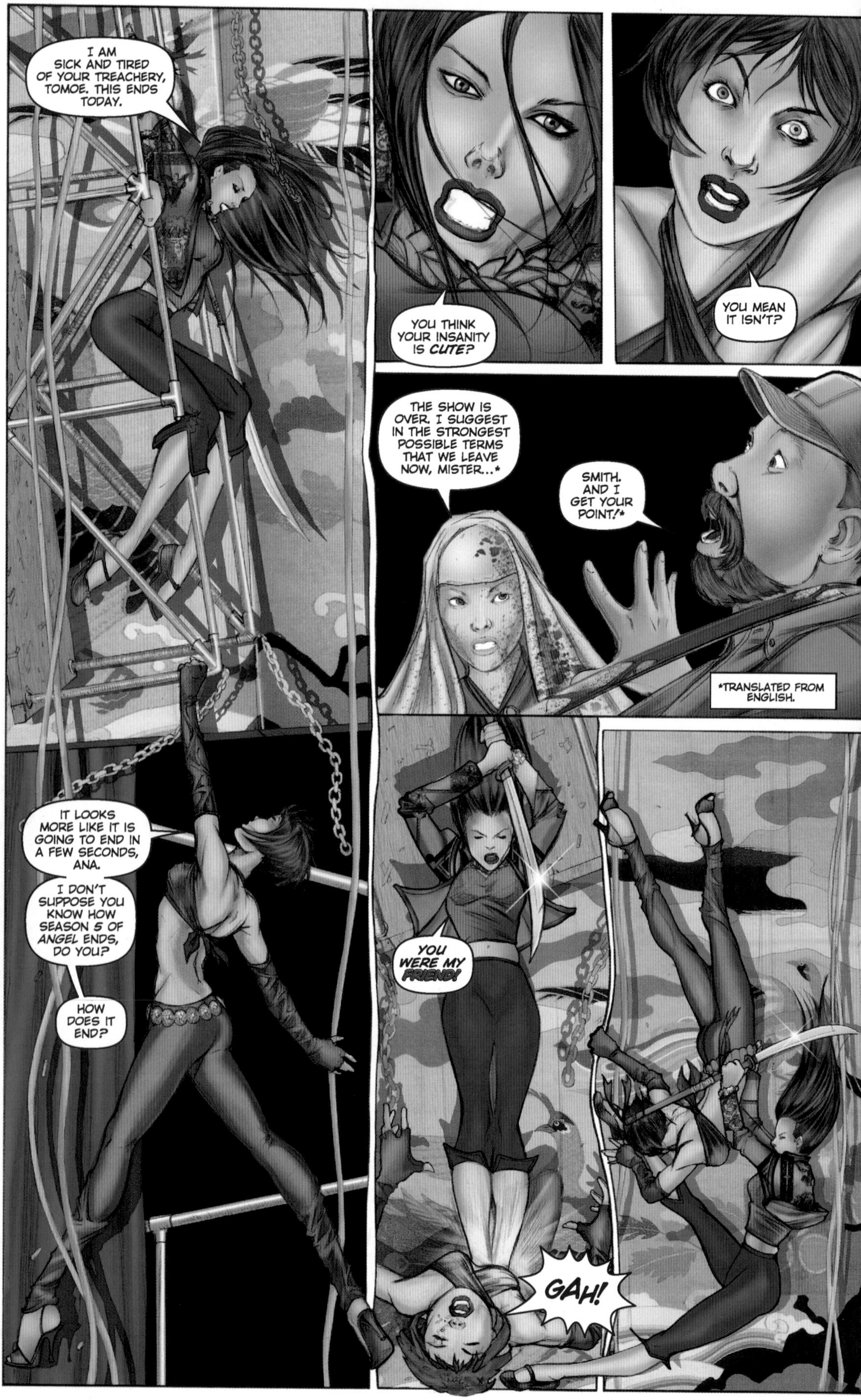
I AM SICK AND TIRED OF YOUR TREACHERY, TOMOE. THIS ENDS TODAY.
YOU THINK YOUR INSANITY IS *CUTE?*
YOU MEAN IT ISN'T?
THE SHOW IS OVER. I SUGGEST IN THE STRONGEST POSSIBLE TERMS THAT WE LEAVE NOW, MISTER...*
SMITH. AND I GET YOUR POINT!*
*TRANSLATED FROM ENGLISH.
IT LOOKS MORE LIKE IT IS GOING TO END IN A FEW SECONDS, ANA.
I DON'T SUPPOSE YOU KNOW HOW SEASON 5 OF ANGEL ENDS, DO YOU?
HOW DOES IT END?
YOU WERE MY FRIEND!
GAH!

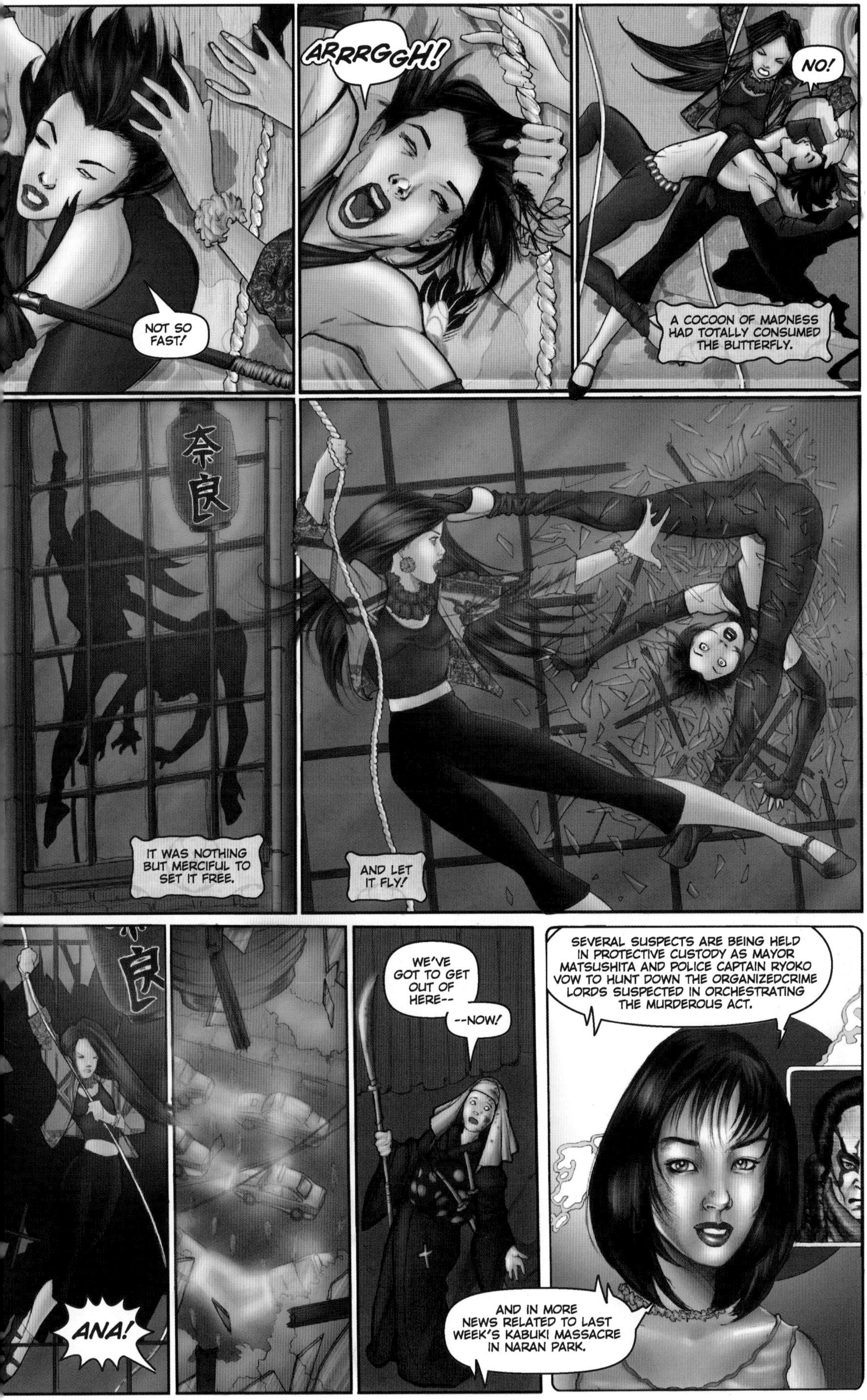
NOT SO FAST!
ARRRGGH!
NO!
A COCOON OF MADNESS HAD TOTALLY CONSUMED THE BUTTERFLY.
奈良
IT WAS NOTHING BUT MERCIFUL TO SET IT FREE.
AND LET IT FLY!
ANA!
WE'VE GOT TO GET OUT OF HERE--
--NOW!
SEVERAL SUSPECTS ARE BEING HELD IN PROTECTIVE CUSTODY AS MAYOR MATSUSHITA AND POLICE CAPTAIN RYOKO VOW TO HUNT DOWN THE ORGANIZEDCRIME LORDS SUSPECTED IN ORCHESTRATING THE MURDEROUS ACT.
AND IN MORE NEWS RELATED TO LAST WEEK'S KABUKI MASSACRE IN NARAN PARK.

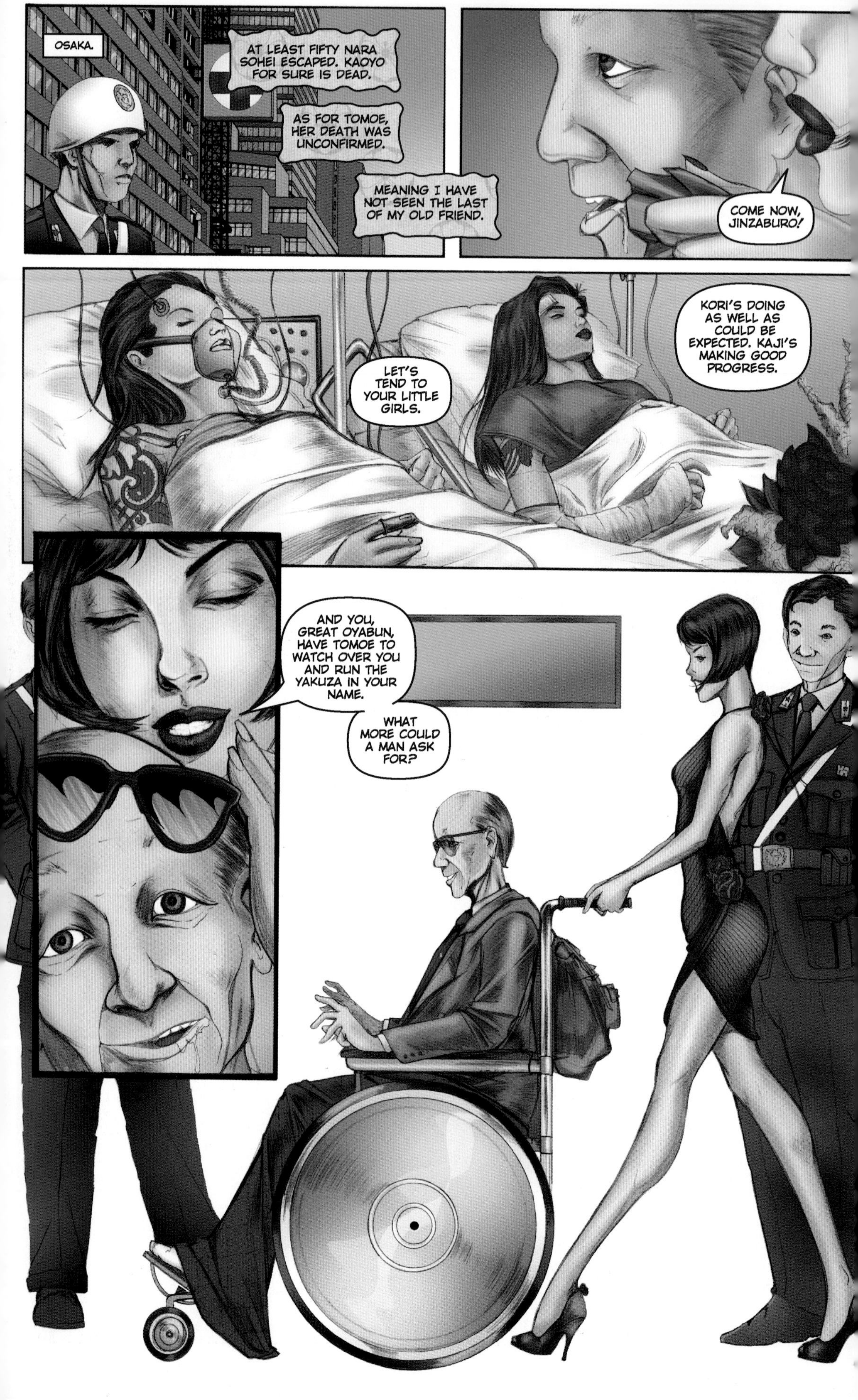
OSAKA.
AT LEAST FIFTY NARA SOHEI ESCAPED. KAOYO FOR SURE IS DEAD.
AS FOR TOMOE, HER DEATH WAS UNCONFIRMED.
MEANING I HAVE NOT SEEN THE LAST OF MY OLD FRIEND.
COME NOW, JINZABURO!
LET'S TEND TO YOUR LITTLE GIRLS.
KORI'S DOING AS WELL AS COULD BE EXPECTED. KAJI'S MAKING GOOD PROGRESS.
AND YOU, GREAT OYABUN, HAVE TOMOE TO WATCH OVER YOU AND RUN THE YAKUZA IN YOUR NAME.
WHAT MORE COULD A MAN ASK FOR?

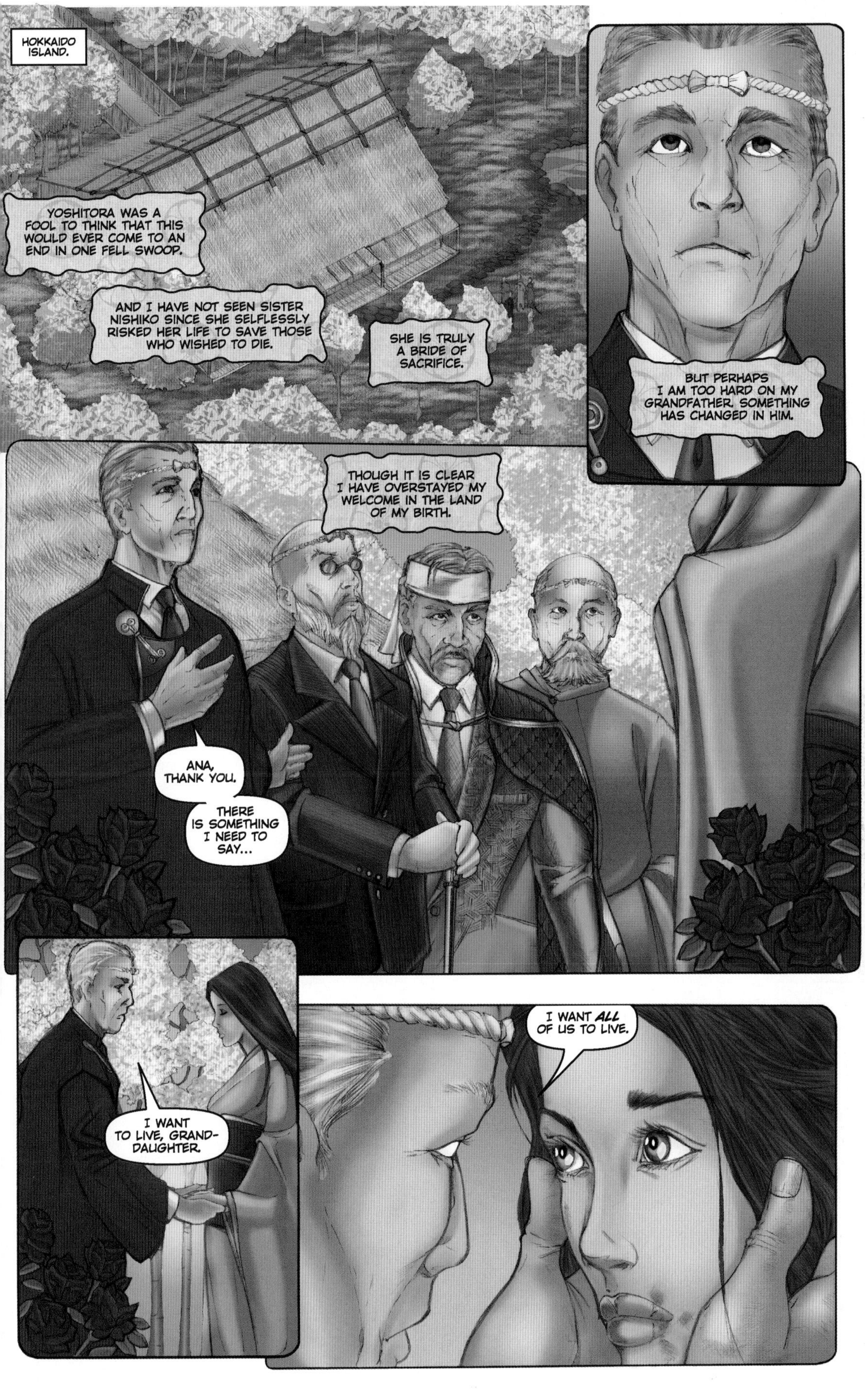
HOKKAIDO ISLAND.
YOSHITORA WAS A FOOL TO THINK THAT THIS WOULD EVER COME TO AN END IN ONE FELL SWOOP.
AND I HAVE NOT SEEN SISTER NISHIKO SINCE SHE SELFLESSLY RISKED HER LIFE TO SAVE THOSE WHO WISHED TO DIE.
SHE IS TRULY A BRIDE OF SACRIFICE.
BUT PERHAPS I AM TOO HARD ON MY GRANDFATHER. SOMETHING HAS CHANGED IN HIM.
THOUGH IT IS CLEAR I HAVE OVERSTAYED MY WELCOME IN THE LAND OF MY BIRTH.
ANA, THANK YOU.
THERE IS SOMETHING I NEED TO SAY...
I WANT TO LIVE, GRAND-DAUGHTER.
I WANT ALL OF US TO LIVE.

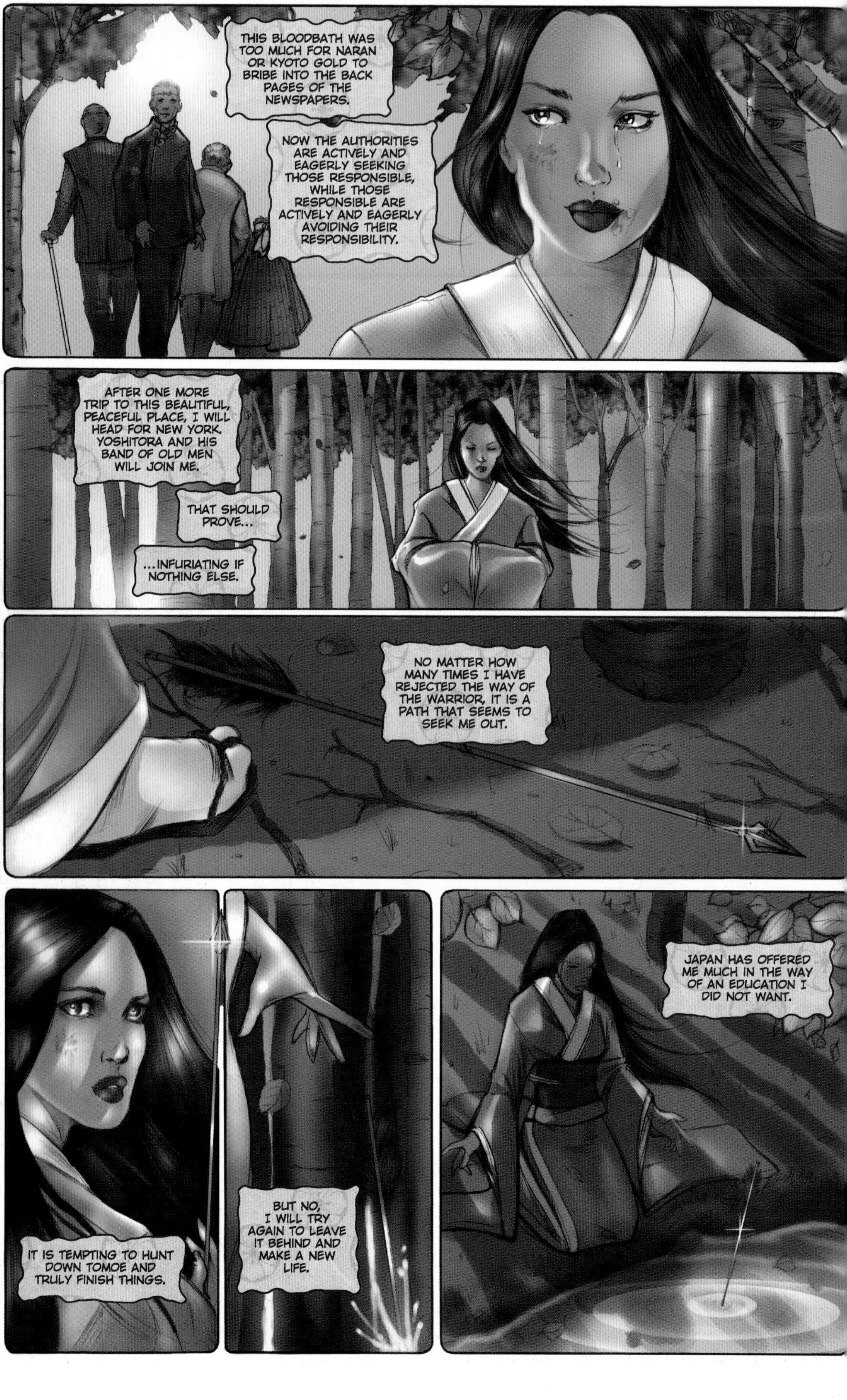
THIS BLOODBATH WAS TOO MUCH FOR NARAN OR KYOTO GOLD TO BRIBE INTO THE BACK PAGES OF THE NEWSPAPERS.
NOW THE AUTHORITIES ARE ACTIVELY AND EAGERLY SEEKING THOSE RESPONSIBLE, WHILE THOSE RESPONSIBLE ARE ACTIVELY AND EAGERLY AVOIDING THEIR RESPONSIBILITY.
AFTER ONE MORE TRIP TO THIS BEAUTIFUL, PEACEFUL PLACE, I WILL HEAD FOR NEW YORK. YOSHITORA AND HIS BAND OF OLD MEN WILL JOIN ME.
THAT SHOULD PROVE...
...INFURIATING IF NOTHING ELSE.
NO MATTER HOW MANY TIMES I HAVE REJECTED THE WAY OF THE WARRIOR, IT IS A PATH THAT SEEMS TO SEEK ME OUT.
IT IS TEMPTING TO HUNT DOWN TOMOE AND TRULY FINISH THINGS.
BUT NO, I WILL TRY AGAIN TO LEAVE IT BEHIND AND MAKE A NEW LIFE.
JAPAN HAS OFFERED ME MUCH IN THE WAY OF AN EDUCATION I DID NOT WANT.

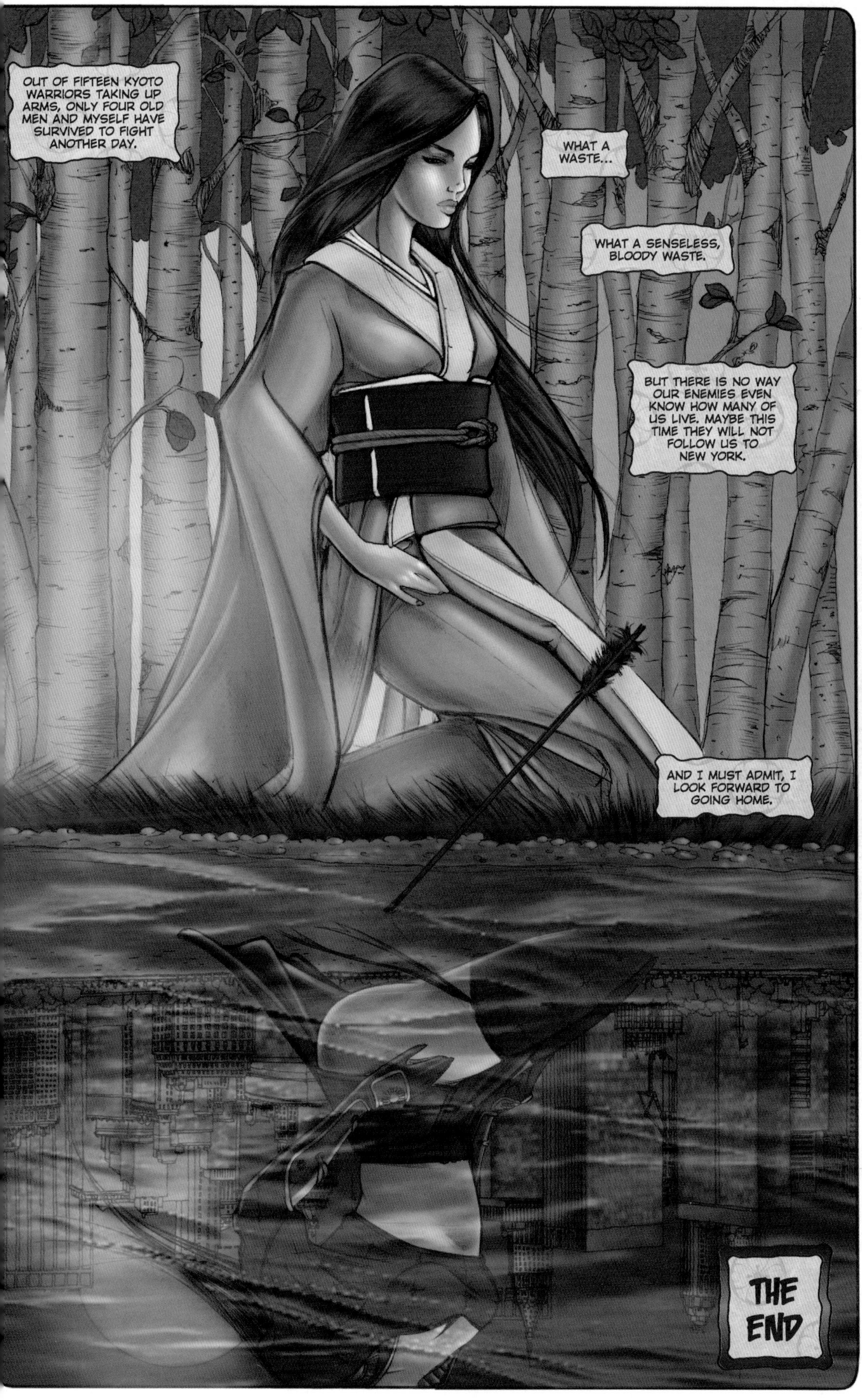

OUT OF FIFTEEN KYOTO WARRIORS TAKING UP ARMS, ONLY FOUR OLD MEN AND MYSELF HAVE SURVIVED TO FIGHT ANOTHER DAY.
WHAT A WASTE...
WHAT A SENSELESS, BLOODY WASTE.
BUT THERE IS NO WAY OUR ENEMIES EVEN KNOW HOW MANY OF US LIVE. MAYBE THIS TIME THEY WILL NOT FOLLOW US TO NEW YORK.
AND I MUST ADMIT, I LOOK FORWARD TO GOING HOME.
THE END

SHI

SHI ACTION FIGURE
Item No. 13-340 | $14.99

The action figures feature up to
18 points of articulation, and are
sculpted by Steve Kiwus.

TOMOE ACTION FIGURE
Item No. 13-341 | $14.99

SHI MINIBUST
The samurai heroine as sculpted by
master sculptor Jeffery Scott, limited to
2,500 numbered pieces, comes with a
certificate of authenticity.
Item No. 10-201 | $44.99

SHI ZIPPO®
Item No. 10-195 | $29.99

SHI COASTER SET
Format: 4 full-color coasters
1/8" thick, packaged in a printed box
ISBN: 1-59617-008-5 | $9.99

SHI POSTER
Poster (22" x 34")
Item No. 10-051 | $9.99

dark horse Deluxe ™
darkhorse.com

For more information or to order direct visit darkhorse.com
or call 1-800-862-0052 Mon.-Sat. 9 A.M. to 5 P.M. Pacific Time
*Prices and availability subject to change without notice